# Feminist Alternatives

Irony and Fantasy
in the Contemporary Novel by Women

# Feminist Alternatives

Irony and Fantasy
in the Contemporary Novel by Women

## Nancy A. Walker

University Press of Mississippi
Jackson and London

93  92  91  90     4  3  2  1

The paper in this book meets the guidelines for
permanence and durability of the Committee on
Production Guidelines for Book Longevity of the Council
on Library Resources.

A version of Chapter Two "Language, Irony, and
Fantasy" appears in *Literature Interpretation Theory* 1,
no. 1–2 (1989): 33–57.

*Library of Congress Cataloging-in-Publication Data*

Walker, Nancy A.
   Feminist alternatives : irony and fantasy in the contemporary
novel by women / Nancy A. Walker.
      p.  cm.
   Includes bibliographical references.
   ISBN 0-87805-430-8 (alk. paper)
      1. American fiction—Women authors—History and criticism.
   2. English fiction—Women authors—History and criticism.
   3. American fiction—20th century—-History and criticism.
   4. English fiction—20th century—History and criticism.
   5. Feminism and literature—History—20th century.   6. Women
   and literature—History—20th century.   7. Fantasy in literature.
   8. Irony in literature.   I. Title.
   PS374.F45W35   1990
   813'.54099287—dc20                                    89-25052
                                                              CIP


British Library Cataloguing-in-Publication data available

For my students at Stephens College

# CONTENTS

Introduction   3

1   Narrative and Transition   14

2   Language, Irony, and Fantasy   38

3   Multiple Narrative: Revising the Self   75

4   Acceptable Fantasies   113

5   Alternate Realities   146

Conclusion   185

Notes   191

Bibliography   207

Index   217

# Feminist Alternatives

Irony and Fantasy
in the Contemporary Novel by Women

# Introduction

In her graceful and perceptive book *Writing a Woman's Life*, Carolyn Heilbrun writes, "Women must turn to one another for stories; they must share the stories of their lives and their hopes and their unacceptable fantasies."[1] There are, Heilbrun notes, "four ways to write a woman's life":

> [T]he woman herself may tell it, in what she chooses to call an autobiography; she may tell it in what she chooses to call fiction; a biographer, woman or man, may write the woman's life in what is called a biography; or the woman may write her own life in advance of living it, unconsciously, and without recognizing or naming the process. (11)

*Writing a Woman's Life* deals with three of these four ways, omitting "an analysis of the fictions in which many women have written their lives" (11).

This is a book about those "fictions"—specifically the contemporary novel—in which women have written their own lives and women's lives they have imagined, and as such it joins many other studies published in recent years. Indeed, the outpouring of critical studies of contemporary women's fiction informs Heilbrun's decision to confine her remarks to other genres. The rich diversity of scholarly studies of women's fiction is exceeded only by that of the fiction itself, as numerous writers have shared their stories with increasingly large numbers of readers, especially since the 1960s. Inevitably, not all of these novels will ultimately be judged to be of lasting merit by readers and critics; as the circumstances of women's lives continue—one hopes—to change, some of these fictions may come to have a primarily historical interest, as does Fanny Fern's 1855 novel *Ruth Hall* at present. In fact, the process of classification into periods has already begun. Nora Johnson, for example, has commented on "the feminist novel, which flourished in the 1960's and 70's," which featured what Johnson calls "the story of the awakening housewife."[2] Johnson refers to such novels as Sue Kaufman's *Diary of a Mad Housewife*, Alix Kates Shulman's *Memoirs of an Ex-Prom Queen*, and Penelope Mortimer's *The Pumpkin Eater*, in which the "meat-and-potatoes sexism" is "deafeningly familiar" (32). The process of developing consciousness and evolving themes can often be charted in the career of a single writer, as in Margaret Atwood's progression from *The Edible Woman* (1969) to *The Handmaid's Tale* (1986).

But whether the authors write of women struggling to get out of "the women's room" (to use Marilyn French's title) or create metafictions such as *The Handmaid's Tale*, the women's novel—by which I mean the essentially realistic novel, as opposed to the popular romance—of the period from the late 1960s to the mid-1980s has several common characteristics, two of which are the focus of this study. One of these characteristics is suggested by Heilbrun's remark that women must share with each other their "unacceptable fantasies"—fantasies unacceptable, that is, except to other women: fantasies of sexuality, freedom, power: alternate worlds in which women are autonomous, self-defining people. The second characteristic, or narrative strategy, is irony, a mode that springs from a recognition of the socially constructed self as arbitrary, and that demands revision of values and conventions. Irony and fantasy represent, respectively, intellectual and intuitive challenges to perceived reality that reflect in the form of narrative the socio-political challenges to the status quo that the women's movement has launched during this period. This is not to suggest that these novels are overtly political; on the contrary, they are typically cast as personal, frequently painful accounts of individual women confronting re-definitions in their lives and thought. But they are political in the way women came to understand politics in the 1960s and 1970s: as an intensely personal and individual experience that radiates outward into common, shared hopes and goals.

It is important to set the novels with which this study deals—fictions by Margaret Atwood, Marge Piercy, Gail Godwin, Margaret Drabble, Fay Weldon, Doris Lessing, Alice Walker, and others—against the popular romance novels which, according to some estimates, account for four out of ten paperback book sales,[3] not least because the popular romance is a recurring metaphor and narrative element in these novels of struggle and change. The popular romances, such as the Harlequins and Silhouettes, are *acceptable* fantasies; they endorse rather than challenge cultural assumptions about women's nature and aspirations, reinforcing what Rachel Brownstein has called the "marriage plot" as the proper script for women's lives. Further, they are wholly unironic texts that do not question their own assumptions or the assumptions of readers, who read them precisely to confirm their own options and choices. Kay Mussell has speculated, in fact, that increased sales of popular romances during the years of the contemporary women's movement may have come about because of, rather than in spite of, the changes in attitude occurring in those decades:

> It appears particularly appropriate, if tragic, that romances should be a dominant form of fictional fantasy in a period of enhanced options and rising expectations for women, for women's niche in culture has at least the potential to be comfortable and rewarding. And many women understand that, for them, autonomous choices may have consequences that they find disquieting or unacceptable. (*Fantasy and Reconciliation* 190–91)

Janice Radway, whose *Reading the Romance* is based largely on interviews with regular readers of romances, comes to similar conclusions. Noting that these readers tend to be conservative women

5

Introduction

who resent what they perceive as attacks on their lives by "women's libbers," Radway posits that the romance provides the possibility of change within reasonable limits:

> Their desire to believe that the romantic heroine is as intelligent and independent as she is asserted to be even though she is also shown to be vulnerable and most interested in being loved is born of their apparently unconscious desire to realize some of the benefits of feminism within traditional institutions and relationships—hence, the high value attached to the simple *assertion* of the heroine's special abilities. With a few simple statements rather than with truly threatening action on the part of the heroine, the romance author demonstrates for the typical reader the compatibility of a changed sense of the female self and an unchanged social arrangement.[4]

The frequency with which contemporary women novelists make reference to popular romances in their work suggests that they are well aware of the tension between the apparent security of the "marriage plot" and the desire for change that many of their own readers feel. The fantasy of "happily ever after" is one that these writers subvert, as their characters grow to view such fantasy ironically. The title character in Gail Godwin's *Violet Clay* (1978), for example, paints cover illustrations for gothic romances, and amuses herself by wondering what happens to the heroines of these books after the conclusion, when the villain has turned into a hero, but the inevitable dailiness of marriage has set in. Violet is herself using cover illustration as a means of fending off confrontation with her true talents as an artist. In Godwin's *The Odd Woman* (1974), Jane Clifford is a professor of literature whose mother once wrote formula stories for *Love Short Stories;* although Jane has been impatient with the lack of variety and reality in her mother's stories, she is as caught in the literature she teaches as are her mother's heroines in their formulaic plots. The most extensive use of the popular romance as a metaphor occurs in Atwood's *Lady Oracle* (1976), in which the central character and narrator, Joan Foster, writes "costume Gothics." Her life as the author Louisa K. Delacourt is a secret from her husband and her friends, and at times it is more emotionally sustaining than her "real" life

6

as Joan Foster. Joan realizes that the other women around her have fantasy lives, which "except for the costumes weren't that different from my own. . . . They wanted multiple orgasms, they wanted the earth to move, but they also wanted help with the dishes." Joan is able to feel a bit superior to these women: "After all, when it came to fantasy lives I was a professional, whereas they were merely amateurs."[5]

The overwhelming need for fantasy, represented in both the popularity of romance novels and the use of the romance as metaphor in the contemporary realistic novel by women, suggests a perception on the part of many women that the daily reality with which they live is insufficient to sustain a sense of self. Suzanne Juhasz has argued provocatively that whether it is formulaic or complex, unambiguous or ironic, the "woman's novel" essentially embodies a fantasy. "The lines of difference," Juhasz writes, "between romance fiction and those novels that strive for social verisimilitude are drawn along the axis of possibility—or lack of it—for psychological reparation and cultural reconstruction." Juhasz points out that whereas in a novel such as *The Awakening* or *The Mill on the Floss*, "the heroine's struggle for selfhood must be thwarted," in popular romances such as the Harlequins, "the heroine gets a self as well as the hero," but in both cases the issue comes from the same origins:

> The difference between the Harlequin romance and a Jane Austen novel has more to do with psychological complexity and depth than with the outlines of the plot. We can situate other romance novels on a continuum between these extremes. They all share a basis in fantasy because they run counter to societal fact in responding to a need that cannot usually be met by the culture as it is.[6]

While Juhasz's essential point is incontestable, it will be my argument in the following pages that it is the combination of fantasy and irony—particularly fantasy viewed ironically—that constitutes a fundamental critique of cultural realities in the contemporary novel by women.

Juhasz's mention of Jane Austen reminds us of the long tradition of irony in women's fiction, in which Austen is perhaps pre-

eminent. Certainly Austen was well aware of the limiting social
construction of womanhood in the late eighteenth century in England, and her novels are filled with statements calculated to call
into question the authority of social convention. The famous first
sentence of *Pride and Prejudice*—"It is a truth universally acknowledged that a single man in possession of a fortune must be in want
of a wife"—undercuts with its very solemnity the surface meaning, as the statement is revealed to be a fervent hope masking the
awful truth that women required husbands for social and economic security. In her posthumously published *Northanger Abbey*,
Austen anticipated, as did other authors of the period, male and
female, the great nineteenth-century debate about the effects of
romance-reading on women. Yet unlike the heroines of Charlotte
Lennox's *The Female Quixote* and Tabitha Tenney's *Female Quixotism*, Austen's Catherine is, characteristically, too sensible to be
ruined by her reading, just as Godwin's and Atwood's characters
are able to emerge from their reliance on such fantasies.[7]

Like Austen, the contemporary woman novelist understands
the power of language to both control and subvert the control of
authority. Not only do irony and fantasy depend for their force
upon a recognition of verbal constructions, but authors must ma-
neuver around the language of dominant discourse in order to de-
construct cultural mythologies, including the myths that women
construct about their own lives. Therefore, a prominent focus in
this study is the use of language in the novels. Another important
focus is identity or selfhood—concepts that are particularly complex in an era in which feminist psychology poses challenges to
Freudian and post-Freudian theories of human development. Dissatisfaction with the self as constructed by others leads women to
imagine alternative selves, a conceptualization that extends into
fantasy in the form of dreams, memory, and even madness. Ultimately, the impulse toward alternate worlds takes some novelists
into the realm of speculative fiction, proposing utopian or dystopian visions that serve as ironic counterpoints to contemporary
reality. Yet none of these novelists forfeits a grounding in that reality; from the dialect of Walker's *The Color Purple* (1982) to the recognizable elements of contemporary society in *The Handmaid's*

# Introduction

*Tale,* the contemporary novel by women locates the reader in a world that she or he knows and is forced to re-evaluate.

Given the large number of novels written by women that deal specifically with women's experience during the past twenty years, the choice of works to include in this study is somewhat arbitrary. Some authors, such as Doris Lessing, Margaret Atwood, and Alice Walker, are too important or too influential to be omitted. Others, such as Fay Weldon and Joanna Russ, use the narrative strategies on which I focus here—fantasy and irony—more overtly and dramatically than do many writers, but they represent tendencies that can be observed in the fiction of many women, and their works embody the full development of those tendencies. The choice of 1969 as the beginning point may seem even more arbitrary, but it allows consideration of two major novels published in that year: Lessing's *The Four-Gated City* and Drabble's *The Waterfall,* each of which provides an important paradigm of contemporary women's fiction. *The Four-Gated City,* the culmination of Lessing's "Children of Violence" series, provides a historical context for the social movements of the 1960s. It also makes cross-cultural references to the United States that remind us that the women's movement crossed national boundaries and allowed women to explore common experiences as women regardless of national origin. Furthermore, Lessing's novel has several affinities with Atwood's 1986 *Handmaid's Tale.* Not only do the two novels share a dystopian vision, but in some ways Atwood's story of Gilead takes up where Lessing's story of Britain leaves off, describing a post-feminist world in which the values espoused by members of Martha Quest's and Offred's mother's generation have been overturned. *The Waterfall* also embodies a sense of both history and futurity. Drabble consciously refers to her literary predecessors as her narrator revises their stories; Jane Gray, in the 1960s, is poised between past and future, and her uncertainty about the coherence and morality of her life anticipates a major theme in subsequent women's novels.

Yet this study is not a history, organized chronologically, of the contemporary novel by women. Fiction that is subversively rather than overtly political does not directly mirror year-by-year changes in theory or political activism; instead, it is the response of indi-

9

vidual writers to their perception of social reality and change. Imaginative responses to the conditions that have prompted contemporary feminism have no fixed progression of either theme or technique, and although it seems certain that these novels have constituted a dialogue among many of their authors as well as for their readers, questions of influence are less important than issues of common purpose and technique. The first chapter introduces the narrative strategies of irony and fantasy as common devices used in this dialogue, and proposes a direct relationship between the women's novel of this period and the urgent need to share stories during a period of social upheaval and hope.

The second chapter deals with the problem of finding a voice with which to convey ironies and fantasies—the difficulty that authors and narrators tell or show us they experience in merely finding the words to express with any precision their unique visions. The search for a language is particularly apparent in the work of writers for whom language as well as gender creates initial barriers. Language represents power, and for the essentially powerless person, acquiring and using language is a step toward understanding both self and power. For the narrator in Kingston's *The Woman Warrior* (1976) there are the problems of a second language, secrecy, family and cultural myths. For Celie in *The Color Purple* there is a lack of education and apparently unresponsive correspondents. Even for those to whom the use of language comes more easily—who are educated and at ease in a native tongue—language may be untrustworthy to define experience, or it may be forbidden. In *The Handmaid's Tale* only the ruling class have access to books, biblical injunctions are distorted, and even Scrabble is a clandestine activity.

But even when language is available and allowable, it proves inadequate to the flux of experience, unable to fix with certainty a self that doubts its own reality. Thus stories are told, re-told, revised, inconclusive. French critic Hélène Cixous maintains that the female text is characterized by just such fluidity:

> A feminine textual body is recognized by the fact that it is always endless, without ending: there's no closure, it doesn't stop. . . . [It is] the

manner of beginning . . . that marks a feminine writing. A feminine text starts on all sides, all at once, starts twenty times, thirty times, over.[8]

The concept of "starting over," which characterizes the lives of many of the narrators and characters in contemporary fiction by women, is represented in the multiple narrative perspectives that so many of these writers use. Aware that creating a self is an act of fantasy, the ironic narrator observes, as does Jane Gray in *The Waterfall*, her own creation and realizes that it is false, incomplete. The third chapter therefore explores the use of the multiple consciousness in the work of Drabble, Weldon, Atwood, and others, emphasizing ways in which fantasy and irony interrelate to underscore the uncertainty of change.

The fourth section of the study deals with fantasy in the form of the dreams and imaginings of characters. Whether awake or sleeping—or on the edge of madness—characters in these fictions dream of alternate realities. In some cases, such as Atwood's *Surfacing* (1972) and Weldon's *Words of Advice* (1977), the central characters must find or invent a past that will allow them to make sense of the present. Atwood's narrator in *Surfacing* must emerge or "surface" from two sets of fantasies before she can live as a fully adult woman: one set of fantasies involves her parents, and the other is composed of the identity as wife and mother that she has created for herself from an affair and an abortion. In Weldon's novel, Gemma reinvents her past as a fairy tale in which she is the princess rather than the beggar-girl. The dream of the "woman warrior" in Kingston's novel allows her narrator to imagine herself as a strong Chinese woman instead of the silent schoolgirl who feels herself to be on the fringes of both American and Chinese culture. The central irony of the novel is that the narrator is empowered by stories of strong women told to her by her now timid, tradition-bound mother; one of the "ghosts" of Kingston's subtitle is that of her mother as a young woman in China, working as a midwife with courage and independence. Erica Jong's *Fear of Flying* (1973), and her more recent novel *Serenissima* (1987), concern dreaming as aspiration rather than as revision or reconstruction. Isadora Wing envisions a life in which women's sexuality is a positive force rather than the means to emotional enslavement to men. The central character in *Serenissima* participates in a dream/fantasy in which she travels back in time to meet William Shakespeare, for whose *Merchant of Venice* she has come to Venice to play a role. Ironically, she ends up playing a role in Shakespeare's own life, and by doing so is able to come to terms with both her aging and her creativity.

By featuring time travel, in the manner of Virginia Woolf's *Orlando, Serenissima* approaches the genre of speculative fiction. Works having elements more clearly within that tradition, in which the fantasy is that created by the author rather than by the character, are considered in the fifth chapter of this study. Atwood's *Handmaid's Tale,* Lessing's *Four-Gated City* and *Memoirs of a Survivor* (1974), and Russ's *Female Man* (1975) all present visions of alternate worlds that examine the multiple ironies of contemporary society. The dystopian elements of all of these novels mark their distance from the innocent optimism of Gilman's *Herland* and Edward Bellamy's earlier *Equality.* Although they are feminist visions, they describe worlds in which feminist principles of dignity, nurturance, and autonomy are negated by anarchic or repressive societies. In Marge Piercy's *Woman on the Edge of Time* (1976), the dystopia of contemporary society, epitomized by the mental institutions in which Consuelo is repeatedly confined, is contrasted to the world of the year 2137, which has many of the benign, communal features of Gilman's Herland. But in an attempt to contact Luciente, her link with this future world, Connie stumbles upon another, Orwellian future that she realizes is also a possible outcome of current trends. These speculative fictions, not surprisingly, focus on issues of particular concern to feminists. In *The Handmaid's Tale,* as in the alternate future that Connie encounters in *Woman on the Edge of Time,* women are completely controlled by men, and are arranged in a hierarchy of value in which even the most privileged have their activities severely limited. In *Memoirs of a Survivor,* even as the culture is giving way to anarchy and barbarism, the narrator is concerned about the fact that traditional gender roles remain intact. The authors use fantasy as a means of exaggerating the ironies, the absurdities, of contemporary sexism.

# Introduction

Lessing's narrator in *Memoirs of a Survivor* notes at one point that "if you have nothing, you are free to choose among dreams and fantasies."[9] On one level, this statement points to an irony in human experience: the less one has, the more one is free to dream, unbounded by determining privilege, much as a child is free to imagine any conceivable future. But the statement also points to the source of certain narrative choices that contemporary women novelists have made. One of the effects of the women's movement has been, paradoxically, to convince women of their own power-lessness while at the same time giving them the courage to try to change that condition. Two of the possible responses to power-lessness are dreaming, which allows temporary transcendence, and adopting the superior stance of irony, which points to absur-dity and its sources. The use of irony and fantasy in the contempo-rary novel by women testifies to the writers' convictions about the necessity of change, not only in the tone and form of the novel itself, but also in women's lives.

# CHAPTER ONE

# Narrative and Transition

As a writer, I feel that the very source of my inspiration lies in my never forgetting how much I have in common with other women, how many ways in which we are all—successful or not—similarly shackled. I do not write about superwomen who have transcended all conflict; I write about women who are torn, as most of us are torn, between the past and the future, between our mothers' frustrations and the extravagant hopes we have for our daughters. I do not know what a woman would write about if all her characters were superwomen, cleansed of conflict. Conflict is the soul of literature.[1]

These comments by Erica Jong, published in 1980, identify several crucial elements of the contemporary novel by women writers. It is true, as Jong says, that all literature requires conflict, but the particular conflicts, for women, of the period between the mid-1960s and the mid-1980s arose from dramatic alterations in their roles, their relationships, and their involvement in political activity on a scale unprecedented in Western culture. The women's movement aroused anger, raised hopes, and disrupted traditional life patterns in ways that quickly found expression in women's poetry and prose. Jong also refers to the uncertainty

14

of women poised between past and future, between mothers and daughters, frustration and hope. This sense of transition is reflected in the titles of Jong's own Isadora Wing trilogy—*Fear of Flying* (1973), *How to save your own life* (1977), and *Parachutes and Kisses* (1984)—as well in the titles and substance of dozens of novels by women published during the same period. Finally, and most significantly, Jong speaks of the bond she feels with other women, all "similarly shackled" by sexist mythologies—a sharing of experience that provides her with both solidarity and inspiration. In contrast to her college years (she graduated from Barnard in 1963, the year Betty Friedan published *The Feminine Mystique*), when she was told that women could not be writers, the events of the 1960s and 1970s created a climate in which women wrote copiously, using the novel in particular to speak to each other of their anger and their fear and their triumphs, and at the same time bending narrative structures and strategies to their own purposes.

As feminist literary criticism has made abundantly clear, women have not only written and published novels for several centuries, they have been some of the most innovative and imaginative practitioners of the form. Jane Austen, Edith Wharton, Virginia Woolf, Kate Chopin, and many other writers are beginning finally to be viewed not merely as anomalies or accidents but as major figures in the tradition of the novel in English. Yet not until the 1970s and 1980s can it be said that the female novelist—in England, Canada, and the United States—claimed significant contemporary attention, as opposed to posthumous re-evaluation. Many of the writers commonly agreed to be "major"—such as Doris Lessing, Margaret Atwood, and Margaret Drabble—are women, and, increasingly, they are women of color: Alice Walker, Toni Morrison, Maxine Hong Kingston. That they are being regarded with such seriousness owes much to the development of feminist criticism, which in turn grew out of the women's movement itself—a movement that, as many of these writers have testified, provided them with the courage and motivation first to be writers, and then to break out of traditional patriarchal forms and tell the stories of women in their own voices.

15

The relation between art and reality has been debated for centuries, but that relation has taken on new resonances since the 1970s, when feminist critics began to posit that women as writers and readers participate in the creative process more directly than do men. Rachel Brownstein, in *Becoming a Heroine*, argues that young women in particular discover in fictional heroines the possibilities—and more importantly the limitations—of their own lives. Female readers, Brownstein says, have relied on fiction for "structures they use to organize and interpret their feelings and prospects":

> Girls have rushed right from novels, headlong and hopeful, into what they took to be happy endings: the advice they have given their friends, their gossip about their enemies, their suspicions and interpretations of the actions of others, and their notions about themselves have run along lines derived from fiction. Women who read have been inclined since the eighteenth century to understand one another, and men, and themselves, as characters in novels.[2]

Brownstein refers primarily to the traditional novel, written by both men and women, which features the "marriage plot": "finding validation of one's uniqueness and importance by being singled out among all other women by a man" (xv). It is failure in the marriage plot that makes Edith Wharton's Lily Bart a tragic figure, and it is deviation from that plot that dooms Kate Chopin's Edna Pontellier; both *The House of Mirth* and *The Awakening* can be read as cautionary tales.

Contemporary women novelists, aware of the effect of fictions (both literary and cultural) on themselves and their readers, also write cautionary tales, but they subvert the marriage plot. Their characters leave marriages or refuse them altogether; they have affairs and do not drown themselves or turn on the gas; they seek identity in work, their friends, and themselves rather than primarily in men. Margaret Drabble's Jane Gray, in *The Waterfall*, is conscious of both the inevitability of her emotions and her freedom to write the ending of her own story: "There isn't any conclusion. A death would have been the answer, but nobody died. Perhaps I should have killed James [her lover] in the car, and that would

16

have made a neat, a possible ending. A feminine ending?"[3] For James to die—better, for both of them to die—would be to echo or recapitulate the plots of earlier novels by women, such as *The Mill on the Floss,* and thus to submit to the moralism of the marriage plot, in which women were punished for infidelity by the loss of lover or life. But Jane Gray lives in an era of choice, and therefore can choose to avoid the "feminine ending."

By thinking of herself as a character in a novel, Jane Gray, like many other characters in the contemporary novel by women, exemplifies Brownstein's thesis. She is aware of the power of the traditional plot, and moves tentatively beyond it, testing the ways in which life may be plotted outside of traditional fiction, seeking, as Heilbrun says, to "write her own life." Both Beth and Miriam, central characters in Marge Piercy's *Small Changes* (1973), grow up depending on stories to tell them what is possible for their lives. Beth reads indiscriminately, out of a vague sense of dissatisfaction. She reads Frank Yerby and Galsworthy, Huxley and Iris Murdoch: "On such books she formed her notions of what was out there, past Syracuse."[4] Miriam reads for the same reason—"She was never as happy as when she saw a new movie or read a book or saw a story on television that she recognized as usable: a hero, a situation, a motif she could borrow"—but she is conscious that these stories have better roles for men than for women:

> Most plots consisted of a hero going through adventures. Once in a while there was a heroine instead, but her adventures then were men she met and got involved with. Everybody said it was bad for a woman to have affairs with a series of men. Therefore women were supposed to be dull and good. Miriam decided that she would rather be bad and exciting, but she was not sure she would ever get the chance. (97)

Both Beth and Miriam have the chance to be "bad" in Piercy's novel by becoming involved with the 1960s counterculture, including the embryonic women's movement.

Margaret Drabble has written that the novel is the ideal place for women to deal with the issues raised by the women's movement, and she echoes Brownstein when she says that "many people read novels to find patterns or images for a possible future—to know how to behave, what to hope to be like." But Drabble, like Jong, emphasizes the uncertainty of women in a period of transition:

> We do not want to resemble the women of the past, but what is our future? This is precisely the question that many novels written by women are trying to answer: some in comic terms, some in tragic, some in speculative. We live in an unchartered world, as far as manners and morals are concerned, we are having to make up our own morality as we go. . . . There is no point in sneering at women writers for writing of problems of sexual behavior, of maternity, of gynaecology—those who feel the need to do it are actively engaged in creating a new pattern, a new blueprint. This area of personal relationships verges constantly on the political: it is not a narrow backwater of introversion, it is the main current which is changing the daily quality of our lives.[5]

By emphasizing that the contemporary novel by women fuses the personal and the political, Drabble evokes a central rallying cry of the early years of the women's movement: that the personal lives of women *are* political issues.

Like consciousness-raising groups, a central goal of which was to help women see the connection between the personal and the political, the contemporary novel by women has become a forum for issues of deep relevance to women's lives. This is not to suggest that women writers have abandoned art for politics, or that the novel has become merely a soapbox,[6] but rather that for the lay reader (as opposed to the scholar or critic), the most crucial aspect of the novel is on the level of characterization and plot: what kind of person is the central character? What choices does she have/make? What are the consequences of those choices? As novelist Nora Johnson wrote in an essay in the 20 March 1988 *New York Times Book Review*, "my response to this feminist fiction was primal and only half-critical; I listened for cries that matched mine, novelty and hope (however illusory) in the dark night."[7] The novelists themselves have often written with a sense of mission that corresponds to this "primal response." Fay Weldon, for example, began writing her witty, irreverent fictions before there was a recognized women's movement in England, and only later

18

saw that her themes "could actually be organized into an ideology, a movement":

> And yet, you see, the sources of my indignation are for me the same as they are for other women in the Women's Movement who are better fitted to analyse and to see how things can be changed.
>
> I want to lead people to consider and explore ideas that aren't very popular, which many people would rather not think about. But if anybody's to get anywhere, they had better think about it. One *can* transcend one's body: whether it's good to do so is another matter.[8]

Weldon's insistence on exposing painful issues that have caused her "indignation" can be said to characterize the contemporary novel by women, as women embody in fiction the personal and political issues that have affected their lives as well as those of their characters.[9]

It is important to keep in mind, of course, that the embodiment of issues specifically relevant to women's lives in fiction written by women is not a new phenomenon. Jane Austen in the eighteenth century, George Eliot, "Fanny Fern," and Sarah Orne Jewett in the nineteenth, and many others detailed the myriad complexities of female experience in fiction that has had particular resonance for female readers. Indeed, as Annette Kolodny has pointed out, women writers have commonly written within the context of other women's texts. Although Kolodny finds merit in assertions such as those of Harold Bloom that readers and writers alike perceive the meaning of a specific text in light of their experience with other texts, so that, in Bloom's terms, "meaning is always wandering around between texts," she argues convincingly that these texts have been different for women than for men. Kolodny points to the fact that from the 1850s on in American literature, women writers "perceived themselves as excluded from the dominant literary tradition and as writing for an audience of readers similarly excluded."[10] Further, Kolodny extends Brownstein's cultural analysis of the effect of reading on women into the realm of reader-response criticism when she asserts that "women taught one another how to read and write about and out of their own unique (and sometimes isolated) contexts" (465). What distinguishes the women's novel of the contemporary period from earlier fictions, however, is its focus on the inevitability of change and its representation of the variety of women's socio-economic, ethnic, and sexual orientations and experiences.

Logically enough, in fiction that constitutes at least in part a sharing of values and experience during turbulent times, the line between fiction and autobiography has tended to blur. Lily Bart and Edna Pontellier live lives removed from their creators' personal experience, and are distanced from them also by the use of a third-person narrative. But the frequent use of first-person narration in the contemporary novel provides an impression of autobiographical narrative even when this is not actually the case. In addition, as Joanna Frye points out in *Living Stories, Telling Lives,* the use of a female "I" in control of the novel is a way of escaping from the cultural expectations of the marriage plot: "By virtue of speaking as a woman, any female narrator-protagonist evokes some awareness of the disjunction between internal and external definitions and some recognition of her agency in self-narration. To speak directly in a personal voice is to deny the exclusive right of male author-ity implicit in a public voice and to escape the expression of dominant ideologies upon which an omniscient narrator depends."[11] The first-person perspective of Drabble's Jane Gray, Gail Godwin's Violet Clay, Atwood's Offred, and other narrators draws the reader into the realm of the personal, the "real," and even when the author selects a more objective narrative perspective, a sense of intimate confession nonetheless permeates these novels.

Elizabeth Janeway, writing of women's literature since 1945, finds the blurred distinction between fiction and autobiography the most compelling innovation of the period, and she, like many others, ties this narrative tendency to changes in ideology: "The need for women to exchange information about their lives and thus to arrive at shared judgments and conclusions gives such reportage a particular interest in this period of growing awareness."[12] Weldon's 1977 novel *Words of Advice* provides an ironic gloss on such a sharing. Gemma, who was once a naive, impressionable secretary, tells the story of her life to Elsa, who seems to be drifting romantically through life as Gemma once did. "If only," Gemma says plaintively, "we women could learn from each other."[13]

Another reason for the frequent use of pseudo-autobiography is to again underscore the link between the personal and the political. As Judi Roller puts it in *The Politics of the Feminist Novel*, "the use of autobiography seems to mirror the tension which exists in these novels between individualism and modern mass collectivism and between public and private experience."[14] The narrators or characters in these novels frequently attempt to define themselves as women against a backdrop of political upheaval. Martha Quest Hesse, in Lessing's *The Four-Gated City*, seeks a direction for her life in the midst of post-World War II London, and Atwood's Offred struggles to find meaning in the post-apocalypse Republic of Gilead. Both women are at odds with the political and social structures that surround them, and self-definition is in part a direct response to cultural chaos. To write, or appear to write, of direct personal experience is to emphasize isolation while at the same time seeking connection.

For minority women, the problems of selfhood and isolation have been compounded by cultural as well as gender barriers. The women's movement, despite its close ties with the civil rights movement of the 1960s, has been largely a white, middle-class movement. Women of this group could identify closely with the experiences of central characters in works by Drabble, Atwood, or Godwin; but black, Chicana, and Chinese-American women have commonly lacked the advantages of race and class that would make such identification possible. It is no accident, then, that a central issue in the apparently autobiographical narratives of minority women is the struggle to find a voice with which to communicate. Maxine Hong Kingston's *Woman Warrior* opens with the narrator's mother warning her, "You must not tell anyone what I am about to tell you," thus adding the burden of family secrets to the language barrier of the immigrant family.[15] Similarly, Celie, in Walker's *The Color Purple*, writes, haltingly at first, to a God who fails to answer and a sister whose answers are hidden from her. The need for fantasy in these works—the desire to fash-

21

ion an alternative space in which to speak as one's self—is fed by the silencing of racial and cultural oppression.

There would seem to be a paradoxical relationship between the autobiographical mode, with its grounding in the realistic detail of everyday life, and fantasy, and between the grim struggle to achieve selfhood and the superior, often humorous stance of the ironist. Yet the detailing of uncomfortable experience leads easily to the imagining of an alternative way of life, whether better, such as being a warrior-heroine, or far worse, as in the ritualized subjugation of *The Handmaid's Tale*. Further, the very perception that alternate worlds can exist, if only in the imagination, contributes to the double vision implicit in irony. Elizabeth Janeway speaks in part to the first of these issues when she notes that "the drive to create a new world of symbols does not separate itself from dailyness":

> Instead, it works within everyday experience, looking there for clues to a new interpretive paradigm that is already taking shape. Its first manifestation may be felt merely as disturbances in orthodox theory; but as they increase, they point to the existence of an alternative world view that will in time stand forth in its own essential identity.[16]

Just as fantasy may be a way of constructing an unreal world from the specifics of the real, so irony is a way of negating the truth or validity of a received tradition and pointing to its incongruity or absurdity. Both devices, as used by the contemporary woman novelist, allow transcendence of immediate experience even as the main characters tell their lives to the reader.

To stress the uses of irony and fantasy in contemporary fiction by women is not, of course, to argue that these narrative strategies are the sole province of the woman writer. Indeed, both have been staples of the novel since its earliest days as a form, and their power to suggest transcendence of immediate reality has in fact made them natural tools of members of the dominant culture, for whom the superior stance of the ironist and the dreams of the fantasist have come more naturally than they have to members of oppressed groups. For all that we speak of the novel as an essentially realistic mode, authors as disparate as Hawthorne, Melville, and

22

Joyce have written elaborate fantasies, a tendency that has continued in the work of John Barth and Lawrence Durrell; and irony of different kinds permeates the fiction of Twain, James, and many others. Nor can it be claimed that irony and fantasy have only in recent years been employed by women writers; the examples of Jane Austen and Charlotte Perkins Gilman would alone belie such an assertion.

What is striking, however, is the widespread appropriation of these devices by contemporary women writers in fiction that overtly explores the conditions of women's lives, so that traditional narrative techniques become natural and effective modes of expressing the flux and uncertainty of those who envision a new but indefinite social order. What these novels, taken together, convey most clearly is a gender-specific resistance to the status quo of oppression, and within this thematic scheme, fantasy—even when embodied in madness—explores alternative ways of being, while irony questions the fixity of conventional reality. Lilian Furst, in *Fictions of Romantic Irony,* insists on the relativity conveyed by irony. Distinguishing between irony and satire, she asserts that the latter is grounded in a fixed moral vision, whereas irony is characterized by ambivalence:

> The less immediately abrasive art of irony may ultimately be the more disturbing because its upshot is a series of open ends and contradictions. It is an inquiring mode that exploits discrepancies, challenges assumptions and reflects equivocations, but that does not presume to hold out answers.[17]

Neither irony nor fantasy is governed by rules of right and wrong, truth and falsity, and the combined use of them in contemporary women's fiction testifies to a shared consciousness of necessary though unsettling change in women's relation to cultural expectations.

Irony, as the term is used in this study, is intended with its full range of possibilities, including verbal irony, ironies of circumstance, and double narrative perspectives that challenge the immutability of perceived reality. Drabble's *The Waterfall* exemplifies all three types of irony. When Jane Gray comments, "But love is nothing new. Even women have suffered from it, in history," the irony of the word "even" is both apparent to the reader, who may mentally substitute the word "especially," and a comment upon the narrator's obsession with her lover, James, an obsession that can send her into a "total panic" about the extent of her "subjugation" (161). This comment is made by the first-person narrator who, more detached than her self in the third-person narration, assesses that other self, challenging her own and the reader's sense of reality, beginning one chapter by saying of her narrative, "Lies, lies, it's all lies. A pack of lies. I've even told lies of fact, which I had meant not to do" (89). Drabble's use of irony thus allows her to present and challenge reality simultaneously.

D. C. Muecke, in *Irony*, suggests that irony may have a subversive and potentially revolutionary function when he stresses its rarity as a mode of thought: "The ordinary business of the world in which most of us are engaged most of the time could not be carried on in a spirit of irony. . . . [A] sense of irony depends for its material upon a lack of a sense of irony in others, much as scepticism depends upon credulity."[18] The ironist, such as Drabble's first-person narrator, thus stands apart from both herself and most of her culture; irony becomes a method of questioning and of at least an imaginative escape. Fay Weldon's Chloe, in *Female Friends* (1974), uses irony to question a number of the myths that women are raised to believe, from principles of female biology to the existence of God. A central myth is the efficacy of the marriage plot; taught to believe in "happily ever after," Chloe comments wryly, "I remember love's enchantments. Of course I do. . . . the whole self trembles again in the memory of that elation, which so transfigured our poor obsessed bodies, our poor possessed minds. It did us no good."[19] The mere knowledge that love has been a trap does not free Chloe entirely from it, but it constitutes a step toward such freedom because it engages the intellect rather than the emotions.

Situational irony has particular relevance to detachment. As Muecke puts it, "the ironic observer is in a special relationship to what he observes; he is detached from what he observes and this ironic spectacle has . . . an aesthetic quality which, so to speak, objectifies it" (63–64). Thus Chloe presents to the reader of *Female Friends* the ironic spectacle of her mother being in love with her employer for years without reciprocation, so that "her life . . . has settled into a tolerable pattern of exploitation and excitement united" (107). Thus objectified, her life becomes a cautionary tale to the reader as well as to Chloe, who unfortunately cannot heed its message in her own life. A more comically presented ironic situation opens Jong's *Fear of Flying*. Isadora, on her way with her husband to an international meeting of psychiatrists, objectifies her situation:

> There were 117 psychoanalysts on the Pan Am flight to Vienna and I'd been treated by at least six of them. And married a seventh. God knows it was a tribute either to the shrinks' ineptitude or my own glorious unanalyzability that I was now, if anything, more scared of flying than when I began my analytic adventures some thirteen years earlier.[20]

Jong uses irony here not only to challenge the authority of psychiatry, but also to suggest that autonomy arises from the self rather than being conferred by an outside agency—especially an agency derived from patriarchal systems of thought. Isadora's "parachute" in the final novel of Jong's trilogy is her own self-esteem.

Just as women were re-evaluating their lives during the years of the women's movement, so irony as a linguistic device forces a re-evaluation of the meaning of a text. Classically, verbal irony has been viewed as a kind of negation in which the reader participates. That is, the writer makes a statement that the reader perceives, because of context or tone, to be untrue, and the reader then substitutes his or her own version of the statement the author intended. This is the process that Wayne Booth explains in *A Rhetoric of Irony*. Thus when Jong refers to her "glorious unanalyzability," the reader is unwilling to take this at face value and moves back to the "shrinks' ineptitude" of the preceding phrase. Booth maintains that irony gains force from the fact that the reader, having been compelled to replace one meaning with another, becomes committed to that meaning because it is his or her own: "I make the new position mine with all the force that is conferred by my sense of having judged independently."[21]

However, Bertrice Bartlett has suggested a different way of reading irony that is more relevant to the transitional phase that the contemporary women's novel describes. Rather than reject or negate the author's initial statement, Bartlett says, we are invited to observe the contrast between that statement and the one we perceive to be "true": "If we say she has the grace of a swan about someone who has just stumbled and fallen downstairs, we invite contrast between her behavior and the ideal of gracefulness (perhaps especially in women)."[22] The contrast that the reader perceives when rejecting Jong's phrase "my own glorious unanalyzability" points to a shfit in the locus of responsibility for her continued fear. The traditional thinking of the patriarchal culture would blame the woman for failing to overcome her fear, whereas Jong's irony forces us to see that the fault may be that of an inept male authority instead. The irony is compounded by the word "glorious," which seems to erect a self-congratulatory barrier between Isadora and the process of psychoanalysis.

By involving the reader in the construction of meaning, irony reinforces the bond between writer and reader that these novels seek to create. Bartlett notes that irony "redirect[s] the focus of discourse from new information about the world to a kind of shared game between speaker and listener: I point the contrast, you draw the evaluative inference" (5). Fay Weldon, like other authors, frequently makes this process overt by combining ironic statement with a direct address to the reader. In *Female Friends*, Chloe speaks of the power of children to keep women in emotional bondage, and then admonishes the reader: "Oh my friends, my female friends, how wise you are to have no children or to throw them off. . . . Give birth, and you give others the power to destroy you." The irony deepens when she continues, "And never have parents, either" (204). Caught between children and parents, women in traditional roles may become the victims of both, and Weldon's irony invites the reader to observe the contrast between these emotional ties and their complete (and impossible)

26

absence, suggesting that since generations are inevitable, the only solution is the avoidance of their emotional traps. A few sentences later, Weldon interjects one of several ironic parodies of Biblical language: "Blessed are the orphans, and the barren of body and mind" (205). Such statements, which anticipate a similar use of Biblical language in Atwood's *Handmaid's Tale,* attack the role of Christianity in perpetuating patriarchal structures and attitudes.

It is precisely the role of the ironist to subvert such forms of authority. The term "irony" originates in the Greek *eiron,* whom Aristotle defined as the "mock-modest man"—the person who pretends to be or to know less than he actually is or does. The *eiron* is the child who dares in feigned innocence to point out that the Emperor has no clothes; it is Mark Twain using the mask of Huck Finn deciding to go to hell for helping a slave escape from bondage. Irony is a mask that the reader is invited to see *as* a mask in order to view simultaneously the reality underneath it. It becomes the means of complicity between writer and reader. Offred, in *The Handmaid's Tale,* delivers flat statements that invite us to look beyond them for complexity. When she says of her narrative "this is a reconstruction," she not only echoes Drabble's Jane Gray struggling for a conclusion to her story; she also challenges us to consider what she really means—for surely *all* narratives are reconstructions.

By pointing out that irony is the exceptional rather than the normal mode by which we conduct our lives, Muecke suggests that both the use and the perception of irony require exceptional abilities; and in fact the ironist, while pretending innocence, actually adopts a stance of superiority to his or her immediate reality, holding two possible truths in balance at the same time. The relativity implicit in irony—the ability to stand apart from the authority of conventional values and systems—requires an unsentimental intelligence and a courageous wit, qualities not easily compatible with the traditional expectations of women. It is for this reason that the frequent use of irony in the contemporary novel by women is particularly significant: it represents a challenge to traditional values, recognition that the structures that cause and perpetuate women's oppression are arbitrary and therefore subject to change. The ironic stance, which insists upon the contrast between two alternative realities, forces a revision of the self that is objectified in the double narrative employed in so many of these novels.

The fact that irony challenges our notions of reality means that it may be misunderstood. This is what Umberto Eco calls "the quality (the risk) of irony. There is always someone who takes ironic discourse seriously."[23] By inviting the reader to mistrust what is said, the ironic writer causes us to question all reality. Offred calls her story a "reconstruction," and the "Historical Notes" that conclude *The Handmaid's Tale* give the term renewed force by revealing that the story has been reconstructed from cassette tapes by scholars. When Gemma, in Weldon's *Words of Advice*, tells her friend Alice that she is telling Elsa the story of her days as a secretary, Alice responds, "Which version?" Gemma invites Alice to "listen and you'll find out" (130). Jane Gray, in *The Waterfall*, presents side-by-side versions of the story of her relationship with James. The risk that the authors of these novels take is that readers may be impatient at not knowing the "true" story; but the reward is that they present the possibility of change and alternative realities.

Nancy K. Miller has written that "to read women's literature is to see and hear repeatedly a chafing against the 'unsatisfactory reality' contained in the maxim . . . that grants men the world and women love."[24] One major form in which this "chafing" manifests itself is fantasy, as Miller emphasizes. Countering Freud, who posited that whereas men's fantasies chiefly embody "ambitious wishes," women's fantasies are primarily erotic, Miller writes:

> Women writers . . . are writers . . . for whom the "ambitious wish" . . . manifests itself as fantasy within another economy. In this economy, egoistic desires would assert themselves paratactically alongside erotic ones. The repressed content, I think, would be, not erotic impulses, but an impulse to power: a fantasy of power that would revise the social grammar in which women are never defined as subjects; a fantasy of power that disdains a sexual exchange in which women can participate only as objects of circulation. (41)

28

Fantasy—in the forms of dreams and daydreams, madness and utopian vision—is a way of fashioning an alternative reality, of subverting the social order of the marriage plot and imagining power outside of it. The contemporary women's novel employs fantasy in a number of ways to accomplish this subversion while at the same time maintaining an atmosphere of reality that speaks to women's actual lives.

Fantasy and irony, as narrative devices, have several elements in common. Both point to a contrast between different truths or realities, irony by causing a revision of ostensible statements or events, and fantasy by imagining alternative patterns or scripts by which life may be conducted. Also, although both irony and fantasy are ancient literary devices, the combination of the two is closely related to some definitions of the post-modern spirit or temperament. Umberto Eco suggests this in "Postmodernism, Irony, the Enjoyable" when he speaks of the "lost innocence" of postmodernism. He imagines the "postmodern attitude" as that of a man who cannot say to a woman "I love you madly," because "he knows that she knows (and that she knows that he knows) that these words have already been written by Barbara Cartland." The words he wishes to say have been preempted by romantic fantasies of which both people are aware, and the solution, Eco says, is to incorporate the fantasy into the utterance by saying, "As Barbara Cartland would put it, I love you madly." And "both will consciously and with pleasure play the game of irony" (67–68). As a primarily intellectual mode, irony works with the more emotional, intuitive mode of fantasy to acknowledge contrast and change.

Indeed, the writer who uses irony is necessarily involved in some type of imaginative leap that is akin to—even when it does not embody—fantasy. A. E. Dyson, pointing to the complexity of most literary irony, notes that the ironist's real meaning "may exist somewhere between the literal meaning and its logical opposite, in a no-man's-land where we feel our way very delicately and sensitively, among many puzzling nuances of mood and tone."[25] It is such a "no-man's-land" that the reader must traverse, for example, in *The Color Purple*, in which a semi-literate black woman

29

and her missionary sister recreate the epistolary novel in a series of letters that for the most part do not reach each other, so that communication between the two is conjured from their—and the reader's—fervent desire for reconciliation. In more overtly speculative fictions, such as *The Handmaid's Tale*, fantasy is part of the design of irony. As Dyson says about other dystopian novels, such as *Brave New World* and *1984*, "a fantasy world is constructed to carry ironic implications beyond purely verbal manipulation, into the plot and structure of the whole" (xiii). Thus in Atwood's novel the multiple ironies of a society based on a fundamentalist interpretation of Christian doctrine are demonstrated in the imaginative creation of that society.

Whereas many theories of literary fantasy emphasize its negation of actuality and possibility,[26] Rosemary Jackson has proposed that fantasy is heavily dependent upon a social context:

> Fantasy characteristically attempts to compensate for a lack resulting from cultural constraints: it is a literature of desire, which seeks that which is perceived as absence and loss. . . . The fantastic traces the unsaid and the unseen of culture: that which has been silenced, made invisible, covered over and made "absent."[27]

Jackson is speaking here of works of literature that are wholly fantasies rather than those of which fantasy is an element or strategy, but her remarks about the role of fantasy in revealing the "silenced" and "invisible" parts of culture have particular relevance to women's literature. It is through such imagining that women have attempted to break their silence and to become visible, and the contemporary women's novel is both a record of that imagining and a space in which women writers have experimented with narrative structures and devices that embody the relationship between fantasy and selfhood.

Fantasy, like irony, is used in this study in its broadest possible sense. All fiction is in some sense a fantasy, in that it is an imaginative construction, but the pervasive use of fantasy as a plot element, a narrative strategy, or a controlling form in the recent novel by women suggests an overwhelming need for imaginative release from objective reality. On the simplest level, fantasy may be used

30

as a part of the realistic narrative context. In Godwin's *Violet Clay*, for example, the central character is an aspiring artist who earns her living by designing covers for popular gothic romances—themselves fantasies to provide fleeting glamor and excitement to women's lives. But Violet Clay is herself living a fantasy by waiting for some magic to transform her into a "real" artist, a fact that she recognizes in retrospect: "On the morning on which I invite you to enter my life, I was an illustrator, not an artist. I was still spending my skills on other people's visions."[28] The heroines who flee from castles in the cover illustrations that Violet paints have more in common with her than she likes to think; like them, she cannot envision what comes after "happily ever after"; until her uncle's suicide confronts her with his failure and the possibility of her own, she resists the risks she must take in order to prove her gift. Even when Violet takes the first step toward independence by leaving her husband to go to New York, she realizes that the marriage plot offers a security to which part of her wishes to return, and sees herself with "one foot in the door of the Unknown, the other still holding open its place in the Book of Old Plots" (57).

The need to free oneself from the "Book of Old Plots" informs another use of fantasy in these novels: the re-telling or revision of traditional stories, including fairy tales, literary works, and even history itself. In the final section of *The Four-Gated City*, Francis Coldridge, trying to preserve a record of the destruction of western civilization, comments that history is an often erroneous substitute for human memory:

> The mass of the human race has never had a memory. History, the activities of historians, has always been a sort of substitute memory, an approximation to actual events. In some epochs this false memory has been nearer to events; in others very far—*sometimes by design.*[29]

Francis's concern is that historians may, deliberately or not, distort the truth and thus falsify human experience. Contemporary women writers have a different but related concern, which is that the stories or scripts not only *describe* what is assumed to be women's experience, but also attempt to *prescribe* appropriate roles and responses. By re-telling these stories, women question

31

their authority precisely by showing them to be stories, or fantasies. In Weldon's *Words of Advice,* Gemma begins telling the story of her life to Elsa by describing it as a fairy tale: "Princes, toads, princesses, beggar girls—we all have to place ourselves as best we can" (20). Ironically, Gemma distorts her own history to make it more like a fairy tale than it really was, because in a sense she has married the toad rather than the prince and feels that she must explain why she is a victim; but Elsa realizes that Gemma is trying to manipulate her as she has manipulated her own story, and manages to use this knowledge to escape from her own romantic fantasies.

The most radical re-telling of history is the utopian or dystopian novel: the former posits, as did Charlotte Perkins Gilman's *Herland,* a future that has repudiated many of the values and conventions of the past; the latter extends the worst features of contemporary social reality into a grim design. It is significant as a measure of the failure of the socio-political movements of the 1960s and 1970s that the contemporary women's novel tends to the dystopian mode. The disintegration and anarchy that Lessing describes at the end of *The Four-Gated City* and in *Memoirs of a Survivor* stand at one extreme of this dark vision; at the other extreme is the rigid moralism of the Republic of Gilead in Atwood's *Handmaid's Tale.* Both Lessing and Atwood (like Gilman and Orwell before them) extrapolate from the conditions of their respective cultures—postwar Britain and post-feminist America—to write cautionary tales of crumbling cultures that have abandoned the humane values of a Herland. But Atwood is also re-writing a classic text: Hawthorne's *The Scarlet Letter.* In addition to all of the obvious superficial correspondences, such as the color red, the location in Massachusetts, and the identity between religion and government, Offred's story is in many ways the ironic inversion of Hester's: whereas Hester is punished for adultery, Offred is forced into it, both cultures using the same Bible as authority for their laws. Further, the "Historical Notes" section of *The Handmaid's Tale,* like the "Appendix" to *The Four-Gated City,* makes clear that both books are meant as "reconstructions" of reality. Martha Quest writes without knowing whether there is a recipient of her letter—"Is it you I am writing to, Francis?"—just as Offred has recorded her thoughts on cassette tapes, not knowing whether anyone would hear her story.

Another type of revision of history is the revision of one's personal history. One of the most pervasive devices in the contemporary women's novel is the dual narrative voice that represents a duality of consciousness—the second, usually first-person voice interprets, adjusts, revises the initial story. The effect is to reinforce the fact that we invent our own stories, trying to find a coherent pattern, and such an effort reflects the search for identity that many women experienced between the mid-1960s and the mid-1980s. Jane Gray, in *The Waterfall*, continually revises her own story in an attempt to find a coherent morality and set of motivations:

> I will take it all to pieces, I will resolve it to its parts, and then I will put it together again, I will reconstitute it in a form that I can accept, a fictitious form: adding a little here, abstracting a little there, moving this arm half an inch that way, gently altering the dead angle of the head upon its neck. If I need a morality, I will create one: a new ladder, a new virtue. If I need to understand what I am doing, if I cannot act without my own approbation—and I must act, I have changed, I am no longer capable of inaction—then I will invent a morality that condones me. (53–54)

No longer tied to the marriage plot, Jane must invent her own rules to accord with the necessities of her life, and in the process she also revises the traditional English novel, such as *The Mill on the Floss*, in which the heroine accepts the prevailing morality and dies of it. Godwin's *Violet Clay* also features alternating first- and third-person narratives as Violet tries to understand her own past. She is conscious of being a character in a story, and says at one point, "In someone else's story, the heroine would have embraced her setback, welcomed it as a prod to catapult her out of her slough" (73). But Violet is a character in her own, not someone else's story, and therefore must make sense of what she has actually (in Godwin's fiction) done. Revision and interpretation are also the method in Weldon's *Female Friends*. Late in the novel, Grace announces this as the purpose when she says to the nar-

33

rator, Chloe, "There has to be a kind of truth about one's life, doesn't there?" (269), and in the last chapter Chloe speaks of her desire to make coherent the experiences of the novel's central characters:

> What can we tell you to help you, we three sisters, walking wounded that we are? What can we tell you of living and dying, beginning and ending, patching and throwing away; of the patterns that our lives make, which seem to have some kind of order, if only we could perceive it more clearly. (309)

The division of the self into multiple selves to question and revise reality is common in fantasy fiction. As Jackson points out in *Fantasy: The Literature of Subversion*, "the narrator is no clearer than the protagonist about what is going on, nor about interpretation; the status of what is being seen and recorded as 'real' is constantly in question" (34). By questioning the "real," the novel subverts patriarchal authority as women invent selves that they can accept. Nowhere is the division into selves more compelling than in Joanna Russ's *The Female Man*, a work of speculative fiction embodying both utopian and dystopian visions and inhabited by four facets of a single woman. Russ takes the concept of a woman having more than one "self" several steps further than do Drabble, Weldon, and Godwin by creating four parallel universes, each of which is inhabited by a different aspect of the same female consciousness, and each of which represents a different relation to feminism. The unifying consciousness is that of Janet, who comes from an all-female utopia named Whileaway that is similar in some respects to Gilman's Herland. Through the experiences of all four selves, Russ parodies sexist and misogynist cultures in ways familiar to feminist thinkers, and Janet provides the ultimate challenge to the culturally determined "self" when she rejects the concept of gender difference altogether and declares herself to be a man:

> For years I have been saying *Let me in, Love me, Approve me, Define me, Regulate me, Validate me, Support me.* Now I say *Move over.* If we are all Mankind, it follows to my interested and righteous and rightnow very bright and beady little eyes, that I too am a Man and not at all a Woman.[30]

34

Through such ostensibly outrageous statements, Russ keeps the reader off balance with regard to objective reality, yet the instances of sexism that the protagonists' selves endure are easily recognizable to the contemporary feminist: sexual harassment, job discrimination, assumptions of intellectual and biological inferiority.

The four aspects of one woman in *The Female Man* converse as separate individuals, but they also intuit each other as different parts of the same personality. Similarly, Martha in *The Four-Gated City* is able to hear the thoughts of others—especially Mark's wife Lynda, whose madness she begins to understand almost as though they, too, exist in parallel universes. As Martha and Lynda explore paranormal phenomena, "they used their dreams, their slips of the tongue, their fantasies . . . as maps or signposts for a country which lay just beyond or alongside, or within the landscape they could see and touch" (355). Martha's search for an alternate reality takes the form of voices, dreams, memories, and even madness itself—all forms of fantasy. In Kingston's *The Woman Warrior*, the narrator is empowered by her mother's "talk-story" about the female warrior Fa Mu Lan to recreate imaginatively the experience of the warrior and thus to rise above the anticipated fate of a Chinese woman: "She said I would grow up a wife and a slave, but she taught me the song of the warrior woman, Fa Mu Lan. I would have to grow up a warrior woman." [31] The narrator's search for identity as a Chinese-American woman requires her to enter the myths of her heritage, just as the narrator in Atwood's *Surfacing* must undergo a mythological rebirth in order to come to terms with her past.

The line between dreams and fantasies, on the one hand, and madness on the other may be almost indistinguishable in the contemporary women's novel. What can be termed madness may be temporary and fleeting, such as Violet Clay's pantomime of her uncle's suicide or the *Surfacing* narrator's abandonment of reality during her quest; or it may be a continual, inescapable condition, such as Lynda's recurrent bouts of what she terms "acting silly" in *The Four-Gated City*. At times, an entire culture is presented as being "mad": Atwood's Gilead, for example, and the brutality of racial and sexual oppression in *The Color Purple*. The ultimate evocation of an alternative reality is the overturning of what is conventionally considered rational thought, and madness may itself be "divinest sense" or a stage on the journey to self-realization. In Piercy's *Woman on the Edge of Time*, Consuelo, who is repeatedly committed to mental institutions because of behavior that arises from fear or despair, is able to make contact with Luciente, from the year 2137, and thus to observe a culture that creates a positive space for what our culture terms madness—"getting in touch with the buried self and the inner mind."[32]

Barbara Rigney, in *Madness and Sexual Politics in the Feminist Novel*, points out that a double or divided self is common in the feminist novel because a central theme of these works is the forging of a new identity and the concomitant abandoning of a socially approved identity:

> Each novelist [Brontë, Woolf, Lessing, Atwood] indicates that women in particular suffer from more or less obvious forms of schizophrenia, being constantly torn between male society's prescriptions for female behavior, their own tendencies toward the internalization of these roles, and a nostalgia for some lost, more authentic self.[33]

Even when there is little or no suggestion of actual madness, the divided self appears as a common narrative device—the ironic revision of reality that Weldon, Drabble, and others use to structure their fictions. In either case, the central message is change: the need for social change and the recognition that social change begins with individual change—the personal is political, but the reverse is also true. If—to cite deliberately two vastly different novels—Isadora Wing can overcome her fear of flying, and Alice Walker's Celie can emerge as a woman with dignity and self-esteem, these characters become larger and more significant than their individual triumphs, and serve as mirrors and models for readers who have their own fantasies.

The most widely read novels involving fantasy are the popular romances such as the gothic romances that Violet Clay illustrates in Godwin's novel. But these fantasies are diametrically opposed to the elements of fantasy in the novels considered in this study. The popular romance reinforces and validates the marriage plot rather than proposing alternative realities for women. As Kay Mussell writes in *Fantasy and Reconciliation*, "the romance fantasy

36

is retrogressive; it does not promote genuine change or individual growth. Instead, it works as a conservative force, palliating and ameliorating the effects of chaos and change by portraying traditional modes of being and aspiration as more fulfilling and exciting than they may seem in reality."[34] Rather than challenging the *status quo*, popular romance novels "reduce the need to redefine oneself or to experiment with one's own life" (188). Further, such fiction has no trace of irony. Instead of questioning a received tradition of "truth," as does the ironist, the romance reformulates the fairy tale in which the woman's struggle to "become" is presumed to end when her identity is conferred by the man who selects her. Yet the overwhelming popularity of contemporary romance fiction may in its own way be a response to the women's movement of recent years, as Mussell suggests when she notes that whereas for many women the movement has opened new possibilities, for many others it poses a threat, "for it promises to call into question the very basis of decisions made years ago that are difficult to revoke" (xv).

The pervasive use of irony and fantasy as narrative devices in the contemporary novel by women, on the other hand, does call into question assumptions about identity, gender, relationships, and women's potential and achievements. Both devices propose alternatives—irony by pointing to a contrast between conventional surface reality and the possibility of another set of truths, and fantasy by promoting an imaginative recreation of experience. Both devices also suggest and reflect change in fundamental aspects of women's lives during a turbulent period of social and political upheaval. That this change has not been as broad or deep as feminists would want is a cultural truism in the late 1980s, but the fictions that women have written should also have prepared us for this fact. The barriers to women's power and autonomy that the authors portray—barriers that irony and fantasy attempt to surmount or negate—are sufficiently strong and entrenched that, as *The Handmaid's Tale* frighteningly reminds us, they are capable of reversing the trends that the women's movement has set in motion. Yet successive generations of readers will find in these novels women who rebel against oppression in a new kind of cautionary tale.

37

# CHAPTER TWO

# Language, Irony, and Fantasy

In Marge Piercy's *Small Changes,* Beth, one of the two central characters, dissolves in angry tears after an argument with Phil: "Oh, I wish I was better with words!" Beth views words as weapons in the battle for selfhood—a battle in which she, as a woman, is disadvantaged. She has difficulty arguing because "it's crossing taboos. You know, asserting myself, contradicting somebody. . . . I only want to use words as weapons because I'm tired of being beaten with them. Tired of being pushed around because I don't know how to push back."[1] In the Republic of Gilead in *The Handmaid's Tale,* language is all but forbidden because the ruling class recognizes the power of words as weapons that can free people from bondage. Piercy's 1973 novel is set in the 1960s, the turbulent decade in which Offred's mother was an active feminist; Atwood's 1986 novel is set in the late twentieth century after a fundamentalist revolution has repressed not just the women's movement but all expression of freedom and equality. In different ways these two novels suggest the centrality of language to the process of self-realization and the struggle for equality. In fact language—the ability to speak, to tell one's own story—is at the heart of the contemporary novel by women.

Both irony and fantasy, as narrative devices, are interdependent with language in specific, complex ways. Whereas on the simplest level irony is a verbal construction—the reader is invited to question the surface validity of a statement that an author or a character makes—deeper irony, of circumstance or attitude, requires that the author create a context in which ambiguity is tolerable, a linguistic fabric that signals a stance from which she (or he) will approach whatever reality is being depicted. When Atwood opens *The Handmaid's Tale* with the line, "We slept in what had once been the gymnasium," she plunges the reader at once into a world of uncertainty in which everything—including language—will be, as Offred says repeatedly, a "reconstruction": the essential method of irony.

Fantasy is tied to language in several ways, which I will suggest here and explore in more detail later. When authors or narrators in the contemporary women's novel revise the mythologies of their lives, they are in a very direct way addressing the language of those mythologies. When, for example, Gemma, in *Words of Advice*, says of the fairy tale that is her life story, "Princes, toads, princesses, beggar girls—we all have to place ourselves as best we can," she is commenting on the use of language to dichotomize people into the favored and the unfavored.[2] Alternatively, words and stories may free a woman to engage in fantasy that helps to empower her. In *The Woman Warrior*, the story the narrator's mother tells her of Fa Mu Lan allows her to dream of being a woman warrior rather than a wife or a slave. Fantasy may even be a way of avoiding the language of dominant discourse. Lesje, in Atwood's *Life Before Man* (1979), has fantasies in which she is "wandering in prehistory," able to "violate whatever official version of paleontological reality she chooses,"[3] in order to escape from the male museum world she normally inhabits. As Margaret Homans points out, Lesje has failed to appropriate the male language of science: "it is clearly because she is a woman that she is denied access to the legitimate professional and intellectual satisfactions its native speakers should enjoy."[4]

The issue of women's language is the subject of much contemporary debate, and it is an issue that has several dimensions. On the most basic level is the silencing and suppression of women's expression—terms taken from the titles of Tillie Olsen's *Silences* (1978) and Joanna Russ's *How to Suppress Women's Writing* (1983). Both Olsen and Russ describe the multiple barriers to women's writing over time: the conflicting demands of domestic responsibilities, the refusal of the literary establishment to take women's writing seriously, the consequent lack of models for young female writers—and so on in a vicious circle, causing women to feel insecure about their own voices. Such insecurity, as Olsen points out, has often kept women from writing honestly out of their own experience:

> These pressures toward censorship, self-censorship; toward accepting, abiding by entrenched attitudes, thus falsifying one's own reality, range, vision, truth, voice, are extreme for women writers (indeed have much to do with the fear, the sense of powerlessness that pervades certain of our books, the "above all, amuse" tone of others). Not to be able to come to one's truth or not to use it in one's writing, even in telling the truth to have to "tell it slant," robs one of drive, of conviction; limits potential stature; results in loss to literature and the comprehensions we seek in it.[5]

This uncertainty about one's own "truth" is reflected in the dual narratives of Jane Gray in Drabble's *The Waterfall* and Chloe in Weldon's *Female Friends* as they revise their lives, seeking an honest, coherent version.

Another, more complex aspect of women's use of language is the extent to which they can or should forge or reclaim a language of their own, free from the influence of male conceptualizing. Once, like Beth, having found the courage to speak up, what language do women use? How is their expression their own, as women? Alicia Ostriker, writing of American women poets in *Stealing the Language,* asks the same question: "Does there exist, as a subterranean current below the surface structure of male-oriented language, a specifically female language, a 'mother tongue'?" The answer to this question, in Ostriker's view, awaits

40

further research, but she argues that women have indeed been "thieves of language":

> What distinguishes these poets, I propose, is not the shared, exclusive *langage des femmes* desired by some but a vigorous and varied invasion of the sanctuaries of existing language, the treasuries where our meanings for "male" and "female" are themselves preserved. Where women write strongly as women, it is clear that their intention is to subvert and transform the life and literature they inherit.[6]

One of the ways that Ostriker believes women have transformed the literature they have inherited is by revising cultural mythologies, and this has been true in the novel as well as in poetry, in ways to which I have previously pointed: Violet Clay, the title character in Gail Godwin's novel, seeks to escape from the "Book of Old Plots" that would have her give up a potential career in art to be a homemaker. Gemma, in *Words of Advice,* sees her life as a constantly revised fairy tale. And *The Handmaid's Tale* is in some measure a rewriting of Hawthorne's *The Scarlet Letter:* fundamentalist morality can mean that women are forced to be adulteresses just as it can punish them for adultery.

For some critics, such as Hélène Cixous, the *langage des femmes* not only exists, it is necessary for women's emancipation. Cixous maintains that women have been driven away from language just as they have been forced to deny their bodies, and she encourages full expression of the female experience as a powerful subversive force. Masculine language, Cixous believes, has been used for the oppression of women:

> in a manner that's frightening since it's often hidden or adorned with the mystifying charms of fiction; that this locus has grossly exaggerated all the signs of sexual opposition (and not sexual difference), where woman has never *her* turn to speak—this being all the more serious and unpardonable in that writing is precisely *the very possibility of change,* the space that can serve as a springboard for subversive thought, the precursory movement of a transformation of social and cultural structures.[7]

For Cixous, as for many other feminist critics, language is tied intimately to gender: "Woman must write woman. And man, man"

(877). Female writing is bound up in female biology, she maintains, because women have been taught to feel guilty about both, and the courage to claim and proclaim both language and biology is the first step toward "transformation."

For many French feminist critics, language is seen as being in the control of men, with women left out, silenced. In Cixous' terms, language is a decisive and oppositional mechanism:

> For as soon as we exist, we are born into language and language speaks (to) us, dictates its law, a law of death; it lays down its familial model, lays down its conjugal model, and even at the moment of uttering a sentence, admitting a notion of "being," a question of being, an ontology, we are already seized by a kind of masculine desire, the desire that mobilizes philosophical discourse.[8]

For Cixous, the "desire" to enter into philosophical discourse is futile for women, because the discourse is conducted in a language that effectively silences them.

Linguist Deborah Cameron, however, comes to different conclusions about the power of male language. In *Feminism and Linguistic Theory,* Cameron argues against linguistic determinism—the concept that one group has the ability to fix meaning and thus deprive another group of access to the power of language: "Since language is a flexible and renewable resource, and since girls must come to grips with it as their socialisation proceeds, there is no reason in principle why language cannot express the experience of women to the same extent that it expresses the experience of men."[9] However, Cameron recognizes that language is closely tied to the power structures of a society, and that "the institutions that regulate language use in our own society, and indeed those of most societies, are deliberately oppressive to women" (145). When women themselves believe that their own use of language—their own talk—is important rather than trivial, Cameron believes that it will thereby *become* important, and can be a source of autonomy.

The differences between French and American feminist scholars' beliefs about the relationship between women and language—the former seeing women denied a language in which to express their experience, and the latter believing that women are capable of appropriating the dominant discourse for their own purposes—are summarized by Margaret Homans in a 1983 article that attempts to mediate between them. One way in which Homans bridges the philosophical gap is by pointing out that American women novelists themselves address women's exclusion from language as a theme in their fiction, thus providing thematic evidence of the French critics' position:

> A woman novelist's ability to represent verbally her response to exclusion from the dominant discourse does not at all disprove the thesis that women's silence serves as the basis for the operation of language. Such an ability is constantly undermining itself: in the very act of asserting through capacious representation the adequacy of language, these novelists betray their anxieties about its sufficiency.[10]

Thus, even as American critics take the pragmatic and optimistic stance that women are able to take possession of language, as Cameron asserts, the texts of those who write in English proclaim that language is a central problem for women who seek to use it to overcome their oppression.

Yet a belief in the potential power of women's use of language is closely tied to the methods and goals of the women's movement. In both formal and informal ways, the movement has encouraged women to communicate, especially with each other, to understand their commonalities, to overcome isolation and silence. It is not surprising, then, that women's fiction of the period from the mid-1960s to the mid-1980s demonstrates a central concern with language: the ability to use language, tell stories, describe experience, and revise mythologies. Language may be a weapon against male authority, as it is for Beth in *Small Changes;* it may be a way of ordering and giving meaning to experience, as it is in *Female Friends* and *The Waterfall;* it is above all a means of communication with other women.

At the same time, however, language is viewed in these novels and others as untrustworthy, and this is the central irony of its significance: even as women writers and their characters feel compelled to describe their experience, they are aware that language can be used to manipulate, that it can lie, as women themselves have been manipulated and lied to. Thus, in the midst of telling their stories, women express their awareness that the truth they seek to tell of is illusory, and that a fantasy could be as "real" as the observable facts of their lives. Indeed, the perception that language is arbitrary and mutable can be the first step toward liberation. When Beth, in *Small Changes*, overcomes her timidity about language, it is through her participation in a women's theater group in which the members learn together to use their voices as well as their bodies: "They were still learning how they felt and how to express it and create with it" (477).

As a significant issue in the contemporary novel by women, language is addressed in a number of ways that can be grouped in two general categories. One group includes challenges to male-dominated language, either by appropriating male discourse for women's purposes or by altering or subverting it. The second group of approaches is composed of those that emphasize women's exclusion from language—their silence. Writers who challenge the dominant discourse typically do so by employing some form of irony, whereas those who stress women's position outside that discourse are more apt to use fantasy as a concomitant narrative strategy. Both of these approaches and strategies may be combined in a single work, as they are, for example, in the three novels considered in the final part of this chapter: *The Handmaid's Tale, The Woman Warrior,* and *The Color Purple.* In each of these three novels, language is initially a silencing but ultimately a liberating phenomenon.

The initial step in negating the hegemony of oppressive language is to question its authority by making fun of it. Pointing to the absurdity of the official language of a culture is a method used commonly by members of oppressed groups; humor negates the power of hegemonic discourse quite simply by refusing to take that power seriously. Joanna Russ's *The Female Man* provides the clearest and most overt examples of this undercutting of male language and power, and at the same time makes explicit men's attempt to silence women. In fact, *The Female Man* extends into speculative

44

fiction the attempts at silencing that Russ also describes in *How to Suppress Women's Writing,* but in her novel, the (fictional) women fight back effectively. An exchange late in the novel serves as a paradigm of both silencing and the subversion of that attempt. A man in Manland, in one of the four parallel universes in the novel, says to Jael, from the opposing camp of Womanland, "You're on my turf, you'll Goddamn well talk about what I Goddamn well talk about," and Jael thinks to herself: "Let it pass. Control yourself. Hand them the victory in the Domination Sweepstakes and they usually forget whatever it is they were going to do anyway."[11]

Throughout *The Female Man* the various narrators parody the language—especially the clichés—of male discourse. In the chapter titled "The Great Happiness Contest," Russ records a paradigmatic exchange between wife and husband in which the latter reveals his need for domination:

HE: Darling, why must you work part-time as a rug salesman?

SHE: Because I want to enter the marketplace and prove that in spite of my sex I can take a fruitful part in the life of the community and earn what our culture proposes as the sign and symbol of adult independence—namely money.

HE: But darling, by the time we deduct the cost of a baby-sitter and nursery school, a higher tax bracket, and your box lunches from your pay, it actually costs us money for you to work. So you see, you aren't making money at all. You can't make money. Only I can make money. Stop working.

SHE: I won't. And I hate you.

HE: But darling, why be irrational? It doesn't matter that you can't make money because *I* can make money. And after I've made it, I give it to you, because I love you. So you don't *have* to make money. Aren't you glad?

SHE: No. Why can't you stay home and take care of the baby? Why can't we deduct all those things from your pay? Why should I be glad because I can't earn a living? Why—

HE (with dignity): This argument is becoming degraded and ridiculous. I will leave you alone until loneliness, dependence, and a consciousness that I am very much displeased once again turn you into the sweet girl I married. There is no use in arguing with a woman. (117–18)

The very stiltedness of the dialogue, especially the man's final comments, makes it seem absurd, but the reality of the exchange lies in the man's stereotypical assumption that women are dependent and irrational. Russ's technique is to allow the man's words to make overt his normally unspoken attitudes, and thus to make clear his sense of dominance—and finally to render that dominance itself as absurd and powerless as the strutting of a small bully.

In Russ's novel it is Janet, from the all-female planet Whileaway, who strikes at the heart of sexist language when she asserts that if the term "Mankind" is meant to include women (as it so clearly does not), then she will insist on being called a man rather than a woman. "For," she says, "whoever heard of Java Woman and existential Woman and the values of Western Woman . . . ? . . . Stop hugging Moses' tablets to your chest, nitwit; you'll cave in" (140). Thus emerges the "female man" of the title. As Natalie Rosinsky says, "Shocking us into recognition of the absurdity of patriarchal law and so-called truth, Russ's humor enables the reader to distance herself from unexamined experience or belief, to become a healthy renegade." [12]

In most other novels of this period, patriarchal language is attacked more subtly, using irony rather than parody. In both *Female Friends* and *The Handmaid's Tale*, Biblical language is mocked, altered, and called into question as a means of authority. Weldon's narrator comments on women's susceptibility to words: "reading significance into casual words, seeing love in calculated lust, seeing lust in innocent words." [13] Yet the young Chloe, growing up in the pub where her mother works, reads the Bible at night and instinctively questions its validity: "'Remember now thy Creator in the days of thy youth, when the evil days come not—' But supposing they do?" (72). Atwood's Offred, who refers to the Bible as an "incendiary device" [14] because, like other weapons, it is available only to the ruling-class men in Gilead, similarly questions Biblical statements or finds them inadequate. As part of the handmaids' training, they are required to recite Biblical passages that reinforce their submissiveness. After reciting a passage from the Beatitudes—"*Blessed be those that mourn for they shall be comforted*"—Offred undercuts the power of the utterance by thinking,

46

"Nobody said when" (89). Writing of the emotional bondage of women with children, Weldon's Chloe herself rewrites the Beatitudes: "Blessed are the orphans, and the barren of body and mind" (205).

Weldon and Atwood also question the authority of patriarchal language by demonstrating that whatever its stated intention, it all comes from the same reservoir of male discourse. Religious and political dogma blend and become indistinguishable. Speaking of the enforced domesticity for women in the period following World War II—"women have to leave their jobs and return to the domestic dedication expected of all good women in peacetime"— Chloe says, "Hitler is not coming, and neither is God; there is to be neither punishment or salvation. There is, instead, a flurry of sexual activity which will land the schools between 1950 and 1960 with what is known as 'The Bulge'" (114). In Atwood's Republic of Gilead, the birth-rate is dangerously low, which leads to the establishment of the class of handmaids, whose "domestic" duties are a degraded, obscene version of the "flurry of sexual activity" of which Chloe speaks. Biblical and Marxist teachings are blended and distorted in the effort to brainwash the handmaids: "*From each,* says the slogan, *according to her ability; to each according to his needs.* We recited that, three times, after dessert. It was from the Bible, or so they said. St. Paul again, in Acts" (117). Offred's ironic comment "or so they said" casts doubt on the authority of the statement, and forces the reader to note also the use of the pronouns "her" and "his" as yet another evidence of the oppression of women in Gilead.

Both suspicion of and domination by male discourse are consistent threads in Piercy's *Small Changes.* Beth, who begins the novel as a young woman wanting and living in the marriage plot, is nonetheless initially and increasingly resistant to received linguistic tradition. Even in the midst of her wedding, she listens to the jingle of an ice-cream truck rather than hearing the "magic words" of the ceremony: "Magic words that made things happen or go away, recipes like I Love You, and I'm Sorry, and I Pledge Allegiance, and God Bless Mommy and Daddy, and Will You Marry Me, and Fine, Thank You, and I Do" (21). Beth's perception that

47

words are agents rather than merely symbols is what causes her to fear their use as weapons against her later in the novel, but this perception also frees her, for she is able to view the language of the dominant culture ironically, and ultimately to reject it altogether. Even very early in the novel, in the chapter ironically titled "The Happiest Day of a Woman's Life," Beth recasts her sister Nancy's description of her wedding dress, "The train comes away," in terms that suggest marriage as a potentially detachable burden: "That meant the thing that dragged could be taken off, with a little timely help" (12). Later, having escaped her marriage, Beth confronts Dorine's statement, "I feel sometimes as if I'll go through life and never belong to anyone," with, "But you aren't a dog, why do you want to be owned?" (88). Beth's sense of freedom and selfhood is expressed late in the novel in a poem she writes:

Everything says no to me.
Everybody tells me no.
Only I say yes.
I have to say it again and again
like a singer
with only one song.
Yes, Beth! Yes, Beth! Yes, Beth!
Yes! (313)

Elaine Tuttle Hansen identifies Piercy's approach to language in *Small Changes* when she states that "Piercy expresses her mistrust of language but does not advocate or sentimentalize silence on the part of women. While women need to seek alternatives and to reject language and literature when they are used to keep women in their place, they cannot allow themselves to be muted; inarticulateness is not a useful weapon." [15]

Kate Brown, in Doris Lessing's *The Summer Before the Dark* (1973), is, like Beth, conscious that conventional phrases are just that—conventions—and not prescriptions for how one must think or feel. At the beginning of the novel she is "trying on" words and phrases "like so many dresses off a rack"—phrases "as worn as nursery rhymes." And indeed they *are* nursery rhymes for women: *"Growing up is bound to be painful! . . . Marriage is a com-*

48

*promise. . . . I am not as young as I once was."* Kate perceives that such phrases rarely reflect actual feelings, yet have become the common currency of habit:

> Such power do these phrases have, all issued for use as it might be by a particularly efficient advertising campaign, that it is probable many people go on repeating *Youth is the best time of your life* or *Love is a woman's whole existence* until they actually catch sight of themselves in a mirror while they are saying something of the kind, or are quick enough to catch the reaction on a friend's face.[16]

Kate's acknowledgment at this point that people—women—are capable of recognizing the insincerity of their own formulaic utterances is magnified later in the novel when she and her friend Mary are driven to helpless laughter by the jargon referent to homemaking. Each has been patronizingly advised by a child's teacher about the child's "normal" adjustment: "The phrases followed each other: well-adjusted, typical, normal, integrated, secure, normative" (149); subsequently, even the words "wife, husband, man, woman" begin to seem to the two women hilarious clichés, and Lessing notes that "it was a ritual, like the stag parties of suburban men in which everything their normal lives are dedicated to upholding is spat upon, insulted, belittled" (150).

A second way in which women writers deal with male discourse is to appropriate it—to use, as authors and narrators, the language of the dominant culture in order to demonstrate an altered relationship with it. Joanne Frye has identified the novel as "peculiarly susceptible to feminist concern for cultural change": "its capacity to 'represent' the shared experience of women's lives—'differenced' as women experience it, whatever its explanation or cause—while simultaneously resisting external definitions of those lives as they have been encoded within male-dominated expectations."[17] Appropriation of male discourse is the most problematic of the ways in which women deal with it. Lesje, in *Life Before Man,* is an example of one caught in the paradox of male-defined female roles and her own professional life in the male-dominated field of paleontology. As Homans points out, Lesje uses the language of science without being a part of its creation; her

49

creative participation in prehistory exists in fantasies, not in reality. Even her pregnancy is an act of vengeance and desperation—a way to solidify her relationship with Nate and remain in the "marriage plot." Miriam, in *Small Changes,* does appropriate successfully the language of male professional discourse as a computer scientist, but she gives up her professional aspirations in order to remain, like Lesje, in the marriage plot. Beth, in the same novel, does not *fail* to appropriate male discourse, as she initially wishes to do, but chooses instead to express herself specifically as a woman in her women's theater group.

Other female characters, however, do use words as weapons. In Walker's *The Color Purple,* the turning point in Celie's struggle for self-esteem comes when she is finally able to talk back to Mr. ———, the husband who has degraded her and hidden the letters her sister Nettie has written to her over the years. With the support of Shug Avery, Celie finds her voice when Mr. ——— says that she will go to Memphis with Shug "over my dead body." The log jam of Celie's resentment breaks at that moment: "You a lowdown dog is what's wrong, I say. It's time to leave you and enter into the Creation. And your dead body just the welcome mat I need." Shocked at Celie's freely spoken resolve, Mr. ——— is effectively silenced, reversing the pattern of male dominance that he has enjoyed for so long: "Mr. ——— start to sputter. ButButButButBut. Sound like some kind of motor."[18] The image of Mr. ——— as a piece of machinery emphasizes Celie's human transcendence over him.

Perhaps the most common and effective method by which women writers have addressed male discourse is by revising the mythologies it has promulgated. The various myths and stories that have been used as paradigms for success, heroism, and male-female relationships are perceived with skeptical irony by these authors. The efficacy of romantic love is a staple of the traditional fairy tale that is frequently deconstructed in these works. For example, shortly after Celie has confronted Mr. ——— on his own terms, he asks her about her rejection of him and her preference for Shug Avery:

> He say, Celie, tell me the truth. You don't like me cause I'm a man?
> I blow my nose. Take off they pants, I say, and men look like frogs to
> me. No matter how you kiss 'em, as far as I'm concern, frogs is what
> they stay. (224)

By refusing to accept the role of princess, who can turn the frog
into a prince, Celie refuses to identify herself as the nurturer and
savior of men. Fairy tales and their revision permeate Weldon's
*Words of Advice*. Not only is the story of her life that Gemma tells
Elsa a constantly revised fairy tale, but Elsa's naive romantic view
of herself—fed by fairy tales—is finally replaced by a more mature
view at the end of the novel. Gemma, having lost a finger, married
the frog rather than the prince, and developed a psychosomatic
inability to walk, needs to recreate her life as a different fairy tale.
When at the end of the novel Gemma's husband, Hamish, tells
Elsa that Gemma's story has been a fabrication, Gemma responds
in a passage that posits the human need for illusion:

> "One story or another, Hamish," she says. "What's the difference? It is
> all the same. It's the one-way journey we all make from ignorance to
> knowledge, from innocence to experience. We must all make it; there
> is no escape. It's just that love and romance and illusion and hope are
> etched so deeply into all our hearts that they can never quite be wiped
> away. They stay around to torment us with thoughts of what might
> have been." (231)

Gemma recasts her life as a fairy tale in order to lessen the power
that romance and illusion have over her; at the same time, she
suggests that all our stories are fictitious—"One story or another
. . . what's the difference?" By the end of *Words of Advice*, Gemma
has taken the trip from "ignorance to knowledge" and is able to
walk; and Elsa is home having cocoa with her brothers and sisters,
ready to embark anew upon her adult life.

Moving from ignorance to knowledge frequently involves dis-
entangling oneself from one or more mythologies. Jane Gray, in
*The Waterfall*, has to come to terms with the fact that her life is not
a novel by Thomas Hardy or George Eliot, and must write her own
text. The earliest mythology that Jane must free herself from is her

family's concept of respectability, composed of beliefs "in the God of the Church of England, . . . in monogamy, in marrying for love, in free will, in the possibility of moderation of the passions, in the virtues of reason and civilization."[19] When she marries Malcolm, she is still in the clutches of these myths; a "doomed romantic" (91), she believes it is love at first sight when she hears Malcolm sing Thomas Campion's lyrics. Like Gemma a believer in the power of "romance and illusion and hope," Jane later places the blame for her mistake on the literature that perpetuates such ideas: "I blame Campion, I blame the poets, I blame Shakespeare for that farcical moment in *Romeo and Juliet* when he sees her at the dance, from far off, and says, I'll have her, because she is the one that will kill me" (92). A central irony of *The Waterfall* is that Jane does not, in fact, die of love the way that Juliet, Sue Bridehead, and Maggie Tulliver do. In the automobile accident the couple has when stealing away for an illicit weekend, her lover, James, is injured, but Jane walks away with only scratches. Indeed, Jane's guilt and wonder at her escape from both respectability and the old plots cause her to narrate and revise her story. At the end of the novel she revises a twentieth-century mythology—that birth-control pills are liberating and safe—by reporting that use of the pills has caused a blood clot in her leg. The Jane who feels guilty about her happiness with James is glad to have this small price to pay for it—"I prefer to suffer, I think" (256)—yet as she has so ironically shown the reader, her suffering is scarcely equal to her happiness.

However haunted Jane Gray may be by the old mythologies, she sees clearly the dangerous illusions they can foster in women's minds, and by writing of her own fulfillment outside these mythologies, she writes a truly female text in which the sensual pleasures of the female body—childbirth, orgasm—are celebrated as not only natural but also the wellsprings of female creativity. The character Jane is a poet; in *The Waterfall* she is the first-person reviser and shaper of her own story, so that woman and writer are finally identical. As Ellen Cronan Rose has written, "Jane's task as woman and as artist is the same: to acknowledge the existence within her self of the Other and not simply to reconcile but to encompass that division."[20] The woman artist, especially in the period from the 1960s to the 1980s, rejects a belief in stability and certainty—in the creation of art as well as in the middle-class respectability of Jane's parents. As Joanne Creighton comments, "Jane has discovered intuitively what post-structuralists have postulated, that reality is necessarily mediated through language and that different 'codes' create different discourses."[21] Creighton points to one of the passages in which Jane questions the "accuracy" of her own text:

> the ways of regarding an event, so different, don't add up to a whole; they are mutually exclusive: the social view, the sexual view, the circumstantial view, the moral view, these visions contradict each other; they do not supplement one another, they cancel each other out, they destroy one another. (47)

This passage is remarkably similar to one in *The Handmaid's Tale* in which Offred is reminding us once again that what she is telling us is a "reconstruction":

> It's impossible to say a thing exactly the way it was, because what you say can never be exact, you always have to leave something out, there are too many parts, sides, crosscurrents, nuances; too many gestures, which could mean this or that, too many shapes which can never be fully described, too many flavors, in the air or on the tongue, half-colors, too many. (134)

Rose points to the postscript of *The Waterfall* as "a triumph of feminine form," because of both its irony and its refusal to make a "final formulation": "The last dramatic, heroic, 'masculine' statement—'I prefer to suffer'—is followed by the feminine ending, 'I think'" (66). But more than this, Drabble undercuts the suffering of the romantic, mythological heroine with the revisionist stance of the ironist.

As Jane Gray uses her skills as a writer to bring her life into clearer focus and free herself from the old mythologies, so Violet Clay, title character in Godwin's novel, must learn to take herself seriously as an artist and disentangle herself from the myths and stories she has both inherited and created. Violet, like Jane, is able to see herself ironically, revising her own history as she inhabits the present. Violet's grandmother, who had hoped to be a pianist, instead became trapped in the marriage plot and gave up her career. As she tells Violet, she was seduced away from Carnegie Hall by "a subversive, tempting picture":

> The picture was of that lady so feted in our day—her praises were sung in every women's magazine—the accomplished wife and mother who turns her gifts to the enhancement of Home. I saw myself, safe and rich and beautiful, seated at a nine-foot grand in Charles's ancestral home, playing the G Minor Ballade by Chopin, followed by Mozart's sonata with the Turkish Rondo, to a select cultural gathering, after which my two beautiful children would be led in by the servants to say good night.[22]

Such a romantic vision did not materialize, and Violet's grandmother tells Violet her story as a cautionary tale; but Violet insists that she will not make the same mistake: "Don't worry. I have my own plans" (38). However, Violet not only marries rather than going to New York to pursue her career; when she finally leaves her marriage and makes the move, she remains caught in a romanticized image of herself as a victim of circumstance until her uncle's suicide forces her to begin to disengage from the fantasies she has so carefully constructed. As an illustrator of Gothic romances, Violet assumes that she is superior to her material, but like the Gothic heroine, she is waiting to be rescued rather than creating her own future. In order to free herself from the myth of "The Young Woman as Artist" (26), she has to confront her uncle Ambrose's failure as a novelist and hence the potential of her own. Violet's first successful painting is titled "Suspended Woman," which aptly characterizes Violet's situation at the end of the novel: having rejected the "Book of Old Plots," she is poised to begin life on her own terms.[23]

In mocking, appropriating, and revising the language and the stories of a culture that has at the very least discouraged women's participation in its dominant discourse, the contemporary woman novelist creates fiction that is fundamentally ironic in its intent. That is, by questioning the formulations of self and experience that are imposed on women rather than arising from their own perceptions, the writer creates what Lilian Furst calls "an inquiring mode that exploits discrepancies, challenges assumptions and reflects equivocations, but that does not presume to hold out answers."[24] The absence of clear answers both mirrors the historical period during which these novels were written and creates fictions that are not conclusive, because conclusions, like traditional mythologies, do not allow growth and evolution. When these novelists focus on ways in which women are silenced and excluded, the possibility of change takes the form of fantasy. Some forms of fantasy are positive and enabling, such as Kingston's dream of the "woman warrior"; others, like the dystopian vision of *The Handmaid's Tale,* are horrific; all, however, arise from a need for alternative realities. Fantasy theorists frequently note the function of fantasy as a critique of existing norms and structures, challenging not merely facts, but also assumptions. William Irvin, for example, states that "conventions as to factual possibility and impossibility are not the only kind that fantasies deny. There are also beliefs, interpretations, and understandings seemingly based on facts and widely enough accepted to have the status of convention."[25] The use of fantasy in women's fiction is a way of exploring and challenging assumptions about women's lives.

Metaphoric of the silencing of women is the fact that characters in these novels frequently lack names, or have more than one name for more than one identity. The power of names to define women's status and role came into sharp focus during the 1960s and 1970s as feminists sought not only to rid English of sexist and exclusionary terminology (Janet's diatribe against the word "mankind" in *The Female Man* reflects this concern), but also to make clear that such terms as "girl" and "little woman" are demeaning. The fact that women traditionally assume first the names of their fathers and then the names of their husbands means that they go through life without named identities of their own, but instead with names that indicate their status as objects: daughter, wife.[26]

55

The most extreme example of relational naming is "Offred" in *The Handmaid's Tale:* not even a name, this is a tag that the narrator wears to signify that she is the handmaid "of Fred."[27] Significantly, the researchers who report in the "Historical Notes" section of the novel can attempt to discover Offred's identity only by determining which "Fred" her Commander was, and their efforts are inconclusive.

Margaret Atwood's narrator in *Surfacing* is not only nameless, but also obsessed by language and a search for identity—a search that allows her to cast off the fantasies she has constructed about her own life and enter into a primitive world of the imagination in which language is secondary to feeling. By limiting the narrative perspective to that of the unnamed narrator, Atwood allows us only gradually to understand—as the narrator herself confronts it—that she has imaginatively transformed an affair with a married man and the abortion of a child into marriage, childbirth, and divorce. The narrator clearly feels the power of language, and regards naming as a limiting, restrictive act. Of the child she pretends to have borne, she says early in the novel, "I never identified it as mine; I didn't name it before it was born even, the way you're supposed to."[28] The act of getting married, she thinks, ruined the relationship with her "husband": "We committed that paper act. I still don't see why signing a name should make any difference but he began to expect things, he wanted to be pleased" (47). Language is "everything you do" (153), and it "divides us into fragments" (172). The major obstacle the narrator confronts in trying to come to terms with her life and her fantasies is the split between mind and body, between the rational and the intuitive. Midway through the novel she comments that "the trouble is all in the knob at the top of our bodies": "I'm not against the body or the head either: only the neck, which creates the illusion that they are separate. The language is wrong, it shouldn't have different words for them" (91). At the end of the novel, on the verge of accepting Joe because he is "only half formed," she still distrusts language: "For us it's necessary, the intercession of words; and we will probably fail, sooner or later, more or less painfully" (224).

Atwood's narrator resists naming, but the narrator's aunt in *The*

Language, Irony, and Fantasy

*Woman Warrior* has, in the eyes of her Chinese family, lost the right to her name because she has become pregnant and committed suicide. The "no name woman" has been effectively expunged from family history, so that the narrator must flesh out her mother's sparse, confidential story with her own imaginings as she tries to come to terms with the Chinese heritage that silences her. The narrator's Chinese and American identities are at war as she matures; nor can she reconcile her mother's life as a doctor in China and her timid, unadventurous manner in America. The reconciliation between mother and daughter takes place when the narrator's mother calls her by her childhood nickname, "Little Dog": "a name to fool the gods. I am really a Dragon, as she is a Dragon, both of us born in dragon years." [29]

Just as Kingston's narrator, having heard the stories of Fa Mu Lan, has her fantasy of being the woman warrior, so the adolescent Miriam, in *Small Changes,* creates a fantasy self. Having discovered that the best parts in most plots are reserved for men, Miriam makes up stories in which she is Tamar De Luria, an anthropologist who has defended a primitive tribe from white colonialists and in return has been taught their secrets. Like Kingston's woman warrior, Tamar has both male and female characteristics: "Tamar could track people and walk so silently she never broke a twig and climb trees like a cat and scamper over buildings and fight as well as a man" (97–98). Yet "when Tamar danced, men fell in love with her" (98). As the woman warrior sends her infant son home with her husband while she finishes her conquest, so Tamar remains dedicated to the tribe that has taught her its secrets: "Because she never knew when a message would come from her island saying that her people were in danger again and she must return to save them, she could never marry" (98). In these fantasies, triggered by other stories, the female characters take on an autonomy that, as they are aware, is normally reserved for men, and escape, imaginatively and temporarily, the scripts that have been written for them as women. Similarly, Lesje, in *Life Before Man,* uses her fantasies of prehistory to take control as she cannot do in her professional life. She is a scribe, a copyist of the language of paleontology, not a researcher who creates the lan-

57

guage that she copies onto tags in the museum. In her daydreams, however, Lesje "allows herself to violate shamelessly whatever official version of paleontological reality she chooses":

> She mixes eras, adds colors: why not a metallic blue stegosaurus with red and yellow dots instead of the dull greys and browns postulated by the experts? Of which she, in a minor way, is one. Across the flanks of the camptosaurs pastel flushes of color come and go, reddish pink, purple, light pink, reflecting emotions like the contracting and expanding chromatophores in the skins of octopuses. (13)

Fitting neither into the world of her male profession—except as a "minor" expert—nor into the world of women, Lesje wants to merge the two by bringing the colors of emotion into the dry world of her science.

Those women who, like Kingston's narrator, are not part of mainstream culture by virtue of their racial or ethnic backgrounds are more easily and effectively silenced. Kingston's narrator describes at length her refusal to speak during kindergarten and grade school, and links it to the fact that she is Chinese and female: "The other Chinese girls did not talk either, so I knew the silence had to do with being a Chinese girl" (193). Another form that her silence takes is her habit during these years of covering her school paintings with a layer of black paint. Neither her teachers nor her parents understand that in the child's imagination the black paint represents stage curtains behind which her painting waits to be gloriously unveiled. At home, the girl "spread them out (so black and full of possibilities) and pretended the curtains were swinging open, flying up, one after another, sunlight underneath, mighty operas" (192). Celie, in *The Color Purple*, is, like Kingston's narrator, abjured to be silent at the very start of the novel: "You better not never tell nobody but God" (11). Taking this warning literally, she begins, at the age of fourteen, writing letters to God, telling her story to the only one she believes can understand it. In Piercy's *Woman on the Edge of Time*, Consuelo, as a Mexican-American woman living in New York, is at the bottom of the socio-economic scale, a fact that makes it easy for those in

58

control to interpret her despair and rage as madness, and to silence her with drugs. When Geraldo commits her to Bellevue, no one asks to hear her side of the story: "So far no one had heard a word she said, which of course was not unusual." [30] Yet it is Consuelo who is selected for contact by Luciente, from a utopian culture in 2137, who tells her that she is "an unusual person. Your mind is unusual. You're what we call a catcher, a receptive" (41). Considered merely a dangerous psychotic by those who would keep her locked up and drugged, Connie is a sensitive woman who is capable of entering into an alternate reality. [31]

In Lessing's *The Four-Gated City,* the authority of the psychiatric establishment is also challenged, this time by Martha Quest's rejection of it to pursue her own self-examination through empathic union with Lynda. Using both fantasy and irony, Lessing suggests that women's silence is alleviated not by remote institutions but by intimate and intuitive fantasy. The ironically named Dr. Lamb, Lynda's psychiatrist, represents the power of hegemonic culture to label, categorize, and therefore silence those who do not conform to preconceived standards of "normality." Lynda mocks this practice when she tells Martha the joke among psychiatric hospital patients of the "nothing-but":

> You know, it's that point when they get all pleased because they can say: you're nothing but—whatever it is. They've taken weeks and weeks to get to that point, you know, and it's, You're nothing but Electra. You know, that girl who killed her mother? . . . It's nothing but you want to sleep with your father. Nothing-but your brother. . . . I'm nothing-but a depression. [32]

By recognizing the dehumanizing effect of the "nothing-but" labeling, Lynda and Martha can prepare for the joint exploration of "their dreams, their slips of the tongue, their fantasies" (372) that leads Martha to self-realization. As Elizabeth Abel has pointed out, the contrast between Martha's relationships with Dr. Lamb and Mark, and the one with Lynda, points up the sharp difference between scientific objectivity and hierarchy on the one hand, and fluidity and openness on the other. When Martha enters imaginatively into Lynda's world of madness, she "takes the risk of throwing off her rational guard, thereby uncovering a portion of herself":

> The union achieved by Martha and Lynda becomes an emblem of the breakthrough essential to human survival, the transformation of the brain from "a machine which works in division" to the unified and unifying organism invoked by the Sufi tale that forms the dedication of the novel.[33]

In the midst of hers and Lynda's explorations of madness and sanity, Martha articulates the connection between madness and expression, the breaking of silence, when she speaks of their not having words to describe the process they are going through:

> Perhaps it was because if society is so organized, or rather has so grown, that it will not admit what one knows to be true, will not admit it, that is, except as it comes out perverted, through madness, then it is through madness and its variants it must be sought after. (375)

Madness and its "variants"—dreams, daydreams, and fantasies—become subversive ways of overcoming exclusion and silence. "What one knows to be true" but cannot express because it will not be understood or accepted in light of one's marginal position in society emerges in fantasy. Contemporary women novelists use various forms of fantasy to show women attempting to take control of circumstances from which they are excluded, to express what would otherwise be inexpressible. Violet Clay and the *Surfacing* narrator must extricate themselves from fantasies they have devised to avoid confronting painful realities, but to do so they must dream other selves and relations. Kingston's "woman warrior" fantasy, like Martha Quest's approach to madness, is in itself enabling, allowing the woman access to an alternate reality that permits a more complete identity.

In *The Color Purple*, *The Woman Warrior*, and *The Handmaid's Tale*, the central characters are initially silenced by their cultures, but each eventually works her way to freedom through language. The central irony in all three texts is that the very thing that is denied these women—the freedom to speak up, speak out, be heard—becomes the medium through which they define themselves. Celie's letters to God and Nettie, the woman warrior's memoirs, and Offred's voice on cassette tapes all serve as records of an emergence from silence, both in terms of the way in which they relate to others and in the fact of the written record itself. Forms of fantasy work in various ways in these novels: Celie dreams of an eventual reconciliation with Nettie, the *Woman Warrior* narrator imagines herself as a powerful avenger, and Offred dreams of a past in which she had choices while inhabiting a speculative future that is itself the fantasy of the author. Each is aware that her present reality is oppressive, denying her individuality and her autonomy.

In Alice Walker's 1976 novel *Meridian*, she tells the story of the slave woman Louvinie, whose master cuts out her tongue because one of her frightening stories is presumed to have killed his weak-hearted son. Louvinie had been raised in a family of storytellers in West Africa; the loss of her tongue is equivalent to the loss of her spirit: "Without one's tongue in one's mouth or in a special spot of one's choosing, the singer in one's soul was lost forever to grunt and snort through eternity like a pig."[34] Celie, in *The Color Purple*, is silenced by both physical brutality and admonition. Raped by the man she assumes to be her father and warned by him, "You better not never tell nobody but God" (11), Celie keeps her silence in the face of those who oppress her until emboldened by her relationship with Shug Avery. But all the while, in her letters to God and Nettie, she develops her own voice as her own storyteller.

The issue of names, here as in other novels, is a crucial narrative element. Names are closely tied to identity, and the claiming or conferring of a name is an indication of selfhood. Celie's letters to God are unsigned; during the period before she begins writing to Nettie, she feels that she *is* no one, has no particular identity. Shug effectively returns Celie's name to her when she names a song for her:

> Then I hear my name.
> Shug saying Celie. Miss Celie. And I look up where she at.

61

> She say my name again. She say this song I'm bout to sing is call
> Miss Celie's song. . . .
> First time somebody made something and name it after me. (75)

Late in the novel, having achieved a measure of emotional and
economic independence, Celie signs a letter to Nettie in a manner
that shows she has both a name and a place:

> Your Sister, Celie
> Folkspants, Unlimited.
> Sugar Avery Drive
> Memphis, Tennessee (192)

Similarly, Mary Agnes attempts to and finally succeeds in emerging from her nickname, "Squeak." Her real name is a badge of her
personhood and dignity. When her uncle, with whom she tries to
intercede on behalf of Sofia, rapes her, Harpo is sympathetic and
tells "Squeak" that he loves her; but she refuses to be demeaned
by both the rape and her nickname: "She stand up. My name
Mary Agnes, she say" (95). Later, in the same scene in which
Celie finds her voice to talk back to Mr. ———, Mary Agnes wins
this battle for her own name and identity. When she announces
that she, too, wants to go to Memphis to pursue a singing career,
Harpo initially reacts as had Mr. ——— to Celie: "Listen Squeak,
say Harpo. You can't go to Memphis. That's all there is to it":

> Mary Agnes, say Squeak.
> Squeak, Mary Agnes, what difference do it make?
> It make a lot, say Squeak. When I was Mary Agnes I could sing in
> public. (183)

Harpo has not recognized until now the power of names; but the
next time he addresses her, it is as Mary Agnes.

One of the most subtle and ironic instances of naming in *The
Color Purple* involves the relationship between Celie and her husband. Having been forced to marry him, Celie seldom thinks of
him with any affection or intimacy, as reflected in the fact that she
always refers to him as "Mr. ———," without even a last name.
The distance between them is magnified when he brings the ill
Shug Avery, who has been his mistress, home for Celie to care for.

Shug addresses him as Albert, and Celie writes, "Who Albert, I wonder. Then I remember Albert Mr. ———— first name" (51). Yet it is Shug, loved by both Celie and Albert, who fosters whatever tender feelings the couple are able to have for one another. When Albert's father visits and taunts Celie—"Not many women let they husband whore lay up in they house"—they are united in their defense of Shug: "Mr. ———— look up at me, our eyes meet. This the closest us ever felt" (59). Near the end of the novel, Celie and Albert are drawn together by Shug's departure, and he puts his arms around her with tenderness. As they sew together, Celie thinks, "He not such a bad looking man, you know, when you come right down to it. And now it do begin to look like he got a lot of feeling hind his face" (239). In her last letter to God, Celie refers to him as Albert, a fact that marks not only her sense of confidence, but also Albert's new understanding of love that allows her to grant him an identity.

Celie's initial silence is a continual reference point in her letters to God. When Albert's sister urges her to fight for a decent way of life, she writes, "I don't say nothing" (29). When Albert comes home from seeing Shug, Celie has "a million question," but she does not ask them: "I pray for strength, bite the insides of my jaws" (34). When rumors begin to circulate about Shug's illness, "I want to ast, but don't" (48). First meeting Shug, Celie wants desperately to welcome her to the house, but "I don't say nothing. It not my house" (50). Yet in her letters to God and later to Nettie, Celie not only breaks her silence, but creates a vivid tapestry of her life that shows her to be a sensitive, perceptive woman who sees the ironies of her own experience. By using the epistolary form, Walker allows Celie the freedom to shape her existence in vivid, expressive prose. The changes in Celie's style during the course of the novel reflect her growing sense of worth. In the earliest letters her writing is inhibited and cryptic, but as writing increasingly becomes a mode of ordering her experience, her style becomes more fluid and scenic; in short, Celie becomes the novelist of her own life. One evidence of this is that she guards her dialectical speech. In Memphis, Darlene attempts to correct Celie's grammar, but Celie resists: "Pretty soon it feel like I can't think.

My mind run up on a thought, git confuse, run back and sort of lay down" (193). Her resistance to changing her language is essentially rooted in her common-sense integrity: "Look like to me only a fool would want you to talk in a way that feel peculiar to your mind" (194). As Elizabeth Fifer puts it, "By using dialect, the only language she knows, when all public communication is forbidden, she discovers and exploits a powerful tool in her development of awareness through self-expression."[35]

Significantly, Celie gains strength and confidence from a community of women: the resilient Sofia, the loving Shug Avery, and her sister Nettie with whom she dreams of being reunited. Shug is the agent by which Celie's dreams are realized. She awakens Celie to her own sexuality, finds the letters from Nettie that Albert has hidden, and makes possible the pants-making business that gives Celie economic independence. Yet it is ultimately Celie's taking control of language that allows her to put her life together. When she refuses to let Albert stop her from going to Memphis with Shug, she effectively reverses the balance of power in their relationship, becoming the one who teaches him—about sewing, about the larger world, and about love. Having dealt with the sexual oppression in her life, she ultimately addresses racism by using what she has learned from Nettie's letters. Revising the Genesis story according to the Olinka tribe's beliefs, Celie proposes to Albert that the first human beings were black, and that they considered the occasional white child that was born an aberration. "So really Adam wasn't even the first white man. He was just the first one the people didn't kill" (239). When she has achieved her own identity, Celie is in harmony with the natural world, and language seems to be supplied by agencies outside herself. Cursing Albert for his history of meanness, Celie muses, "Look like when I open my mouth the air rush in and shape words" (187).

By questioning the authority of received tradition and her own oppressor, Celie demonstrates her freedom from arbitrary justification for sexual and racial oppression. In significant ways, her life begins anew. Her last letter is addressed not merely to God, but to the entire "Creation" she has told Albert she wishes to enter: "Dear stars, dear trees, dear sky, dear peoples. Dear Everything"

(249). Celie and Nettie, reunited, appropriately, on Independence Day, "totter toward one nother like us use to do when us was babies" (250), and this last letter ends with a declaration of youth and hope: "I think this the youngest us ever felt" (251).

Kingston's novel, like Walker's, opens with an admonition to silence: "'You must not tell anyone,' my mother said, 'what I am about to tell you'" (3). This highly autobiographical work also shares with *The Color Purple* a focus on cultural marginality: both Celie and Kingston's narrator—the latter a first-generation Chinese-American woman—are excluded from the language of the dominant culture by their racial and ethnic origins. King-Kok Cheung wisely cautions against readers or critics taking these two texts as representative of the authors' respective cultures, pointing out that Walker and Kingston are imaginative writers rather than cultural historians. Further, Cheung reminds us that the sources of sexism and silence are quite different in the cultures from which their authors come:

> [B]lack silences, deepened by the history of slavery, are not the same as Chinese American silences, which were reinforced by anti-Asian immigration laws. Celie's repression is much more violent and brutal than Maxine's, and her resources are at the beginning much more limited. Celie expresses herself tentatively at first because she lacks schooling; it is in school that Maxine becomes totally incommunicative (because she has to learn a second language).

But Cheung agrees that language becomes for both characters an empowering force, and that "gender and ethnicity—inhibitive forces when these texts open—eventually become the sources of personal and stylistic strengths."[36]

Celie's husband Albert, angered by her defiance of him, attempts to reduce her to nothingness: "You black, you pore, you ugly, you a woman. Goddam, he say, you nothing at all" (187). Kingston's narrator experiences a similar humiliation when her parents reflect the traditional Chinese belief that girls are worthless: "Better to raise geese than girls" (54). Both Walker and Kingston also avoid traditional linear narrative. Celie's and Nettie's letters to each other are hidden and misdirected, so that they do not follow a pattern of response and exchange, and Walker leaves it to the reader to fill in the gaps between the episodes Celie narrates. The five sections of *The Woman Warrior* are free-standing narratives that overlap and enrich each other rather than following a clear narrative continuum.

Yet Celie's progress toward freedom from oppression unfolds as a steady, gradual process, mirrored in the increasingly confident style in which she writes and in the actions and attitudes she records. Kingston's work, on the other hand, is what Suzanne Juhasz has called "circumstantial, complex, and contextual": "In their form, women's lives tend to be like the stories they tell: they show less a pattern of linear development toward some clear goal than one of repetitious, cumulative, cyclical structure," which is similar to Hélène Cixous's description of a "feminine text" as one that "is always endless, without ending: there's no closure, it doesn't stop. . . . [A] feminine text goes on and on and, at a certain moment the volume comes to an end but the writing continues."[37] As part of this unfinished circularity, Kingston constantly alters the form of her narrative, which makes it difficult to classify as fiction or autobiography.[38] Roberta Rubenstein has identified the five major sections of the book as follows:

> The first three of the five major divisions of *The Woman Warrior* might be viewed respectively as a morality tale, a fairy-tale epic, and a series of "ghost stories" and adventures completed by the reconciliation between mother and daughter. The fourth section, "At the Western Palace," is a tragedy, and the final one, "Song for a Barbarian Reed Pipe," is a combination of confession and legend.[39]

While such identifications should be viewed as suggestive rather than fixed, Rubenstein's comments indicate the complexity of *The Woman Warrior*'s formal characteristics.

Language, irony, and fantasy are interdependent in *The Woman Warrior*, for it is the multiple ironies of her life that the narrator must resolve, and it is through fantasy that she finds the language to do so. Two sets of related ironic circumstances affect the narrator's life. Juhasz identifies one set of ironies when she states that *The Woman Warrior* "is about trying to be an American, when you are the child of Chinese emigrants; trying to be a woman, when

66

you have been taught that men are all that matters; trying to be a writer, when you have been afraid to speak out loud at all."[40] All of these paradoxes serve initially to silence the narrator. As her aunt, the "no name woman," "gave silent birth" (13), so the young narrator is silent in school—a Chinese girl among Americans. "It was when I found out I had to talk in school that school became a misery, that the silence became a misery" (193). Because she is uncertain of either her Chinese or her American identity, she retreats into silence in the face of "Chinese communication," which is "loud, public" (13). Even as an adult, though she is "getting better," the narrator notes that "a telephone call makes my throat bleed and takes up that day's courage" (191).

Speaking of the work of Margaret Atwood, Toni Morrison, and Alice Walker, Margaret Homans has noted that these writers "differentiate between the linguistic exile they experience as minorities and that which they experience as women,"[41] and so does Kingston. In the public, "American" world of school, her ethnic identity, not her gender, silences her; but at home in the immigrant community, girls are by tradition considered useless: "When one of my parents or the emigrant villagers said, 'feeding girls is like feeding cowbirds,' I would thrash on the floor and scream so hard I couldn't talk" (54). Her inarticulate rage brings the response that she is a "bad girl," which the narrator suggests might be an advantage: "Isn't a bad girl almost a boy?" (56).[42] Since she cannot transform herself into a boy, she fantasizes being a woman warrior, and through relating such fantasies, emerges from her silence.

The second set of ironies—and the one that eventually gives Kingston's narrator her language—consists of multiple versions of "truth" that relate to her history, her identity as a Chinese-American woman, and her role as a writer. Confronted at every turn by contradictions, the narrator must, like the reader of an ironic text, formulate her own version of reality. When the narrator reaches puberty, her mother tells her the story of her aunt in China, who disgraced the family not only by bearing an illegitimate child, but also by drowning herself in the family well. The story is, as Rubenstein says, a "morality tale," meant to warn the young girl about sexuality and family honor; yet she is simultaneously admonished never to tell it to anyone else—to deny, in fact, the existence of the aunt:

> "Don't tell anyone you had an aunt. Your father does not want to hear her name. She has never been born." I have believed that sex was unspeakable and words so strong and fathers so frail that "aunt" would do my father mysterious harm. (18)

The story of the "No Name Woman," who both existed and did not exist, introduces Kingston's narrator to the power of both language and silence.

As she must revise and recreate the story of her aunt, so the narrator must reconcile the story of her mother's heroic actions as a woman doctor in China with her docile, hard-working American presence. Brave Orchid, who rid her medical school of ghosts and delivered babies in pigpens, is in America a woman surrounded by ghosts, who tells her daughters that they are not worth feeding. The confusion of her mother's two selves mirrors the split between a Chinese identity and an American identity: "Those of us in the first American generations have had to figure out how the invisible world the emigrants built around our childhoods fits in solid America" (6). Yet it is the stories of this "invisible world"—her mother's "talk-story"—that ultimately allows the narrator to create herself by telling her own story. As Rubenstein puts it, "Rejecting her mother's entrapment in a culture that devalues females, yet identifying with Brave Orchid's talent—and in tribute to her—Kingston became a storyteller, committed to giving expression to the muted females of her culture" (179–80).

However, it is not only members of Chinese-American culture for whom Kingston's narrator speaks up. As difficult as speech remains for her, she tells her employer at an art supply store that she does not like his calling a color "nigger yellow"; her voice is a "bad, small-person's voice that makes no impact," but she nonetheless says the words (57). Later, she loses a job when she confronts an employer with the fact that the restaurant he has chosen for a banquet is being picketed by members of NAACP and CORE: " 'I refuse to type these invitations,' I whispered, voice unreliable" (58). As unreliable and ineffectual as her spoken voice may be, however, Kingston's written language uses myth, fantasy, and memory to penetrate the ironies of identity and avoid the madness that overtakes Moon Orchid when she arrives from China to find her husband remarried and thoroughly Americanized. In the final section of *The Woman Warrior*, "A Song for a Barbarian Reed Pipe," the narrator says, "I thought talking and not talking made the difference between sanity and insanity. Insane people were the ones who couldn't explain themselves" (216). The closest the narrator comes to madness is the eighteen-month "mysterious illness" she suffers after physically and emotionally abusing a young Chinese girl who refuses to speak. Having gone to the extreme of castigating someone so like her younger self, she retreats from life to stay in bed: "It was the best year and a half of my life" (212).

By returning to the narrator's childhood, the final section of *The Woman Warrior* underscores the circularity of the search for truth in the midst of ironic paradox and contradiction. Fittingly, the book ends with a "talk-story" begun by the mother and finished by the daughter. The mother tells of her own mother outwitting bandits by having the family take everything they owned with them when they went to the theater. The narrator completes the story by imagining that at the theater her grandmother has heard the songs of Ts'ai Yen, a female second-century poet who brought songs to China from her barbarian captivity. Both parts of the story speak to the transforming power of fantasy and language. The narrator's grandmother decides that "our family was immune to harm as long as they went to plays" (241); and the narrator reports that Ts'ai Yen's "Eighteen Stanzas for a Barbarian Reed Pipe" was adopted by the Chinese because "it translated well" (243), the statement that concludes the book and testifies to the narrator's translation of her own experience into a meaningful whole.

If *The Color Purple* and *The Woman Warrior* show women emerging from silence into language as part of their authors' feminist desire for women to claim autonomy, Atwood's *The Handmaid's Tale* posits a future culture in which such feminist dreams have been replaced by a fundamentalist patriarchy that divides women into rigid categories based on function: Wives, Marthas (servants),

Feminist Alternatives

Econowives, Handmaids (surrogate mothers for the children of
Commanders and their Wives), Aunts (who train the Handmaids),
and Unwomen—those from whom language has removed gender
because they are unfitted for any other category. Atwood's dystopian novel—which has been called a "futuristic feminist nightmare" and a "science-fiction fable"[43]—is in significant ways a
cautionary tale: a message from the future to those of us in the
present who may be able to prevent the Republic of Gilead from
coming to pass.[44] Six years before *The Handmaid's Tale* was published, Atwood commented on the writing of fiction in a way that
seems to anticipate the novel:

> What kind of world shall you describe for your readers? The one you
> can see around you, or the better one you can imagine? If only the
> latter, you'll be unrealistic; if only the former, despairing. But it is by
> the better world we can imagine that we judge the world we have. *If
> we cease to judge this world, we may find ourselves, very quickly, in one
> which is infinitely worse.*[45]

The element of contrast between one reality and another that Atwood suggests here is the method of irony.

Indeed, in addition to being a fantasy, *The Handmaid's Tale* is essentially an ironic text in a more fundamental way than are most
other works considered here. At every point Atwood invites the
reader to question the validity of the narrative. Not only is Offred
an unreliable narrator, in the sense that she is enmeshed in the
experience she describes and has an imperfect understanding of
the culture that controls her, but she constantly reminds the reader
that her story is a "reconstruction." Early in the novel, remembering the horror of having her five-year-old daughter taken from
her, Offred speaks of the "truth" of her story:

> I would like to believe that this is a story I'm telling. I need to believe it.
> I must believe it. Those who believe that such stories are only stories
> have a better chance.
>    If it's a story I'm telling, then I have control over the ending. Then
> there will be an ending, to the story, and real life will come after it. I
> can pick up where I left off.
>    It isn't a story I'm telling.

70

It's also a story I'm telling in my head, as I go along.

Tell, rather than write, because I have nothing to write with and writing is in any case forbidden. But if it's a story, even in my head, I must be telling it to someone. You don't tell a story only to yourself. There's always someone else.

Even when there is no one. . . .

I'll pretend you can hear me.

But it's no good, because I know you can't. (39–40)

In this deceptively simple passage, Offred addresses the relative "truths" of our actual experiences and the stories we tell ourselves about them, the prohibition of language in Gilead, and the story-teller's need for an audience.

Later, Offred announces, "This is a reconstruction. All of it is a reconstruction." If she ever escapes to tell her story, she realizes that will be a reconstruction also, "at yet another remove." And, as the author of her own story, she understands the limitations of language in conveying experience: "It's impossible to say a thing exactly the way it was, because what you say can never be exact . . ." (134). Having announced that language cannot tell the whole truth, Offred begins to alter her story deliberately. When her Commander asks her to kiss him, she imagines stabbing him while she does so: "I think about the blood coming out of him, hot as soup, sexual, over my hands." But she immediately corrects herself:

In fact I don't think about anything of the kind. I put it in only after-wards. Maybe I should have thought about that, at the time, but I didn't. As I said, this is a reconstruction. . . . He was so sad.

That is a reconstruction, too. (140)

Later, after three paragraphs describing her first sexual encounter with Nick, the Commander's chauffeur, Offred begins again: "I made that up. It didn't happen that way. Here is what happened" (261). By constantly inviting the reader to question what she says, Offred compels the reader to participate in the process of irony by questioning and revising the language of the text.

Atwood creates the ironic framework in other ways, as well. Offred tells most of her story in the present tense, giving it the im-

71

mediacy of direct experience; she speaks as one imprisoned, remembering the past but knowing no future beyond the present moment. Yet the reader learns in the "Historical Notes" coda that Offred's "manuscript" was itself reconstructed from voice recordings on cassette tapes found in an Army surplus footlocker in what had been Bangor, Maine. The "soi-disant manuscript" was thus recorded after Offred's escape on the "Underground Female-road," rather than at the time of her life as a handmaid. To further cast doubt on the authenticity of Offred's story, Atwood has Professor Pieixoto note that the tapes were in no particular order, so that he and his associate have guessed at their proper sequence: "all such arrangements are based on some guesswork and are to be regarded as approximate" (302). Not only the order, but also the language of Offred's narrative is made dubious by Pieixoto's comment about "the difficulties posed by accent, obscure referents, and archaisms" (302). Atwood thus not only deepens the irony of Offred's text, but also comments on the nature of "truth."

The exclusion from language that Celie and Kingston's narrator suffer is, in *The Handmaid's Tale,* magnified and made part of the repressive culture of Gilead. Women—even the Aunts—are denied books, paper, pens; only the Commanders may read even the Bible, and the shops are identified by pictures rather than by names: "they decided that even the names of shops were too much temptation for us" (25). In a society governed by The Word, words are themselves forbidden. Because biblical language is used for oppression rather than for redemption, hymns with the word "free" in them are banned, as are popular songs, and biblical language is altered and mixed with political slogans. Like Celie in *The Color Purple* deciding that God "must be sleep" (163), Offred attempts her own version of the Lord's Prayer, but finally concludes, "I feel as if I'm talking to a wall" (195).

Yet perhaps because of the prohibition of language, Offred, who had previously worked in a library, is fascinated by words, by puns and word-play. Waiting for the household to assemble for the evening Bible-reading, Offred thinks: "The Commander is the head of the household. The house is what he holds. To have and to hold, till death do us part. The hold of a ship. Hollow" (81). By such word associations, she exposes the hollowness of the concepts of home and family in Gilead. When Offred plays with word associations while remembering the past, she points up the contrast between freedom and oppression for women. Passing what was once a movie theater that had Humphrey Bogart festivals, she thinks of Lauren Bacall and Katharine Hepburn, "women on their own, making up their minds": "They wore blouses with buttons down the front that suggested the possibilities of the word *undone*. These women could be undone; or not. They seemed to be able to choose. We seemed to be able to choose, then" (25). Later, remembering how she had loved books, Offred thinks of her job in the library:

> It's strange, now, to think of having a job. *Job.* It's a funny word. It's a job for a man. Do a jobbie, they'd say to children when they were being toilet trained. Or of dogs: he did a job on the carpet. You were supposed to hit them with rolled-up newspapers, my mother said. I can remember when there were newspapers, though I never had a dog, only cats.
>
> The Book of Job. (173)

The word "job" leads Offred inevitably back to newspapers and books, and the Book of Job is a fitting metaphor for the suffering she endures in Gilead.

The story of Job, however, is a story of survival, and language enables Offred to survive. Telling her story is, in Rubenstein's words, "the self-generated act that opposes the obligations of procreation" (103). By creating an ironic fantasy, Atwood doubly compels the reader to participate in the creation of meaning. It is, finally, in the interaction between writer and reader, between reader and narrator, that the meaning of *The Handmaid's Tale* exists and that Offred triumphs as the author of her own story. Linda Hutcheons, writing about the shift from the lyrical to the narrative mode in Atwood's fiction, has suggested that although writing "can only employ the static counters of language, [it] is capable of being resurrected in the equally dynamic process of reading, the bringing to life of the dead black marks on the white page."[46] Atwood herself feels strongly about the interaction among

73

writer, text, and reader, and has described the writer as one who says, *"There is a story I have to tell you, there is something you need to know"*:

> All writers play Ancient Mariner at times to the reader's Wedding Guest, hoping that they are holding the reader with their glittering eye, at least long enough so he'll turn the next page. The tale the Mariner tells is partly about himself, true, but it's partly about the universe and partly about something the Wedding Guest needs to know; or at least, that's what the story tells us.[47]

Officially denied language in Gilead, Offred escapes to tell her story, however "reconstructed," and tells us something we need to know about the human capacity for survival.

# CHAPTER THREE

# Multiple Narrative: Revising the Self

      In *The Handmaid's Tale*, Atwood creates a situation in which Offred's story must perforce be a reconstruction on several levels: from imperfect memory to cassette tapes to transcription and translation many years later. In the process, Offred's precise identity—her real name, her history—becomes lost, so that there is an ironic tension between the candid, even confessional revelation that is Offred's narrative on the page, and the "real" Offred that the experts in Gileadean Studies attempt in vain to identify. In its presentation of such an extreme discontinuity between selves or identities, Atwood's novel serves as a paradigm of the difficult search for identity in the contemporary novel by women. Indeed, contemporary women's narratives reveal a deep awareness of the "self" as fluid rather than fixed, and this awareness leads in turn to the revision of narrative as a revision of self: a socially created identity becomes replaced by or juxtaposed to an alternative identity that views the socially created self ironically. The emphasis on fluidity—on "becoming" rather than "being"—both mirrors the social and ideological upheaval of the 1960s and 1970s and contributes to a feminist critique of social constructions of female identity.

It can be argued, of course, that the novel as a form in Western culture arises from and belongs to an ideology that individuates human beings—a post-Enlightenment view that the person is as valuable and interesting for his (and occasionally her) uniqueness as an individual as for his representation of common experiences and values. The realistic novel in particular, by emphasizing the growth and development of the individual character, brings the concepts of "self" and "identity" to the foreground, as the unique qualities of the individual are etched against the backdrop of the larger culture. The classic novel of self-development, the *bildungs-roman*, is traditionally the story of a young man achieving maturity by testing himself against the values of his society and emerging as a distinct individual. This pattern of individuation may be seen even more clearly in the autobiography, at least as autobiography has been traditionally defined. George Gusdorf, for example, writes that "autobiography . . . requires a man to take a distance with regard to himself in order to reconstitute himself in the focus of his special unity and identity across time."[1] The concept that the author of an autobiography consciously stands apart from his life in order to "reconstitute" a self to present to the reader is remarkably similar to the novelist's creation of character in fiction.

However, the presentation of a "self," whether in fiction or in autobiography, is a somewhat different matter for women than for men. When Gusdorf says that "autobiography is not possible in a cultural landscape where consciousness of self does not, properly speaking, exist" (30), he could be speaking as well of the traditional realist novel, a pre-condition of which is the assumption that each individual is set apart from all others by possession of unique consciousness and characteristics. Yet conventional notions of the self are postulated on the experience of the dominant—male—culture, and fail to take into account the circumstances in which women and members of other non-dominant groups encounter the concept. Because women and other minorities are systematically discouraged from thinking of themselves as

76

unique and autonomous, their relationship to selfhood must be approached in a different way. Indeed, Judith Kegan Gardiner calls into question the use and validity of the terms "self" and "identity" when applied to women:

> "Identity" is a central concept for much contemporary cultural and literary criticism, which, along with its even vaguer terminological twin, the "self," has become a cliché without becoming clear. The word "identity" is paradoxical in itself, meaning both sameness and distinctiveness, and its contradictions proliferate when it is applied to women. . . . [T]he quest for female identity seems to be a soap opera, endless and never advancing, that plays the matinees of women's souls. A central question of feminist literary criticism is, who is there when a woman says, "I am"? [2]

The fact that feminist literary criticism does concern itself so frequently with questions of self and identity suggests that women writers raise these questions in provocative ways in their work; and yet the very terminology available to the critic derives from a concept of selfhood that is at least oblique to women's experience.

Gardiner suggests that feminist psychology offers a means of describing women's relationship to concepts of the self that in turn has implications for women's narrative strategies. By applying Nancy Chodorow's theories of female personality to identity theory, Gardiner proposes that "for every aspect of identity as men define it, female experience varies from the male model." Most fundamentally, Gardiner concludes that female identity is a "process" (349), and that "primary identity for women is more flexible and relational than for men" (354). One result of this less fixed, more fluid concept of identity is women's "manipulation of identifications between narrator, author, and reader" (349); another is a blurring of the distinctions between genres, particularly between fiction and autobiography. Two of Gardiner's examples are Kingston's *The Woman Warrior* and Mary McCarthy's *Memories of a Catholic Girlhood*, and others come readily to mind: Erica Jong's Isadora Wing trilogy, Nora Ephron's *Heartburn*, Maya Angelou's *I Know Why the Caged Bird Sings*. Such fluidity of genre and of the relationship among author, narrator, and reader suggests that identity, for the woman writer, is constantly in the process of being evaluated and revised.

What characterizes the contemporary novel by women, however, is not merely a fluidity of identity, but a consciousness of the ironic distance between the self as formulated externally, by cultural heritage, and the self as an internal process of redefinition and discovery. Perhaps the most striking instance of this distance and the attempt to address it imaginatively is Kingston's *Woman Warrior*, in which the conflict between Chinese and American cultures underscores the difficulty of developing a concept of self with which the narrator can live comfortably. As Margaret Miller points out in "Threads of Identity in Maxine Hong Kingston's *Woman Warrior*," the very concept of individuality that permeates Western thought and gives rise to the novel is alien to traditional Chinese culture, in which the "process of maturation is not one of differentiation from other members of the group," but rather is intended to "ensure group continuity, to embody group norms."[3] The individual person—particularly the individual woman—is a link between past and future generations, between ancestors and descendants, and thus is bound by tradition in ways more cogent and imperative than in Western culture. The struggle to derive a sense of selfhood while mediating between the Western emphasis on personal uniqueness and the Oriental emphasis on connectedness is responsible, Miller suggests, for the structure of *The Woman Warrior*, in that rather than using the chronological narrative of the traditional autobiography, Kingston "reflects the Chinese emphasis on kinship rather than on individual identity by defining herself in terms of her place in a kinship line" (17). But even more significantly, Kingston's narrator re-tells and revises her ancestral history, recreating the stories of her aunt, the "no name woman," and her mother, Brave Orchid—the first a victim and the second a heroine, poles between which Kingston's narrator must steer in order to find her own identity and worth as a Chinese-American woman.

Despite cultural differences, however, in creating the series of five narratives that comprise *The Woman Warrior*, Kingston is very much in consonance with other contemporary female novelists, who deal with the process of finding or creating an identity in the context of contemporary Western culture. The revision of self and history, the emergence of the ironic voice, and the fantasy of an alternative reality are common narrative elements. One concrete, easily observable evidence of the multiple identities that characterize these novels is the multiplicity of names by which central characters are known. Kingston's narrator is called both "Biggest Daughter" and "Little Dog" by her family. As Miller points out, Chinese seldom refer to each other by real names, even within the family: "instead each person is known by a name which marks the important thing, his or her position within the family" (16). Significantly, the narrator's actual first name is never used; instead, she imagines the identity of the "woman warrior"; and she knows that "Little Dog" is a subterfuge to fool the gods, because she was actually born, as was her mother, in the year of the Dragon.

Like Kingston's narrator, Atwood's narrator in *Surfacing* is nameless; each lacks a clearly defined "self" that can be named. And as Kingston's narrator imaginatively transforms herself into the woman warrior, so Miriam, in Piercy's *Small Changes*, tries to escape the restrictions of her life as a young woman by imagining herself to be "Tamar De Luria," an anthropologist who has learned witchcraft and hypnotism—powers that give the young Miriam the illusion of dominance in a world in which women are powerless. Martha Quest Hesse, in *The Four-Gated City*, disengages herself from both the mask of "Matty"—the self-mocking identity that she had developed as a defense—and her married name Hesse, both of which represent assumed selves that she must shed on her way to self-discovery. Early in the novel, in response to a stranger's question, she names herself Phyllis Jones, "with an imaginary history of wartime work in Bristol," and realizes that individual identity can be both assumed and bestowed: "People filled in for you, out of what they wanted, needed, from—not you, not you at all, but from their own needs."[4] The name Hesse is easy to discard, because she can see it objectively: "it was a name acquired like a bracelet from a man who had it in his possession to be given to a woman in front of lawyers at the time of the signing of the marriage contract" (38). The first step toward achieving a true "self" is Martha's realization that she is essentially a "soft dark receptive intelligence" that has "nothing to do with Martha, or any other name she might have had attached to her" (38).

If, as Gardiner suggests, female identity is a continual process rather than achievement of stasis, represented on the most superficial level by the assuming and shedding of names, then the constant revision of one's personal history is a logical thematic and narrative element of these novels. Not only does fiction blend into autobiography, but the fluidity of the individual self requires constant revision of the "truth" about one's life story. Two dramatically different novels illustrate the possibilities of such revision: *Surfacing* and Russ's *The Female Man*. Atwood's novel presents two personal histories for the narrator: one a set of fabrications and distortions that the narrator has developed as a socially acceptable story, and the other the "real" story that emerges as the layers of the first are peeled away.

The namelessness of the *Surfacing* narrator is deeply significant. Not only is she on a quest to understand her past and thereby to develop a sense of her own present and future; she also lies to the reader and—more importantly—to herself about the central facts of her life as an adult woman: marriage and motherhood. So deeply has she buried her experiences with adultery and abortion that even her private thoughts and memories are for much of the novel permeated by the fictitious husband and child that she has invented to hide these experiences even from herself. Caught between the prevailing morality of the 1950s and the greater personal freedom of the 1970s, she is very much a character of the 1960s, unable to reconcile the values of her upbringing with the imperatives of love and necessity. The narrator's friend Anna wears a mask of make-up without which she is never seen—"her artificial face is the natural one"[5]—but the narrator's mask is a psychic one that must be removed gradually as she becomes able to confront the truth.

So solid is the structure of lies that the narrator of *Surfacing* has developed that the reader initially has no reason to doubt that she has been married and divorced, and has decided to let her former

80

husband keep the child she has borne. Early in the novel, the narrator even allows the French Canadian friends of her parents to believe she is still married:

> I'm safe, I'm wearing my ring, I never threw it out, it's useful for landladies. I sent my parents a postcard after the wedding, they must have mentioned it to Paul; that, but not the divorce. It isn't part of the vocabulary here, there's no reason to upset them.
>
> I'm waiting for Madame to ask about the baby, I'm prepared, alerted; I'll tell her I left him in the city; that would be perfectly true, only it was a different city, he's better off with my husband, former husband. (27)

In order not to disturb her parents' friends, the narrator is prepared to tell lies even about her own lies. Later, she has a brief, unbidden memory of her husband carving his initials into a fence, teaching her to carve her own and suggesting a permanence about their relationship that the ensuing time has negated. She maintains that it was she who ended the relationship: "I was what's known as the offending party, the one who left, he didn't do anything to me. He wanted a child, that's normal, he wanted us to be married" (55). Not until later in the novel does the narrator acknowledge to herself that the reverse of this has been true: her married lover wanted neither her nor the child. Unable to live with the pain of the truth, she has invented her own: "I needed a different version. I pieced it together the best way I could" (69).

Yet in retrospect, the narrator provides clues throughout *Surfacing* that the personal history she initially presents is a fabrication. In the third chapter, she refers to "my husband and child, my attractive full-color magazine illustrations, suitable for framing" (34), which suggests that they are a fantasy. Later, she notes that her current lover, Joe, does not know about her child, and will not find out by stumbling across photographs of it, because none exist. She further acknowledges that she did not select a name for her child before it was born: "I never identified it as mine" (39). The truth of the abortion is prefigured in the language Atwood uses in the third chapter: "I have to behave as though it doesn't exist, because for me it can't, it was taken away from me, exported, deported. A section of my own life, sliced off from me like a Siamese twin, my own flesh canceled" (56). By thus hinting at the reality of her narrator's past, Atwood maintains the tension between her two selves as the narrator gradually revises her invented version, replacing it with another truth as she can bear to acknowledge it.

The image of the Siamese twins is representative of the concept of duality that pervades Atwood's writing, a concept that is frequently rendered imagistically by twins. Even her titles, such as *Double Persephone* and *Two-Headed Poems*, suggest duality of identity. Early in *Surfacing*, the narrator reports that Anna, an amateur palm-reader, has asked her whether she were a twin. When the narrator says she is not, Anna persists: "Are you positive . . . because some of your lines are double" (10). Later in the novel, she thinks, "I'd allowed myself to be cut in two. . . . The other half, the one locked away, was the only one that could live; I was the wrong half, detached, terminal" (129). The self that is "locked away" is the one in touch with her own reality, the one the narrator must re-discover in order to be whole. In her book *Violent Duality*, Sherrill Grace argues that Atwood consistently embraces the notion of duality:

> The speaker in her poems, or the protagonist in her novels, swings back and forth between a solipsistic extreme, withdrawal into the self, and an absorption or submergence in objective reality, the false perceptions of others or the natural world. . . . Freedom, Atwood implies, does not come from denying or transcending the subject/object duality of life; it is not duality but polarity that is destructive. Freedom comes from accepting the duality or, to use the more precise scientific term, duplicity which we share with all living things. . . . Atwood explores the concept of duplicity thematically and formally, always with an ironic eye to its common meaning of deceit.[6]

Freedom, for the narrator of *Surfacing*, comes when she accepts the duality of her biological and intellectual selves. For most of the novel, she is dominated by her intellect, which has created the fabric of lies with which she has shielded herself from her own past. She is unable to feel, because love has betrayed her, and it is in recognition of the split between mind and body that, at the beginning of the second section of the novel, the narrator comments on the assumed polarity of mind and body: "The trouble is all in the knob at the top of our bodies. I'm not against the body or the head either: only the neck, which creates the illusion that they are separate" (91) It is only when Atwood's narrator retreats almost entirely into an animalistic state near the end of the novel that she can leave the ironic detachment of her intellect behind, and begin again to trust her emotions.

The *Surfacing* narrator's emotions are closely tied to her creativity, and another dimension of her divided self occurs in her professional life. Like the title character in Godwin's *Violet Clay,* the narrator has studied to be an artist, but works as an illustrator, fashioning images to order rather than creating them to meet her own artistic needs. As she describes herself:

> I'm what they call a commercial artist or, when the job is more pretentious, an illustrator. I do posters, covers, a little advertising and magazine work and the occasional commissioned book. . . . I can imitate anything: fake Walt Disney, Victorian etchings in sepia, Bavarian cookies, ersatz Eskimo for the home market. (60–61)

As the reader gradually learns, her married lover was one of her art teachers, and it was he who discouraged her from pursuing a career as an artist:

> For a while I was going to be a real artist; he thought that was cute but misguided, he said I should study something I could use because there has [sic] never been any important women artists. . . . [S]o I went into Design and did fabric patterns. (60)

The art teacher's sexism effectively hides from the narrator a tradition of women artists, and without knowledge to the contrary, she is forced to agree with him: "But he was right, there never have been any" (60).

By the end of the novel, however, the narrator's process of self-revision has caused her to shed the "civilized" world and its intellectual structures—what she calls "the word games, the winning and losing games" (223). She burns the illustrations she has been working on, and destroys her paints and brushes: "this is no longer my future" (206). The narrator's fantasy of regressing on the evolutionary scale, which occupies the last few chapters of the novel, is an imaginative analogue to her rejection of the world that has victimized her, and the proclamation that begins the final chapter—"This above all, to refuse to be a victim" (222)—is a signal that she is prepared to be a creator rather than being created to meet the needs of others. Having finally acknowledged to herself the earlier abortion, she now believes herself to be pregnant again— "shape of a goldfish now in my belly" (223)—and even a relationship with her lover Joe may be possible because he seems not to have hardened into a mold: "he is only half formed, and for that reason I can trust him" (224). If Atwood's narrator is not to be a victim, she must create her own reality.

Despite the visionary qualities of *Surfacing*, it is a novel clearly grounded in its time period. The homemade "art" film that Joe and David are making, the counterculture resistance to capitalism, the narrator's guilt-producing back-room abortion, and the denial of her professional aspirations all tie it to the 1960s. In contrast, *The Female Man* ranges over time and space to challenge social constructions of women, using both ironic and speculative modes. Whereas *Surfacing* details the painful progress of a single woman toward freedom from the culture that would create and thus constrict her, *The Female Man* holds up to ridicule the fundamental concept of social prescription of women's behavior. Russ achieves the freedom to launch this critique by using the methods of speculative fiction: parallel universes, travel in time and space, and multiple consciousness. As Tom Staicar has noted, science fiction as a genre has increasingly attracted feminist authors precisely because of that freedom:

> Only science fiction allows the freedom to create a "laboratory" world where one can experiment with matriarchal societies that dominate entire nations, group marriages, radical approaches to child rearing, and other feminist speculations about alternatives to existing sex roles and living arrangements.[7]

It is such a "laboratory world" that Charlotte Perkins Gilman created in *Herland* in the early part of the century, transferring her concept of female nurturance to an all-female culture of the future. But Russ exploits more fully the possibilities of the genre, creating four characters that are actually four different manifestations of the same consciousness in order to expose the arbitrary nature of values and attitudes. Further, as Thomas F. Dillingham has pointed out, a critical central concept of *The Female Man* is that "'gender' is not biologically or psychologically determined, but rather is an ideological product of the dominant forces of society."[8]

The four female "characters" in Russ's novel illustrate the force of social ideology in the construction of female identity, and simultaneously undermine that force by underscoring its absurdity. Joanna, who lives in the late 1960s, most closely resembles the *Surfacing* narrator, precisely because of the period in which she lives; her feminist consciousness exists in tension with the conditioning of her upbringing:

> There is the vanity training, the obedience training, the self-effacement training, the deference training, the dependency training, the passivity training, the rivalry training, the stupidity training, the placation training. How am I to put this together with my human life, my intellectual life, my solitude, my transcendence, my brains, and my fearful, fearful ambition?[9]

Jeannine is equally a product of her era—the 1930s. Intelligent but directionless, she looks to marriage as the panacea for her life that she knows it will not be. Unlike Joanna, she is unable to identify the source of her unease: "I have everything and yet I'm not happy. Sometimes I want to die" (150). The other two avatars of the central consciousness are from other, vastly different worlds. Janet, who, with her all-female planet Whileaway, was introduced in Russ's earlier story "When It Changed" (1972), is outspoken and assertive, unafraid to confront sexism when she encounters it, as when she breaks the arm of a man who makes persistent sexual—and sexist—advances to her at a party. Jael, the fourth character, comes from a future world in which the "war between the sexes" has become an actual war between Manland and Womanland. Jael's contempt for men is expressed in her inversion of the concept of woman as sexual plaything: in her house in Vermont lives Davy, a beautiful young man more pet than companion, whose actions are controlled by the household computer.

It is Jael, who works for the Bureau of Comparative Ethnology and whose specialty, appropriately enough, is disguises, who has brought the four women together, and who makes it clear that each one is an aspect of the same woman. Having decided to search for her other "selves," Jael confronts Jeannine, Joanna, and Janet with their similarities: "What you see is the same genotype, modified by age, by circumstance, by education, by diet, by learning, by God knows what" (161). It is tempting to regard these four incarnations of the same woman as representing a historical progression of consciousness of a sort, with Jeannine and Joanna standing for two stages of pre-feminist awareness and Janet and Jael predicting alternative futures—one peaceful and one warlike. But Jael—and through her, Russ—emphasizes not historical development but rather identity beneath a facade of differences:

> We ought to think alike and feel alike and act alike, but of course we don't. So plastic is humankind! Do you remember the story of the Doppelganger? This is the double you recognize instantly, with whom you feel a mysterious kinship. An instant sympathy, that informs you at once that the other is really your very own self. The truth is that people don't recognize themselves except in mirrors, and sometimes not even then. (162)

The plasticity of human beings—their tendency to adopt the attitudes and behaviors of the society in which they live-—conceals their sameness, and hides them even from themselves.

The central thematic focus of *The Female Man* is thus the ironic disparity between surfaces and essences, and this theme is approached not only in the merged identities of the four "J's," but also in the novel's attack on stereotypes of women—its exposure of both the absurdity and the power of these superficial images by the use of hyperbole and oversimplification. The latter device, for example, is used to point up the dangers of Freudian constructions of women when the character Laura says matter-of-factly, "I'm a victim of penis envy so I can't ever be happy or lead a normal life" (65). More commonly, Russ uses exaggeration to make her point. At the party where Janet ultimately breaks the host's arm after her verbal rejections of his advances have failed, a group of women epitomizes in their names as well as their behavior the force of cultural stereotyping:

> Sposissa, three times divorced; Eglantissa, who thinks only of clothes; Aphrodissa, who cannot keep her eyes open because of her false eyelashes; Clarissa, who will commit suicide; Lucrissa, whose strained forehead shows that she's making more money than her husband; Wailissa, engaged in a game of ain't-it-awful with Lamentissa. (34)

Using what Natalie M. Rosinsky calls the "literalization of metaphor,"[10] Russ addresses the language of social intercourse, exaggerating it to the point of absurdity to make clear its subtext. In a disembodied piece of text, for example, an unidentified male voice addresses a woman who has evidently announced herself a feminist:

> Burned any bras lately har har twinkle twinkle A pretty girl like you doesn't need to be liberated twinkle har Don't listen to those hysterical bitches twinkle twinkle twinkle I never take a woman's advice about two things: love and automobiles twinkle twinkle har. (49)

Janet, in particular, is bothered by the pervasive insistence that the term "man" includes women, and thus it is she who contributes the book's title when she decides that to be included in human experience she will have to become a "female man" (140).

Despite their vast differences in tone and narrative technique, *Surfacing* and *The Female Man* share a central thematic concern with the disparity between appearance and reality. Atwood's narrator must experience depths—figuratively and literally—before she can "surface" as an emerging self. Russ, by using the techniques of speculative fiction, calls into question conventional notions of identity in order to force a recognition of the social construction of women's identities. Both novels, in being visionary, order re-visions of women's selfhood and suggest the possibility of change.

In an essay titled "Towards a Fully Human Heroine: Some Worknotes," published in 1973, Gail Godwin expresses her dissatisfaction with depictions of women in fiction: "One day I mean to write a novel with a heroine I would like to meet, a heroine I can be proud of, the kind of heroine I look for—usually in vain—in other people's novels."[11] Godwin describes the sort of heroine she has in mind:

> She would be the subject of her own destiny, not the object of "Blind Destiny" nor a character in somebody else's destiny.
>
> She would have an inner life that was wide and deep and complex—one that would tempt the novelist to explore it at the risk of getting lost, rather than editing it or shutting part of it behind doors.
>
> She would live anywhere on this planet (or another), but always within her moral center, carefully furnished by herself, consisting of items she needed and liked to see around. She would refurbish it and springclean it and throw away or replace items when they wore out. (28)

Godwin's ideal heroine, who furnishes and maintains her own "moral center" rather than being created by someone else, directs her own life story instead of being a character in someone else's story. Yet the central character of Godwin's *The Odd Woman*, published the following year, cannot develop a life outside the literature she teaches. A college professor, Jane Clifford is presented as a woman who "liked to be in control,"[12] but she is actually controlled by stories written by other people. Jane's family, most fundamentally, expects her to play a certain role in their drama; going home for a funeral, Jane sees them waiting at the airport for her, "never doubting she had any choice but to fall back from the sky into their nets of family and region and social standing and—most compelling weave of all—their image of her, Jane, their Jane" (89).

Jane's immersion in the literature of her professional life causes her to see herself as a character rather than a creator. On her bad days, she plays the game of wondering, "If Jane Austen were putting me in a novel, how would she define me?" (27). A specialist in nineteenth-century literature, Jane frequently yearns for the solid identity of nineteenth-century characters, as opposed to the more ambiguous personalities of contemporary literature, but wonders about the validity of the old-fashioned hero:

Was there, then—had there ever been—such a thing as a basic personality, or was that only a bygone literary convention? Could there exist a true, pure "character" who was nobody but himself—subject, of

course, to the usual accidents of existence—but capable of subordination of his (her) terrain as he progressed through time and space, cut-
ting a swath of chapters that would be meaningful in retrospect? (27)

Even Jane's relationship with her lover, Gabriel Weeks, takes on
the character of fiction rather than being the space in which she
has a "real" life. Gabriel, whose relationship with his wife Ann
remains a mystery to Jane, is as much a fantasy as he is an actual
lover with whom she spends an occasional weekend. She re-
hearses the conversations she will have with him before they
meet; she constantly uses the word "mysterious" when referring
to him. More in love with the idea of an affair than with Gabriel
himself, Jane is unable to enjoy full sexuality with him. Susan E.
Lorsch refers to Jane's "prefabricated fantasy affair" with Gabriel,[13]
and indeed her whole life has the slightly unreal quality of a character in a literary text. Four years later, in *Violet Clay,* Godwin created a heroine more nearly like her ideal conception: Violet Clay,
like so many other characters in contemporary women's fiction, is
finally able to escape from what she terms the "Book of Old Plots"
and become the creator of her own life.

A common motif in the contemporary novel by women is the
story that must be revised or rejected: the fairy tale, myth, romance, plot, even history that defines and limits women's lives
and choices. Rachel Blau DuPlessis, in *Writing Beyond the Ending,*
sees this revisionary critique as a major thread in the work of
twentieth-century women writers:

> There is a consistent project that unites some twentieth-century women
> writers across the century, writers who examine how social practices
> surrounding gender have entered narrative, and who consequently
> use narrative to make critical statements about the psychosexual and
> sociocultural construction of women. . . . Writing beyond the ending
> means the transgressive invention of narrative strategies, strategies that
> express critical dissent from dominant narrative.[14]

Writing "beyond the ending" of the enclosed plot of traditional
fiction—especially in the contemporary novel—necessitates an
ironic vision and an ability to imagine beyond the limits of the
standard narrative. Such standard narratives may be the family

histories that one seems doomed to repeat; they may be the mythologies of a particular culture; or they may be generalized stereotypes and expectations for women's nature and behavior.

Godwin's Violet Clay, for example, has to free herself from her
family pattern of woman-as-victim. Her grandmother, beguiled by
cultural prescriptions for domesticity, gave up her career as a mu-
sician; her mother, more dramatically, drowned herself after her
husband's death, leaving Violet an orphan. When Violet loses her
job as illustrator for Gothic romances—a job which itself represents a selling-out of her own artistic talent—she initially feels
stuck in the family role: "The grooves of my mind were more accustomed to the concept of Violet Clay as victim than as vic-
tress." [15] Yet Godwin's narrator is capable at the same moment of
stepping aside from her own narrative and addressing the reader
from the perspective of her later awareness:

> As any of you know who have been there, there is a certain point on
> the road downward from your homes where you find yourself deriving
> more comfort from imagining the worst than imagining what steps
> you would have to take to make things better.
>     I was near this point. (78)

Godwin's double narrative perspective—the alternation between
the chronology of Violet Clay and Violet's ironic commentary on
her past self—reinforces the concept of revision: Violet is both in
and apart from her own story. The fact that the character Violet
paints covers for popular romances underscores aptly the danger
of her being stuck in the "Book of Old Plots." This element of the
novel also has its origins in Godwin's own life: for several years
when she was a child, her mother wrote love stories for pulp
magazines as a means of supporting herself and her daughter. As
Godwin describes it, the basic plot of these stories never varied:
"1. Girl meets man. 2. They fall in love. 3. Complications arise.
4. But are overcome. 5. Proposal or marriage." [16] Early in *Violet
Clay*, Violet fantasizes beyond the end of the romance she is cur-
rently illustrating, trying to imagine what comes after the word
"always." In Violet's vision of her romantic heroine's future, the
marriage becomes routine and stale and the heroine dissatisfied,

wondering, "Why oh why had nobody prepared her for what came after the last page?" (19). By the end of her own story, Violet's painting "Suspended Woman" has become a metaphor for her own sense of possibilities outside the standard plot.

The metaphor of the popular romance as a possible life story that must be rejected is explored most fully in Atwood's *Lady Oracle,* in which the narrator actually has two identities: she is both Joan Foster and Louisa K. Delacourt, "two people at once, with two sets of identification papers, two bank accounts, two different sets of people who believed I existed." [17] Under the name Louisa K. Delacourt, Joan writes Gothic romances, a profession hidden from her husband, and one which is an analogue for her constant revision of her own life. Joan revises her life in several different ways in the course of Atwood's novel. Like Miriam, in Piercy's *Small Changes,* she is overweight as a child and adolescent; when, at nineteen, she loses weight in order to claim an inheritance from her Aunt Lou and leave home, it is "like being born fully grown at the age of nineteen: I was the right shape, but I had the wrong past. I'd have to get rid of it entirely and construct a different one for myself" (157). Joan's initiation into writing popular fiction happens through the agency of a Polish emigré whom she meets after she moves to London; in order to send money to his relatives in Poland, Paul writes romances with hospital settings under the name "Mavis Quilp," [18] and he encourages Joan to begin her career as Louisa. *Lady Oracle* has three narrative threads: the narrator's account of her present life in Italy, her retrospective account of her past, and passages from the romances she writes. In some senses, each of these is a fiction. Joan's identity as Louisa K. Delacourt is an overt though understandable lie; it is common for authors of popular romances to use pseudonyms. Her life in Italy, too, is invented: having staged her own death in Canada in order to escape her life there, she is in hiding from the very past that she has in some ways invented. Truth is, for Joan, a poor substitute for illusion: "This was the reason I fabricated my life, time after time: the truth was not convincing" (167).

Godwin's Violet Clay is tempted by old plots, but Joan Foster is unable to live her life apart from some fictional construction. "All my life I'd been hooked on plots," she says near the end of the novel (342); she considers writing a realistic novel, but rejects the idea: "I longed for happy endings" (352). Joan is haunted by her mother, whom she could never please, and by her former fat self, the latter the recurring image of the Fat Lady. It is not until the romance novel she is writing and her own life come together that the Fat Lady is exorcised. In her story, the heroine has been drowned, as Joan has pretended to do, but reappears to the hero as the Fat Lady, representing Joan's fear that her husband, Arthur, would reject her if he knew of her real past. It is only when she sees her actual fear embodied in her fiction that Joan is able to let go of the Fat Lady image: "The woman began to fade, like mist, like invisible ink, like melting snow" (355). With this ghost of her past gone, Joan is able to free herself of her mother as well: "I would never be able to make her happy. . . . Maybe it was time to stop trying" (363). At the end of *Lady Oracle*, Joan is preparing to confront the reality of her past and present:

> I won't write anymore Costume Gothics. . . . I think they were bad for me. But maybe I'll try some science fiction. The future doesn't appeal to me as much as the past, but I'm sure it's better for you. I keep thinking I should learn some lesson from all of this, as my mother would have said. (379)

By acknowledging that the future is a better place to live than the past, Joan announces her readiness to attempt life without illusion.

The "Book of Old Plots" that Violet Clay manages to escape in Godwin's novel includes, for a number of women writers, both the myths and fairy tales that are passed from generation to generation and the less overt but equally powerful life patterns adumbrated in the traditional novel of which Rachel Brownstein and Rachel Blau DuPlessis speak—life patterns resolved by marriage or death, and from which real and fictional women depart at peril of isolation and depression. The plots of contemporary women's fiction frequently subvert these patterns by refusing to adhere to or resolve them. In *Small Changes*, the stories of Beth and Miriam intersect at the point that each woman is on the verge of departing from the pattern that has seemed scripted for her in early life, and in a sense they revise each others' stories. By dividing the novel into three sections—The Book of Beth, The Book of Miriam, and Both in Turn—Piercy causes the two narrative threads to counterpoint each other, and forces the reader to observe the irony inherent in the contrast between the characters' life patterns.

Beth, whose story begins the novel, comes from a highly traditional middle-class background. Growing up in the 1950s and early 1960s, she sees no realistic future beyond marriage to her high-school boyfriend, even though she instinctively distrusts this plan for her life. The marriage is, predictably, a disaster; Beth soon finds herself "tired of the whole mythology of love and marriage,"[19] and escapes to Boston, where she is quickly drawn into the late 1960s world of university radicalism. Eventually Beth acknowledges and accepts the fact that she is a lesbian, and leaves her conventional background far behind by living happily with another woman and her children. Miriam, in contrast, goes to college and enters the male-dominated field of computer science. Her involvement with the counterculture begins early, yet effectively ends when she marries the highly conventional Neil and settles into conventional marriage and motherhood. The trajectory of each woman's life thus apparently departs radically from its early patterns, and whereas Beth is self-confident and fulfilled at the end of the novel, Miriam feels dissatisfied and trapped in a marriage to a man who has begun to be unfaithful to her.

Elaine Tuttle Hansen has suggested that in *Small Changes* Piercy has tried to appropriate the dominant discourse in two ways: by using and revising the traditional *bildungsroman* in Beth's story, and legitimizing the female soap opera in Miriam's story. Beth's escape from a constricting marriage parallels the male hero's escape from the constraints of his culture; by the end of the novel Beth has essentially reversed the life plot dictated for her by creating a non-traditional family and a new identity. As Hansen observes, Beth's story "is clearly presented as a romantic journey from darkness to light, a narrative of revolution and rebirth into a new and higher state."[20] Miriam, on the other hand, vacillates between her need to take risks for change and growth and her equally compelling desire for conventional stability; like the typi-

93

cal soap opera, her story is never resolved, but merely repeats the same set of conflicts: "the soap-opera heroine is caught in pre-determined circumstances, unable to choose or act on her own" (217). The final chapter reinforces this sense of repetition and lack of conclusion. Narrated by a new character, Helen, who is having an affair with Miriam's husband, this final chapter ends with the dreams of the romantic heroine that we know will not be fulfilled, as Helen thinks, "He was beginning to love her, he was wanting her, and soon she would not be alone any more" (542). The irony of the ending reverses the conclusion of the popular romance: instead of the secure promise of "happily ever after," we have Helen's self-deluding fantasy.

Yet in spite of Piercy's appropriation of the male story of individuation and the soap opera's ceaseless spiraling to no conclusion, neither Beth nor Miriam undergoes essential, radical change in the novel. From early life, Beth has resisted conformity while Miriam has yearned for it. The ironic chapter titles that begin "The Book of Beth" and "The Book of Miriam" are only the first indication of the plots they will fulfill. The first chapter of Beth's story is titled "The Happiest Day of a Woman's Life," a title ironically at odds with Beth's response to her wedding day. She feels "like a dress wearing a girl" (12), and is aware that the trappings of wedding dress and makeup cause her "to appear as little like Beth as could be arranged" (15). In this same chapter we learn that Beth has always wanted to go to college—has aspirations to be a lawyer—but that these aspirations have not been taken seriously by her family and friends. Her commitment to the marriage she is about to embark on is as false as the social conventions she is forced to endure. The initial chapter of Miriam's story similarly foreshadows her later behavior and decisions. Titled "You Ain't Pretty So You Might as Well Be Smart," the chapter establishes Miriam's fervent desire to please others: to be pretty like her sister Allegra instead of overweight, to play the piano in a manner that would satisfy her music-teacher father. She lives her most satisfactory life in a fantasy world; even when she first meets Phil, Piercy notes, "It was exactly like a daydream. It was a fantasy, so she knew just how to behave" (100). The skeptical realist Beth and the dreaming Miriam are thus presaged in the reader's initial ac-quaintance with them, and the ultimate message of *Small Changes* has less to do with the revision of standard plots than with the imperatives of individual destinies.

Isadora Wing, in Erica Jong's *Fear of Flying*, also struggles to free herself of cultural mythologies, and her story, like that of Miriam, ends in process, with no clear plot resolution, but in Jong's novel the ending suggests possibilities for positive change rather than continuation on a treadmill. In a dialogue with herself toward the end of *Fear of Flying*, Isadora attempts to talk herself out of the clichés that restrict her independence:

ME: Why is being alone so terrible?
ME: Because if no man loves me I have no identity.
ME: But obviously that isn't true. You write, people read your work and it matters to them. You teach and your students need you and care about you. . . .
ME: None of that makes a dent in my loneliness. I have no man. I have no child.
ME: But you know that children are no antidote to loneliness.
ME: I know.[21]

As the dialogue between Isadora's two selves proceeds, her more objective self presents models of authors that she might emulate:

ME: Think of Simone de Beauvoir!
ME: I love her endurance, but her books are full of Sartre, Sartre, Sartre.
ME: Think of Doris Lessing!
ME: Anna Wulf can't come unless she's in love . . . what more is there to say?
ME: Think of Sylvia Plath!
ME: Dead. Who wants a life or death like hers even if you become a saint? (278)

The tension between Isadora's ironic intellect and her emotional need for love and security pervades *Fear of Flying*. At the same time that her liaison with Adrian Goodlove is the culmination of the fantasy of the ideal man she has had since she was sixteen, she is drawn to the ordinariness of life with her methodical husband,

Bennett. In France with Adrian, she yearns for the stability of the cultural stereotype:

> To be that good little housewife, that glorified American mother, that mascot from *Mademoiselle*, that matron from *McCall's*, that cutie from *Cosmo*, that girl with the Good Housekeeping Seal tatooed on her ass and advertising jingles programmed in her brain. (253)

But Isadora recognizes this as "a fantasy straight out of an ad-man's little brain" (253), just as her adventure with Adrian is a different sort of fantasy—and one with its own imperfections. Adrian is not Isadora's salvation, either; as he remarks at one point, "I told you I'm an anti-hero. I'm not here to rescue you—and carry you away on a white horse" (122).

Vacillating between two kinds of fantasies, Isadora imagines herself as two contrasting fictional characters: Alice in Lewis Carroll's *Alice in Wonderland* and Beatrice in Dante's *Inferno*. As Joan Reardon has written, "illustrating the progress of Isadora Wing's 'growing up female,' Erica Jong uses the journey of Alice and Dante through fantasy and dream into a 'wonderland' and an 'inferno' from which her heroine eventually emerges with a clearer perception of herself."[22] The objective, rational "me" that is Isadora understands that to be defined as either a little girl or the idealized lover—as either Alice or Beatrice—is to remain a character in someone else's story. Her journey through Europe with Adrian partakes of both the absurd strangeness of Alice's adventures and the horror of the inferno. "My conversations with Adrian," she says at one point, "always seemed like quotes from *Through the Looking Glass*" (83). Adrian reminds her of the Cheshire cat, his smile becomes a "beautiful smirk" (249); like the cat, he disappears, to meet his wife and children in Cherbourg, whereupon she realizes that she is "nobody's baby now" (271). References to the *Inferno* appear in conjunction with several of Isadora's relationships. When her first husband, Brian, is hospitalized for mental illness, he accuses her of betraying him: "How could I have locked him up? Didn't I know that I would go to the Seventh Circle—the circle of the traitors? Didn't I know that mine was the lowest crime in Dante's book?" (205). When she is in the stage of fantasizing about Adrian Goodlove before their journey together, she recites to herself a list of famous lovers that begins with Dante and Beatrice and ends with "Me and Adrian?" (166). But Isadora and Adrian are not destined to be great lovers, and as she leaves Paris to try to find Bennett, Isadora realizes that "People don't complete us. We complete ourselves" (299).

The final chapter of *Fear of Flying* is titled "A 19th-Century Ending," and indeed it takes place in a Victorian hotel in London with a concierge that reminds Isadora of Bob Cratchit. But Jong's title is ironic, for the novel does not have the neat resolution of the nineteenth-century novel; instead, it ends as Bennett enters the hotel room to find Isadora washing her hair, having returned from her sojourn with Adrian Goodlove. "Life has no plot," Isadora thinks (311). And yet as Reardon suggests, *Fear of Flying* is governed by a structure that is female rather than male: the length of the menstrual cycle. Although a good deal of the novel involves flashbacks to Isadora's earlier life, the actual time span of the novel is twenty-eight days. "The twenty-eight days of the novel chart the various biochemical changes, the physical experiences of ovulation and flow as well as the psychological movements of relaxation and tension which explain, at least in part, Isadora Wing's actions" (315). During the last part of her trip with Adrian, Isadora fears—for no particular reason—that she may be pregnant, but as soon as he leaves her in Paris, her menstrual flow begins, freeing her from that worry as she is now free from him. The novel is thus built on the rhythms of female biology rather than on the actual mythologies from which Isadora has begun to extricate herself.

Jong's use of women's biological rhythms as a controlling metaphor in her Isadora Wing trilogy represents a deeply feminist response to cultural mythologies that idealize women as children or lovers, virgin or temptress or muse. To rejoice not just in sexuality, but also in pregnancy, childbirth, and motherhood, as Isadora does in the trilogy, is to posit a model of female selfhood that is natural rather than stereotypically imposed. Writing about sexuality in novels by women between 1969 and 1979, Ann Barr Snitow suggests that one reason why earlier women writers seldom addressed female sexual experience in any direct way was their awareness that women were so often defined solely as sexual beings. "They tried to break the equation that linked them to private domestic and sexual experience. They wanted to be visionary artists, not limited women."[23] For women to write freely about sexuality, this suggests, they required the sense that addressing the topic would not limit and stereotype them. Part of this assurance came from birth-control methods that removed the necessary link between sex and pregnancy; and Snitow further suggests that an increasing community of female writers and readers by the late 1960s needed to share experiences—including sexuality—with one another. The freedom—and the need—to write openly about sexuality was an initial stage during the period that Snitow considers; the more recent stage goes beyond mere sharing of experiences as sexual beings to an embracing of all that it means to be female. Ursula LeGuin has recently written of the relationship between motherhood and artistry, refuting the notion that women can either have babies or write books by pointing to many instances in which women's artistic production has been enhanced by their engagement with children:

> To push mothers back into "private life," a mythological space invented by the patriarchy, on the theory that their acceptance of the "role" of mother invalidates them for public, political, artistic responsibility, is to play Old Nobodaddy's game, by his rules, on his side.[24]

It is precisely this celebration of female gender that French feminist critic Hélène Cixous argued for in the 1970s. In "The Laugh of the Medusa," Cixous urges, "Write your self. Your body must be heard."[25] In "Castration or Decapitation?" she similarly calls for distinctively feminine texts. "Women who write," Cixous notes, "have for the most part until now considered themselves to be writing not as women but as writers. Such women may declare that sexual difference means nothing, that there's no attributable difference between masculine and feminine writing."[26] But Cixous sees signs of an emerging literature that affirms women's unique selfhood:

> In particular we ought to be prepared for what I call the "affirmation of difference," not a kind of wake for the corpse of the mummified woman, nor a fantasy of woman's decapitation, but something differ-

ent: a step forward, an adventure, an exploration of woman's powers: of her power, her potency, her ever-dreaded strength, of the regions of femininity. . . . There is work to be done on female sexual pleasure and on the production of an unconscious that would no longer be the classic unconscious. (52)

For Cixous, the "classic unconscious" is cultural, and "when it talks it tells you your old stories, it tells you the old stories you've heard before because it consists of the repressed of culture" (52). But the unconscious—and hence its stories—can also be shaped by "what is outside culture, by a language which is a savage tongue that can make itself understood quite well," when women "set out into the unknown to look for themselves" (52). Setting out into the unknown is the *Surfacing* narrator's quest, just as it is Isadora Wing's fantasy of the "zipless fuck"; in both cases, the women search for men and end up finding themselves in quite physical ways, attuned to their own rhythms.

It is important to observe that Cixous' insistence that women write as women does not imply an endorsement of woman as "other" in a culturally negative sense; indeed, she is emphatic about the power and strength of the feminine text. In this sense, and in her suggestion that women attend to an unconscious different from the "classic unconscious," her thinking is consonant with that of feminist archetypal critics, who urge a re-evaluation that would allow women to find that which is valid for them in such a heritage. Such thinking marks a stage beyond the severe dichotomizing of the early stages of the contemporary women's movement, in which whatever could be ascribed to the patriarchy was all-powerfully destructive to women, and women were assumed to have no common store of experience and knowledge that could operate as a generative force. Annis Pratt describes the dangers of such an oversimplified approach:

In their rejection of women's otherness, . . . feminist scholars tend to take not only norms prescribing subordination for women but all descriptions of femininity as myth, or untruth. Because some stories and symbols describing feminine experience have proven sexist, they dismiss all of them and thus they throw out the crucial archetypes along with the sterotypical images. This tendency to consider as tainted by patriarchy everything found in cultural repositories leads, paradoxically, to assumptions like [Simone] de Beauvoir's that women are to be defined wholly in terms of their otherness and not in terms of their intrinsic being.[27]

Searching more than three hundred novels written by women between 1700 and 1978 for recurring elements of plot, characterization, and theme, Pratt was struck by two opposing tendencies— one in which "women characters showed a kind of mindless, tacit accommodation to gender norms," and another in which the texts contained "strands of a more fully human potential self that contradicted gender norms." The tension between these two tendencies, Pratt observes, "produced an ambivalence of tone, irony in characterization, and strange disjunction in plotting" (95).

In the women's novel from the mid-1960s through the mid-1980s, these three elements—the ambivalent tone, irony, and disjunctive plotting—are intimately related. Distrustful of the self constructed as "other," the author or narrator vacillates between or among more than one view of self embodied in the central character(s), as Isadora Wing vacillates between Alice and Beatrice and ends as neither. This multiple perspective, in its function as revisionary mode, requires irony, as culturally constructed images are tested against a deeper reality in women's experience. And both revision and this multiple narrative perspective cause the novel to be organized in circles or spirals rather than in straightforward chronology, and often to end without resolution but with a sense of starting all over again. Another narrative element common in these novels, exemplified most forcefully by *The Female Man*, is a whole or partial setting in another time, as I shall discuss in more detail in a later chapter. Atwood's *The Handmaid's Tale* and Lessing's *Memoirs of a Survivor* are set in future, post-apocalyptic worlds, as are parts of Lessing's *The Four-Gated City* and Piercy's *Woman on the Edge of Time;* Jong's *Serenissima* involves travel in the past. This narrative device is another means of underscoring distrust of contemporary observable reality, especially its fixity, and forces the reader to realize the arbitrary nature of codes and conventions.

Three novels will serve to illustrate some of the possibilities offered by multiple narrative perspective in revising the self and

100

the mythologies that inform its construction. Fay Weldon's *Words of Advice* deals directly with fairy tales, and the same author's *Female Friends* addresses history and cultural mythologies. Margaret Drabble's *The Waterfall* details a woman's attempt to reconcile her intellectual and biological selves and move toward wholeness.

The fairy-tale motif enters Weldon's *Words of Advice* on several levels, as Weldon suggests that women tend to view their lives in terms of the stories they are told as children. Victor, a forty-four-year-old antique dealer, and his nineteen-year-old mistress, Elsa, are invited to spend a weekend with Hamish and Gemma, a millionaire couple who want Victor's advice about the disposition of some family heirlooms. For Elsa, the weekend promises access to a dazzling world of wealth and the opportunity to sleep with Victor in a real bed rather than the couch in back of the antique shop; she also has vague plans to "forget" to take her birth-control pills so that she can become pregnant as a means of snaring the married Victor. Some of her expectations are dashed immediately when, instead of sharing a room with Victor, Elsa is consigned to a tower, like Rapunzel, and expected to do Gemma's typing. A poor typist, Elsa thinks of the peasant girl in the story of Rumpelstiltskin who, having boasted of her weaving skills, is locked in the castle to weave straw into gold, promising her first-born child to Rumpelstiltskin, who can accomplish this miracle. Elsa's sense of being doomed to some such fate strikes her early in the novel:

> Elsa has the sensation that some fixed pattern of events has moved into place and is now firmly locked, and that whatever she says or does now in this household will be according to destiny, and not in the least according to her own desire.[28]

And in fact Hamish becomes her Rumpelstiltskin, doing the typing that she is supposed to do, and trying to impregnate Elsa so that he and Gemma, who are childless, can keep the baby. We are never certain whether Elsa is in fact pregnant, but at the end of the novel she has escaped from Hamish and Gemma, and is at home drinking cocoa with her brothers and sisters, Victor having been reunited with his wife.

101

Elsa's strand of the narrative is told in the third person. Gemma's story, which she tells to Elsa as "words of advice," is narrated in the same way, but as a recollection of the past—or, rather, as one version of her past. Gemma begins by announcing to Elsa that she will tell her a fairy tale, and as she reaches the end, in response to Hamish's comment "I hope it's true," Gemma says merely, "It will do" (224). Gemma's story, Weldon notes, is "like any tale told in retrospect, heightened in the telling, purified of pain, reduced to anecdote and entertainment" (62); yet this comment must be seen as part of Weldon's pervasive irony, because Gemma's story partakes of the violence and pain common to the fairy tale, including having her ring finger cut off with an ax, and marrying the frog instead of the prince. Elsa's and Gemma's stories are similar in several ways: both women are from poor families, and as young women earn their living in London by working as clerk-typists; Elsa's current gullibility mirrors that of the young Gemma; and both have loved, unwisely, the wrong man: Victor and Mr. Fox, respectively. Indeed, Gemma is as much as the princess imprisoned in the tower as Elsa imagines herself to be: she has lost the use of her legs and is confined to a wheelchair, and in fact it was her physical helplessness that caused her to accept Hamish's marriage proposal. Yet the "frog" turned out to be quite wealthy, and Gemma now takes an ironic view of her own life, able to see it in the context of self-fabrication: "Princes, toads, princesses, beggar girls—we all have to place ourselves as best we can" (20).

The third story in *Words of Advice* is that of Janice, Victor's estranged wife. In contrast to Gemma's ironic self-awareness, Janice has spent the years of her marriage unwittingly playing a role in order to meet Victor's expectations of her. Victor had expected to marry a virgin, "someone as pure and helpful as his own mother"; thus Janice, after a sexually promiscuous youth, "silently and instinctively made herself as rigid, plain, clean, orderly and respectable as possible" (154), and has, in Weldon's view, become a type rather than an individual:

Behold wild Janice, married! What we have here, ladies and gentlemen, is no woman, but a housewife. And what a housewife! Note her rigid, mousy curls, kept stiff by spray; her quick eyes, which search for

102

dust and burning toast, and not the appraisal or enquiry of the opposite sex; the sharp voice, growing sharper, louder, year by year.
(154–55)

But after Victor has left her, tired of the person he has created in a
sort of reversal of the Pygmalion story, Janice reverts to her former
behavior by having an affair with a Polish carpenter who comes to
fix her wardrobe. She seems content to have Victor gone, so that
she can shed the mask she has been wearing. She imagines saying
to Victor, "Go to Elsa, then, while I, Janice, remember who I am.
While there's still time: before my hair is iron grey, like my heart,
and there is no turning back" (155). Yet when Victor and Janice
meet at Hamish and Gemma's house, their respective naughtiness
attracts them once again to each other, and they leave together in
Victor's Volvo, presumably to take up their life together in a somewhat altered form.

By the end of the novel, all three women have escaped from the
stories that have shaped their lives. Elsa has been awakened from
her dream of Victor and is at home in the world of her childhood,
awaiting the next stage of her progress to maturity. Janice has
abandoned her false identity as a rigid, self-denying housewife.
Gemma's emergence into the world of reality is the most painful,
perhaps because she has constructed her own fairy tale rather
than fitting herself into someone else's story, as have Janice and
Elsa. When Gemma says spitefully to Elsa late in the novel, "You're
just a two-bit player in other people's dreams" (231), there is an
ironic truth to her statement. But in spite of Gemma's ability to
acknowledge that she has invented several versions of her past,
she is shaken when Hamish insists upon telling Elsa the unglam-
orous truth about her past and thereby removes the possibility of
illusion from her. In her anguish, Gemma enunciates the central
truth of Weldon's novel: "It's just that love and romance and illusion and hope are etched so deeply into all our hearts that they
can never quite be wiped away. They stay around to torment us
with thoughts of what might have been" (231). Yet the truth has
freed Gemma from self-delusion, and she is able to overcome the
psychosomatic paralysis of her legs and leave her wheelchair.

A pervasive underlying theme in *Words of Advice* is the need for women to help each other. The story of her life that Gemma tells to Elsa, however falsified, is intended as a cautionary tale against innocence and ignorance. "If only," Gemma says, "we women could learn from one another" (183). The wife of the Polish carpenter with whom Janice has an affair echoes the same sentiment after she discovers her husband in Janice's bedroom. Angry not at Janice but at her husband, she says, "I only wish women would stick together a bit" (160). Ultimately, it is Gemma who frees Elsa from being the princess in the tower and owing her terrible debt to Hamish/Rumpelstiltskin; free at last from her own fairy tale, "herself transcended," Gemma urges Elsa to escape: "Run, Elsa! Run for all you're worth. Don't fall. Please don't fall the way I did. You can do it; go so far and then draw back. I know you can. You must! You must run for me and all of us" (233). As Elsa runs, she looks back to see Gemma taking her first steps out of the wheelchair where her own fantasy had confined her.

The title of Weldon's novel *Female Friends* similarly suggests female closeness and support, but the title is revealed to be heavily ironic and women's ability to help each other in meaningful ways a fantasy. Caught not in fairy tales but in actualities, the three central characters in *Female Friends* are unable to heed each others' advice about their lives; nor does Chloe, the narrator, believe that their stories can serve as cautionary tales for readers: "If there are lessons to be learned by others, I would be glad, but also surprised. For who bothers to learn by another's experience?"[29] The only worthwhile lesson, Chloe asserts wryly, is not to expect too much from life:

> Pretty little sister, on your feather cushion, combing out your silken hair, don't discredit what your elder sister says. Much less your grandmama. Listen carefully now to what she says, and you may not end as tired and worn as she. . . . The good times come, and no sooner here than gone. . . . So treasure your moments of beauty, your glimpses of truth, your nights of love. They are all you have. (309–10)

As she does in *Words of Advice,* Weldon here warns against fantasy, the happily-ever-after ending, and suggests that life is more coincidental than plotted.

104

Chloe's mother, Gwyneth, is presented in *Female Friends* as the major source of misleading mythologies, including platitudes, truisms, and old wives' tales. A widow, raising her daughter alone during World War II, Gwyneth imparts to Chloe her small store of wisdom, accumulated from "dubious sources, magazines, preachers and sentimental drinkers." Although Gwyneth's "words of advice" come from her ignorance rather than from malice, they are in many ways similar to the maxims that the Aunts use to coach the Handmaids in Atwood's *The Handmaid's Tale*, "false and occasionally dangerous." So Chloe grows up being told that red flannel is warmer than white flannel, and that "marriages are made in heaven," but also, "marry in haste, repent in leisure." Such contradictions do not bother Gwyneth, who "retreats from the truth into ignorance, and finds that the false beliefs and half-truths, interweaving, make a fine supportive pillow for a gentle person against whom God has taken an irrational dislike" (45). Gwyneth lives in a fantasy of love for her employer, Mr. Leacock, and her willful imagination translates an occasional stolen kiss into a mutual grand passion. Preferring fantasy to truth, Gwyneth never declares her love:

> Gwyneth believes she has only to speak the words and Mr. Leacock will be hers; and forever procrastinates, and never quite speaks them. Thus, lonely women do live, making the best of what they cannot help: reading significance into casual words: seeing love in calculated lust: seeing lust in innocent words: hoping where there is no hope. (108)

The perspective in this passage is that of the mature Chloe, whose ironic narrative provides the dominant tone of the novel as she alternately reassesses the past lives of herself and her "female friends" Grace and Marjorie, and describes their situations during a two-day period in the 1960s.

Of the three central female characters, Chloe is the ideal ironic narrator. In both her childhood and her present, she is an outsider, positioned to see that things are not what they seem. When the three meet as children during the relocation of children to rural areas outside London during the war, Grace and Marjorie are from middle-class backgrounds, but Chloe's mother, widow of a miner, works as a barmaid at the Rose and Crown pub; Marjorie lives with Grace and her family, local gentry, while Chloe and her mother inhabit a small room behind the pub. In the present of the novel, Chloe lives outside London with her husband, while Grace and Marjorie live in the city. Chloe is at once mother-figure and oracle. Of the five children who live in her house, only two are her own; one is Grace's and two are the offspring of Patrick Bates, who has been the lover of all three women and is the father of one of Chloe's children. She serves as confidante and adviser to Marjorie and Grace, and in her first-person narratives frequently exhorts readers to beware the traps that life may set for them—traps that she and Grace and Marjorie have fallen into.

By juxtaposing first- and third-person narratives in rapid succession, Weldon contrasts the complex and often painful events of Chloe's life with her stoic, cautionary pronouncements. Despite, for example, Chloe's tendency to accumulate other people's children, she advises the reader to avoid children altogether: "Oh my friends, my female friends, how wise you are to have no children or to throw them off" (204). Chloe's husband, Oliver, openly seduces their French maid, Françoise; when he presents Chloe with the age-old excuse that his sexual urges are stronger than he is, she responds coolly, "It must be dreadful to be a man, and be so helpless in the face of one's own nature" (266). It is Chloe's ability to adopt the ironic stance of her first-person narrative within the alternate reality of the third-person narrative that finally frees her from Oliver and her fantasy of the perfect marriage. *Female Friends* ends at the point of transition, in the present tense: "As for me, Chloe, I no longer wait to die. I put my house, Marjorie's house, in order, and not before time. The children help. Oliver says 'But you can't leave me with Françoise,' and I reply, I can, I can, and I do" (311). The "I do," echoing the marriage vows, signals the ending of the marriage and the beginning of Chloe's new life.

Agate Nesaule Krouse finds the relationships among women in *Female Friends* a strongly positive theme in the novel: "Men come and go, but the relationships between women endure."[30] It is true that Chloe, Marjorie, and Grace stay in touch with one another, and that Marjorie gives her house to Chloe so that she can leave Oliver at the end of the novel, but Weldon makes it clear that much of the time these "female friends" merely tolerate each other. They are thrown together by accident and shared adversity more than by affection. As children, Marjorie and Chloe arrive in Ulden, where Grace lives, by mistake: the train was supposed to stop in Egden. At the end of the novel they are brought together by Marjorie's mother's death. In between these two occasions, they lie to each other, criticize each other, and fail to follow each others' advice. Further, the influence of mothers on daughters seems to be primarily negative because it encourages endurance and conformity rather than independence. As Chloe muses toward the end of the novel, "What progress can there be, from generation to generation, if daughters do as mothers do?" (306). So great is the weight of received traditions and mythologies that it requires enormous struggle to break free, and one can only wish, Weldon suggests, that friends will help. Late in the novel, Marjorie says, "We were none of us all that much help to each other. . . . We should interfere more in each other's lives, and not just pick up pieces" (288). In *Female Friends,* as in *Words of Advice,* Weldon enunciates clearly the need for women to care for and learn from each other, but at the same time posits that female selfhood must be arrived at individually, despite yearnings for sisterhood.

The multiple narrative perspective that in Weldon's novels demonstrates her characters' ability to view themselves and the stories that would control them ironically is used in Margaret Drabble's *The Waterfall* to question the validity of identity itself and to explore the relationships between truth and fiction, reality and fantasy. It is this exploration that has led Michael Harper to call *The Waterfall* a postmodern novel, in which "there are no 'individuals' at all in the sense of independent, solid 'selves' like the characters of old-fashioned 'realistic' fiction but instead mere collections of inconsistent behaviors and interpretations determined finally by language and social practice."[31] *The Waterfall* consists of a third-person narrative that is continually revised by a first-person narrative as Jane Gray attempts to find a story that will represent accurately her experience and emotions. The reader is left to mediate imaginatively among the multiple "truths" about Jane Gray; as author of her own story, Jane claims the freedom to tell and re-tell the narrative as a means of metaphorically claiming control of her life. In a 1972 interview with Nancy S. Hardin, Drabble explained how she came to let her character seem to control her own narrative:

> I'd been wanting to write the first section of that book for a long time and I wrote it and I was intending to turn it into a novel. When I'd written it, I couldn't go on because it seemed to me that I'd set up this very forceful image of romantic, almost thirteenth-century love. Having had the experience [of] describing the experience, one had to say what is this about? I thought the only way to do it was to make Jane say it.[32]

Drabble's consciousness that one must, in the twentieth century, ask questions about "romantic, almost thirteenth-century love" caused her to write *The Waterfall* as, on one level, an inquiry into fictional modes. Jane, as a writer, is acutely aware of literary history—particularly the tradition of the women's novel, in which women paid a steep price for passion, especially adulterous passion such as that which Jane shares with her cousin Lucy's husband, James. Jane makes specific reference to Sue Bridehead in Hardy's *Jude the Obscure* and Maggie Tulliver in George Eliot's *The Mill on the Floss,* and wonders whether she will go mad, like Sue, or drown herself, like Maggie: "Those fictitious heroines, how they haunt me."[33] The endings of these earlier novels will not do in a post-Freudian era, when we "guess dimly at our own passions"; "In this age, what is to be done?" (162). Freed from the endings of old novels, Jane has the dilemma of creating a story that will fit the realities of twentieth-century experience, and the structure of *The Waterfall,* with its constant revising and beginning again, is Drabble's resolution of that dilemma.

Caryn Fuoroli has proposed that *The Waterfall* is flawed because Drabble is unable to control her own narrative. By using the alternative first-person narrative, Fuoroli argues, "Drabble fails to maintain the authorial distance and control that would allow us as readers to evaluate Jane."[34] Fuoroli seems to want *The Waterfall* to conform to the pattern of the *bildungsroman,* in which the central issue is the growth and development of the main character as measured against a standard established by the author and reflecting social norms; what she finds missing in the novel is "some authorial direction which gives a sense of a developing character against which to measure Jane's own narration" (112). But this misses Drabble's point: Jane's life cannot be enclosed by either social convention or the structure of the conventional novel. Instead, her story is what Cixous describes as a "feminine text," which "starts on all sides at once, starts twenty times, thirty times, over."[35] Not only does Jane's story begin many times, as the third-person narration is revised by the first-person narrator, but Jane is also concerned about endings. After the automobile accident in which James is injured as they are leaving on an illicit vacation together, Jane comments as author on this part of her story:

> There isn't any conclusion. A death would have been the answer, but nobody died. Perhaps I should have killed James in the car, and that would have made a neat, a possible ending.
>
> A feminine ending?
>
> Or, I could have maimed James so badly, in this narrative, that I would have been allowed to have him, as Jane Eyre had her blinded Rochester. But I hadn't the heart to do it, I loved him too much, and anyway it wouldn't have been the truth because the truth is that he recovered. (248)

Although she is drawn to the "neat" conclusion of the traditional novel, with its accompanying punishment or reward, Jane's fidelity to the "truth" wins out. Yet she continues to be haunted by this lack of closure: "We should have died, I suppose, James and I. It isn't artistic to linger on like this. It isn't moral either. One can't have art without morality, anyway, as I've always maintained" (249). In view of the story Jane tells us, the irony of this statement is obvious, and is made more so by Jane's explanation a few paragraphs later of why she is concluding her story by telling of a trip that she and James took to Yorkshire, even though the story is "irrelevant"—"and it must be irrelevant because the only moral of it could be that one can get away with anything, that one can survive anything, a moral that I in no way believe" (252).

But the trip to Yorkshire to see the waterfall of the title is not, in fact, the ending of the novel; Jane is compelled to offer a post-script in which she marks the distance between her story and the traditional woman's plot. She notes that because of a blood clot she has ceased taking birth-control pills. The clot is "the price that modern woman must pay for love":

> In the past, in old novels, the price of love was death, a price which virtuous women paid in childbirth, and the wicked, like Nana, with the pox. Nowadays it is paid in thrombosis or neurosis: one can take one's pick. I stopped taking those pills, as James lay there unconscious and motionless, but one does not escape decision so easily. I am glad of this. I am glad I cannot swallow pills with immunity. I prefer to suffer, I think. (256).

Ellen Cronan Rose has pointed out that this postscript "success-fully resists its own impulse to make a final formulation. The last dramatic, heroic, 'masculine' statement—'I prefer to suffer'—is followed by the feminine ending, 'I think.'"[36] By refusing to con-clude her narrative with a "neat" ending, Jane Gray reinforces the concept that life is a continuing process of new beginnings and equivocal endings.

The development of Jane's ironic voice is a measure of her de-tachment from more than the plot of the traditional novel; she has also achieved distance from many of the myths and conventions that had prevented her from being the author of her own life. It is the consciousness of the first-person narrator that assesses and re-vises not just the story she tells, but the stories she has been told. Jane's parents have raised her with a rigid sense of respectability:

> They believed, or so they said, in the God of the Church of England, and in a whole host of other irreconcilable propositions: in monog-amy, in marrying for love, in free will, in the possibility of moderation of the passions, in the virtues of reason and civilization. (51)

As a child, Jane is distrustful of these pieties, but dares not voice her distrust: "I felt all the time afraid that any word of mine, any movement, my mere existence, might shatter them all into frag-ments" (51–52). Only with James does she feel that she is herself, and not someone's construction of her, but at first she is not sure whether what she terms his "recognition" of her represents "salvation or damnation," and it is this uncertainty that leads to the announcement that she will reconstruct her story—an announcement that dictates the narrative structure of the book:

> I must make an effort to comprehend it. I will take it all to pieces, I will resolve it to its parts, and then I will put it together again, I will reconstitute it in a form that I can accept, a fictitious form: adding a little here, abstracting a little there, moving this arm half an inch that way, gently altering the dead angle of the head upon its neck. If I need a morality I will create one: a new ladder, a new virtue. If I need to understand what I am doing, if I cannot act without my own approbation—and I must act, I have changed, I am no longer capable of inaction—then I will invent a morality that condones me. Though by doing so, I risk condemning all that I have been. (53–54)

This passage, occurring barely a fifth of the way into the novel, proposes Jane's position as creator rather than created. The story she ultimately tells may be "fictitious," but it will be a story that she can live with and in; and because the moral structures she has inherited from her parents and from the traditional plot are not sufficient to allow her to "condone" herself, she will create new ones.

It is "that most disastrous concept, the concept of free will" (51) which gives Jane the most difficulty, because she recognizes that it can be deceptive. When she has assumed she was acting out of free will, she realizes, she was instead being compelled by stories. When she fell in love with her husband, Malcolm, for example, she succumbed to the romance of the Thomas Campion lyrics he was singing and not to the person he was. She blames the poets for devising stories of love and tragedy: "I blame Shakespeare for that farcical moment in *Romeo and Juliet* where he sees her at the dance, from far off, and says, I'll have her, because she is the one that will kill me" (92). Instead of free will, Jane chooses to believe in fate, or what she terms "Necessity"—operating on an instinct that derives from one's most basic needs, as she does in her relationship with James. It is this instinctual, rather than culturally determined, need for James that has led one critic to state that she and James "live out an obsessive fairy tale in which she is the imprisoned maiden," and that the narrative "locates itself within the constrained world of the fairytale."[37] But it is precisely in *removing* herself from the world of fairy tales that Jane is able to move toward self-knowledge.

Perhaps the most important single sentence in *The Waterfall* is Jane's comment about her story that "There isn't any conclusion." Having always felt that "people could not change, that they were predetermined, unalterable, helpless in the hands of destiny" (243), she now knows that it is her power to revise her own story—not merely the story of her life with James, but any story in which she may find herself enmeshed. Her ironic consciousness of the relativity of truth is embodied in the last phrase of the novel—"I think"—which is at once a statement of that relativity and an assertion of intellectual control.

CHAPTER FOUR

# Acceptable Fantasies

The frequent use of a multiple narrative perspective by contemporary women novelists is closely related to the sense of divided self that affects contemporary women so directly, as they deal with the simultaneous demands of home and career, family and employment, past and future, myth and reality. Such division is at best disorienting, and at worst calls into question the reality of the self. Fay Weldon, in whose fiction multiple narrative is a standard device, has written amusingly and perceptively about the self-division of the woman writer. In "Me and My Shadows," she interviews herself, declaring that to split herself in two is "a simple task," and describes to her "interviewer" the parts of herself:

> A lives in a kind of parody of an NW [London] lady writer's life. Telephones ringing, washing machine overflowing, children coming and going, and so on. B does the writing. B is very stern, male (I think), hard working, puritanical, obsessive and unsmiling. C is depressive, and will sit for days staring into space, inactive, eating too much bread and butter, called into action only by the needs of the children. A knows about C but very little about B. B knows about A and C and in fact controls them, sending them out into the world but otherwise despising them. C is ignorant of A and B—and although A and B leave

113

her notes, advising her at least to tidy the drawers or sort the files so as not to waste too much of the lifespan, C has not the heart or spirit to act on them.[1]

The splitting of the self into several parts, here described by Weldon as even a duality of gender, suggests conditions of multiple personalities and schizophrenia—mental states in which the psyche constructs alternate realities. Virginia Woolf's "Angel in the House," like Weldon's "A," is an imaginative rendering of an alternative self that is feminine in the traditional sense, at odds with the task of writing. At its extreme, such division of the self into parts results in neurosis or psychosis; more commonly, it is expressed in dreams and fantasies.

If the sense of the divided self is one reason for the frequent use of dreams, fantasies, and madness in these novels, another is the concept of boundaries to be transgressed, lines to be crossed, if only in the imagination. It is no accident that Woolf's angel is *in the house*, or that Weldon's "A" brings the writing self "B" cups of coffee: both inhabit the enclosed spaces of domesticity, rather than ranging over the wide spaces of human possibility. As a number of critics have noted, women's fiction tends to be enclosed, bounded by rooms, walls, gender restrictions—even the body itself. Roberta Rubenstein, for example, asserts that "the body is . . . the template for figurative expressions of boundary conceived as enclosure (or its opposite) in temporal as well as spatial terms. Thus, rooms, walls, houses—including the more emotionally saturated meanings associated with 'home'—are tropes for inner experience, as are imprisonment, escape, flight, and homelessness."[2] Similarly, Mickey Pearlman writes that authors from Edith Wharton to Sue Miller write "of the usually imprisoning psychological and actual spaces of American women, of being trapped, submerged, ovewhelmed."[3] Dreams, fantasy, and madness become ways of transcending boundaries, either temporarily or as part of a journey to autonomy and wholeness.

Patricia Meyer Spacks makes much the same point in *The Female Imagination* when she argues that female fantasy should be seen as a positive rather than a negative force:

# Acceptable Fantasies

The idea that women may find their most significant freedom through fantasy or imagination need not imply any commitment to madness. Saner visions of the imagination as salvation, which underlie many pre-twentieth-century novels about and by women and at least a few autobiographies, substantiate the possibility that the liberated inner life may create new freedoms of actual experience.

The difficulties of feminine freedom . . . inhere in the actualities of feminine experience. To arrive at freedom . . . through direct self-presentation or fictional creation, is to triumph over actuality.[4]

Miriam's adolescent fantasy of being the invincible "Tamar de-Luria" in *Small Changes*, like the fantasy of the "woman warrior" in Kingston's book, are at least temporarily empowering because they allow the characters to escape imaginatively the boundaries of their lives as young women—they permit images of freedom and power denied by the characters' immediate social context. Atwood's narrator in *Surfacing* and Martha in Lessing's *The Four-Gated City* go through periods of self-willed detachment from reality in order to emerge whole and sane.

Mira, in Marilyn French's *The Women's Room* (1977), is an ideal example of Spacks's contention that women seek in books acceptable patterns for their own lives. As an adolescent, Mira gives up on the sugary neatness of "girls' books" and turns to "Jane Austen and Fanny Burney and George Eliot and Gothic novels of all sorts, Daphne du Maurier and Somerset Maugham and Frank Yerby and John O'Hara. . . . she drowned in words that could not teach her to swim."[5] All of this reading "felt like a kind of insanity to her, something she couldn't help, but something that was not good" (30). Nonetheless, it provides an escape: "Sometimes she felt she was reading to escape from life, for the escape, at least, occurred" (29). When French enters *The Women's Room* as the first-person author of Mira's story, she addresses the issue of the fantasy as an alternate reality:

I was on my way to saying that Mira had lived all her life in fairy-tale land and when she went through the doorway, her head was still full of fairyland images, she had no notion of reality. But obviously she did, fairyland was her reality. So if you want to stand in judgement on

115

her you have to determine whether her reality was the same as other people's, i.e., was she crazy? (13)

As the novel unfolds, the reader, thus invited to judge Mira, concludes that she is not crazy, but merely desperate to transcend the boundaries of her life. But Mira is not as certain: at the end, the first-person narrator reports that "the story has no ending," or boundary, but neither has Mira found an alternate world in which to live, and is wondering whether she is going mad. (683)

The fact that dreams and fantasies are so commonly a part of the stories that contemporary women novelists tell suggests that women's fantasies, like their reliance on stories for acceptable life patterns, are widely shared experiences. Such a supposition is supported by Erica Jong's comments on her sense of identity with her readers' fantasies:

> From the courage the women's movement gave and from the reinforcement I received from grateful and passionate readers, I learned the daring to assume that my thoughts, nightmares, and daydreams were the same as my readers'. I discovered that whenever I wrote about a fantasy I thought was wholly private, bizarre, kinky—(the fantasy of the Zipless Fuck in *Fear of Flying* is perhaps the best example of this)—I invariably discovered that thousands of other people had experienced the same private, bizarre, kinky fantasy.[6]

Inherent in exposing what Carolyn Heilbrun calls women's "unacceptable fantasies" to the world is the danger of being considered insane, and many characters in these novels, like Mira, came to doubt their own sanity because their imaginations depart so far from the boundaries of socially constructed reality. Jane Gray in *The Waterfall* is so immersed in her fantasy-come-true relationship with James that she imagines he might be killed while on holiday with his family. After detailing her attempts to discover the precise moment at which he will return to England, Jane comments, "I recount these things as proof of my madness."[7] Her affair with James exists outside the boundaries of respectability—an illicit dream from which she continually expects to be awakened by disaster. Isadora Wing's fear of loneliness, which causes her to create

116

and live out fantasies of relationships with men, leads her to doubt her own sanity and has driven her to one psychiatrist after another. Near the end of the novel, she pulls herself out of self-pity: "I was dimly aware that being able to get up and wash was at least a sign of life. Real lunatics just lie there in their own piss and shit."[8] The ability of Jane and Isadora to see themselves with ironic detachment saves them from actual madness.

Dreams and fantasies can enclose as well as liberate the female character. Jane Clifford, in Godwin's *The Odd Woman*, remains in her world of literature and wonders whether she has dreamed up her lover, Gabriel. Even at the end of the novel, fearing that an intruder is trying to enter her house, she imagines talking to him as she would to one of her students, believing that "he was not yet beyond words."[9] The irony of Jane's statement is that she herself cannot get beyond the words of the stories she teaches. In Atwood's *Lady Oracle*, Joan Foster's life is patterned on the Gothic romances she writes as Louisa K. Delacourt. Having faked her own death by drowning in the manner of a romantic heroine, Joan has still not come to terms with the direction of her life. She does not have "any definite plans," and stays on in Rome to visit in the hospital the reporter who has found her hiding place and whom she has wounded with a Cinzano bottle; he has become in a sense her wounded hero: "there is something about a man in a bandage," she thinks.[10] And Gemma, in Weldon's *Words of Advice*, is trapped physically as well as emotionally by the fairy tale she makes of her life.

More commonly, however, dreams and fantasies represent the possibility of change rather than stasis and entrapment, and demonstrate the characters' need to project lives beyond immediate reality. Adolescent fantasies of power, such as those in *The Woman Warrior* and *Small Changes*; Celie's dreams of Nettie in *The Color Purple*; Lesje's fantasies of her own version of prehistory in *Life Before Man*—all embody urgent desires to revise objective reality into a form consonant with autonomy. The revelation of their characters' dreams and fantasies reflects the novelists' consciousness that the parts of life normally hidden from public view may

117

be significant keys to identity and aspiration. Margaret Atwood has commented on the revelatory nature of the contemporary women's novel as a source of its energy:

> In recent years, much of the energy of women novelsits—and they have been energetic—has come from the sense that they were opening forbidden doors, saying the hitherto unsayable, raising to the level of art, or at least the written word, material that was considered either too dirty or too abnormal or just too trivial to merit inclusion.[11]

The most obvious and paradigmatic example of Atwood's point is Isadora Wing's fantasy of the "zipless fuck," a sexual encounter of pure eroticism, having no reference to relationship or commitment. Isadora is certain that her husband Bennett, a psychiatrist, would cast aspersions on such a fantasy from a purely professional point of view: "A fantasy is only a fantasy, and *everyone* has fantasies. Only psychopaths actually act out all their fantasies; normal people don't." But Isadora understands the power of fantasy in her own life: "I have more respect for fantasy than that. You are what you dream. You are what you daydream" (34).

As Isadora dreams of a future of sexual freedom, Offred, in *The Handmaid's Tale*, must dream of previous autonomy from her position as sexual slave in the Republic of Gilead. Dream and memory are structural elements in the novel: alternating chapters are titled "Night" (and in one case "Nap"), as Offred's memories of her mother, her husband, and her child are counterpointed to her present existence. She remembers her feminist mother and her friends burning pornographic books and magazines, "their faces . . . happy, ecstatic almost."[12] In the chapter titled "Nap," she dreams of the command she once had of her own body:

> I used to think of my body as an instrument of pleasure, or a means of transportation, or an implement for the accomplishment of my will. I could use it to run, push buttons of one sort or another, make things happen. There were limits, but my body was nevertheless lithe, single, solid, one with me. (73)

Offred's dream turns into an nightmare about the loss of her husband and daughter, and in the next "Night" chapter she dreams of making love to Luke during her pregnancy and then of the possible fates he might have suffered since they have been separated. By the time of the fifth "Night" section, midway through the novel, having re-lived in dreams her earlier life, Offred attempts to come to terms with the present: "I must forget about my secret name and all ways back. My name is Offred now, and here is where I live. Live in the present, make the most of it, it's all you've got" (143). By the time of the next "Night" chapter, she has difficulty remembering the faces of her family: "they slip away from me, ghosts at daybreak" (193). Part of confronting the present is acquiescing to Serena Joy's plan to have Nick, the chauffeur, impregnate her as the Commander seems unable to do, and their first, forced sexual encounter occurs in the next-to-last "Night" section, which prepares for the ambiguity of Offred's removal from the Commander's house in the "black van" that could mean either salvation by the underground Mayday resistance group, as Nick assures her it is, or a different kind of imprisonment—or death—as a traitor. The ambiguity of the ending signals another dreamlike state as Offred steps into the van, "into the darkness within; or else the light" (295).

Offred's imprisonment in Gilead is continually contrasted to the relative freedom women enjoyed before the fundamentalist takeover that has relegated them to choiceless categories—Handmaids, Aunts, Marthas, Unwomen. During a shopping trip, Offred remembers that one of the shops was once a movie theater that featured Humphrey Bogart film festivals. She recalls Lauren Bacall and Katharine Hepburn, "women on their own, making up their minds." In these films the women wore "blouses with buttons down the front that suggested the possibilities of the word *undone*. These women could be undone; or not. They seemed to be able to choose" (25). Films, like books, are the sources of adolescent fantasies in many of these novels, providing potential life scripts that reinforce traditional female roles. For the young Joan, in *Lady Oracle*, the ideal is the woman who suffers for love, and her favorite film is *The Red Shoes*, in which the heroine is torn between marriage and career:

119

> I adored her: not only did she have red hair and an entrancing pair of red satin slippers to match, she also had beautiful costumes, and she suffered more than anyone. . . . I wanted those things too, I wanted to dance and be married to a handsome orchestra conductor, both at once—and when she finally threw herself in front of a train I let out a bellowing snort that made people three rows ahead turn around indignantly. (87)

Joan's life becomes a sort of parody of the plot of *The Red Shoes* as she remains caught in the world of fantasy: her career as Louisa K. Delacourt remains hidden from her husband, and instead of a romantic suicide, her "death" is a fraud—part of her unsuccessful attempt to write the script for her own life. In contrast to Joan's immersion in fantasy, the title character in Alice Walker's *Meridian* views such fantasies ironically. At seventeen, Meridian is a mother, a deserted wife, and a high-school dropout. Harsh reality has replaced fantasy for Meridian, and the resultant distance she feels from other young girls allows her to see clearly their own reliance on fantasy: "They simply did not know they were living their own lives—between twelve and fifteen—but assumed they lived someone else's. They tried to live the lives of their movie idols; and those lives were fantasy." The "movie idols" are further removed from the lives of these young black girls because they are white: Rory Calhoun, Ava Gardner, Bette Davis, Slim Pickens. At seventeen, Meridian has already moved by necessity past the world of such fantasies; she considers the gender-role stereotyping in such film fantasies: "So they moved, did the young girls outside her window, in the dream of happy endings: of women who had everything, of men who ran the world. So had she."[13]

Perhaps the most devastating account of youthful fantasy in contemporary fiction is Toni Morrison's *The Bluest Eye*. Pecola Breedlove, having absorbed her family's sense of inferiority, longs for the blue eyes of Shirley Temple until the longing, coupled with a still-birth after she is raped by her father, ends in madness. Morrison juxtaposes the desirable blue-eyed image of the dominant culture to Pecola's undesirable ugliness—a lack of physical attractiveness acknowledged even by her friends, Claudia and Frieda McTeer. But this is only one of many ironic juxtapositions in a

120

novel that addresses both the power and the danger of fantasy. The bland "Dick and Jane" litany that opens the novel becomes obscene when it is connected with the house where Pecola's mother, Pauline, works for a white family, preferring the white child to her own daughter. Pauline's own youthful fantasies of a "Presence, an all embracing tenderness with strength and a promise of rest"[14] have resulted in a destructive marriage to Cholly, whose own humiliation by whites has caused him to hate women. Before her first child is born, Pauline attempts to escape the loneliness of her marriage by going to the movies, where "her memory was refreshed, and she succumbed to her earlier dreams." In addition to the romance in films starring Clark Gable and Jean Harlow, Pauline is introduced to the standards of physical beauty that will later affect her daughter Pecola. Morrison refers to the concepts of romantic love and physical beauty as "probably the most destructive ideas in the history of human thought. Both originated in envy, thrived in insecurity, and ended in disillusion" (97). Pauline is vaguely aware of the distinction between fantasy and her own reality—"Them pictures gave me a lot of pleasure, but it made coming home hard" (97)—but it is Pecola's tragedy to become so enmeshed in the fantasy of the blue eyes that she never achieves this kind of adult perception.

Pecola learns of Shirley Temple not from films, but from her image on Frieda's milk cup when she lives briefly with the McTeer family as a foster child. Claudia, unlike Frieda and Pecola, sees the irony and injustice of the black Bojangles dancing with the blond Shirley Temple. To Claudia, Bojangles was "*my* friend, *my* uncle, *my* daddy, who ought to have been soft-shoeing it and chuckling with me. Instead he was enjoying, sharing, giving a lovely dance thing with one of those little white girls whose socks never slid down under their heels" (19). It is while staying with the McTeers that Pecola begins menstruating, and this event is immediately linked to her ability to bear children. When Pecola asks how this is accomplished, Frieda replies that "somebody has to love you" (29), with a childlike simplicity that cannot anticipate the mixture of hatred and guilt that provokes Cholly to rape and impregnate Pecola. Following the stillbirth, Pecola, having prayed incessantly for blue eyes, seeks the assistance of Soaphead Church, who out of his own powerlessness assures her that a magic spell will give her the blue eyes she seeks. Touched by her simple, straightforward request, this molester of little girls gives her what he believes to be faith in her own beauty. As he writes to God immediately afterward, "No one else will see her blue eyes. But *she* will. And she will live happily ever after" (143). But the only happiness Pecola finds is in removal from reality in madness, talking to an imaginary friend who assures her that hers are indeed the bluest eyes. Near the end of *The Bluest Eye*, Claudia comments on the destruction that fantasy has caused:

> The damage done was total. She spent her days, her tendril, sap-green days, walking up and down, up and down, her head jerking to the beat of a drummer so distant only she could hear. Elbows bent, hands on shoulders, she flailed her arms like a bird in an eternal, grotesquely futile effort to fly. Beating the air, a winged but grounded bird, intent on the blue void it could not reach—could not even see—but which filled the valleys of the mind. (158)

Adolescent fantasies often gain their power from the absence of real information about life, love, and sexuality. Coming of age in the 1960s, the female characters in these novels frequently have mothers who are reticent about sexuality in particular. Meridian's mother "never even used the word. . . . Having told [Meridian] absolutely nothing, she had expected her to *do* nothing," with the result that Meridian's teenage pregnancy "came as a total shock" (60–61). Isadora's mother, in *Fear of Flying*, despite her championing of certain "bohemian" ideas, merely cautions Isadora to "play hard to get," and Isadora suspects that "she disapproved of sex, that it was basically unmentionable" (153). So Isadora derives her ideas of female sexuality from books: "I learned about women from men. I saw them through the eyes of male writers. Of course, I didn't think of them as *male* writers. I thought of them as *writers*, as authorities, as gods who knew and were to be trusted completely" (154). From D. H. Lawrence, Isadora learns what an orgasm is, and that women worship the "Phallos." Shaw teaches her that "women never can be artists"; Dostoevsky, that women

122

have no religious feeling, and Swift and Pope that they have too much religious feeling—"and therefore can never be quite rational." She learns from Faulkner that women are earth mothers, and from Freud that they suffer penis envy. But even as an adolescent, Isadora sees the ironic conflict between the lessons of these "authorities" and the reality of her own life:

> What did all this have to do with me—who went to school and got better marks than the boys and painted and wrote and spent Saturdays doing still lifes at the Art Students League and my weekday afternoons editing the high-school paper . . . ? What did the moon and tides and earth-mothering and the worship of the Laurentian "phallos" have to do with me or with my life? (154)

By the end of *Fear of Flying* Isadora has long since discovered her own sexuality, and is writing her own books, but she still has doubts about who she really is, repeating to herself a litany of identity: "Isadora White Stollerman Wing . . . Isadora Zelda White Stollerman Wing . . . B.A., M.A., Phi Beta Kappa" (252).

Adolescence is no easier for Kingston's narrator, caught between her Chinese ancestry and her American life, but her fantasy is fed not by the films and books of American popular culture, but instead by tarditional Chinese "talk-story," which gives her an empowering sense of female possibilities within a cultural heritage of heroism. The narrator's mother tells the children stories as they fall asleep, so that they cannot tell "where the stories left off and the dreams began, her voice the voice of heroines in my sleep."[15] The story of Fa Mu Lan, a young girl who takes her father's place in battle, convinces her that she "would have to grow up a woman warrior" (24), a destiny that she fulfills by writing her own story to dispel the childhood ghosts. The narrator's fantasy includes a fifteen-year period of rigorous training and apprenticeship, during which she grows from child to adult. In contrast to the narrator's mother's reaction to her first menstruation—which is to tell her the story of her aunt, the "no name woman" whose illicit pregnancy caused family disgrace, and to warn her, "don't humiliate us" (5)—in her fantasy, the onset of menstruation is regarded as a positive event by the old couple who

123

conduct her training. The woman merely tells her, "You're now an adult. . . . You can have children," and the narrator is not deflected by female biology from the rigors of her warrior schooling: "Menstrual days did not interrupt my training; I was as strong as on any other day" (36). Indeed, the fantasy of the woman warrior allows the narrator to remain essentially female even while adopting the traditionally masculine role of warrior, rather than suffering a division of self. After marrying her childhood sweetheart, she gives birth to a son in a moment stolen from battle, and her husband takes the child to live with his parents while she completes the task of liberating her people from tyranny before returning home in glory.

Joanne Frye has pointed out that the woman warrior fantasy begins and ends in the subjunctive: "The call would come from a bird," Kingston begins, and the fantasy concludes with the narrator imagining that "the villagers would make a legend about my perfect filiality" (24, 54).[16] Whereas most of the woman warrior fantasy is narrated in the past tense, as though it were the speaker's actual history, the subjunctive, with its implicit "if," both announces and concludes the story, and is also used within the narrative to reinforce the concept of fantasy. Immediately after the narrator begins menstruating, she looks into the old couple's water gourd and sees her family attending a wedding, her mother expressing delight at her daughter's happiness. This part of the narrative is in the past tense, but Kingston changes to the subjunctive and then to the future in the next paragraph:

> Yes, I *would* be happy. How full I *would* be with all their love for me. I *would* have for a new husband my own playmate, dear since childhood, who loved me so much he was to become a spirit bridegroom for my sake. We *will* be so happy when I come back to the valley, healthy and strong and not a ghost. (37) [italics mine]

The change in verb forms moves the narrator from the contingency of "would" to the certainty of "will." Just as importantly, the narrator's declaration that at some future time she will cease being a ghost is one of the passages that links the fantasy to her actual life, in which she not only feels surrounded by ghosts but also senses that she herself—as a girl in a culture that values only boys, as a Chinese in an English-speaking country—is insubstantial. Another passage that demonstrates the grounding of the woman warrior fantasy in the narrator's own reality is that in which she fights her last battle—this one with the baron who rules her own village and has enslaved her brother. She announces to him that she is a "female avenger," and then the narrator slips into the vernacular to report the baron's response:

> Then—heaven help him—he tried to be charming, to appeal to me man to man. "Oh, come now. Everyone takes the girls when he can. The families are glad to be rid of them. 'Girls are maggots in the rice.' 'It is more profitable to raise geese than daughters.'" He quoted to me the sayings I hated. (51)

The sayings that have so enraged the narrator in her "real" life are brought into her fantasy to be avenged, as she beheads the baron with her sword.

Kingston's fantasy is thus closely tied to the realities she wishes to surmount, rather than removed from them. Further, the end of the woman warrior story is followed immediately by the statement, "My American life has been such a disappointment" (54), plunging the reader again into the narrator's difficult childhood. As is the case in other novels, fantasy is not in itself a solution to the young girl's problems of selfhood, and the juxtaposition of fantasy to uncomfortable reality underscores this fact. Late in *The Woman Warrior*, the narrator finds another temporary escape from her struggle in the form of a "mysterious illness" that lasts a year and a half with "no pain and no symptoms." That the illness is psychosomatic is suggested by the fact that it follows immediately the narrator's harassment of a schoolmate who, like the narrator earlier, refuses to speak in school. The irony of her action—as though she is punishing her younger self—seems not to be lost on the narrator, who says of her illness, "the world is sometimes just" (211). She spends the eighteen months of her illness "like the Victorian recluses I read about," watching soap operas and ringing a bell for assistance (211). "It was," she says, "the best year and a half of my life. Nothing happened" (212). Neither fantasy nor withdrawal is the solution to Kingston's narrator's problems, but the telling of her own story constitutes the taking of control over the pattern it makes.

The mysterious illness from which Kingston's narrator suffers is similar in some ways to the periodic spells of disassociation that Alice Walker's Meridian experiences, beginning in her childhood. The first of these episodes occurs while Meridian is standing in the middle of the Sacred Serpent, a formation atop an Indian burying ground on her father's farm. As Kingston's woman warrior fantasy is inspired by her mother's talk-story of Fa Mu Lan, Meridian's reverie seems to be fueled by stories of her great-grandmother, Feather Mae, who as a young woman experienced a kind of ecstacy while standing in the pit formed by the serpent's tail. The young Meridian, "seeking to understand her great-grandmother's ecstasy," stands in the center of the pit and feels as though she is leaving her body and flying: "And in this movement she saw the faces of her family, the branches of trees, the wings of birds, the corners of houses, blades of grass and petals of flowers rush toward a central point high above her and she was drawn with them, as whirling, as bright, as free, as they" (58). Meridian's sense of freedom and oneness with the universe is repeated when she visits an ancient altar on a mountain in Mexico, where she feels like "a speck in the grand movement of time" (59). While a student at Saxon, having given her son away, Meridian has a recurring dream: "She dreamed she was a character in a novel and that her existence presented an insoluble problem, one that would be solved only by her death at the end" (117). Shortly thereafter, she begins to have the strange feeling that "a small landslide had begun behind her brows, as if things there had started to slip" (117), and this sensation is followed by a period of temporary blindness and paralysis which, instead of being frightening—the "worry part of her brain had been the landslide behind her brows and . . . no longer functioned"—is as pleasurable as the inexplicable moments of ecstasy: "She felt as if a warm, strong light bore her up and that she was a beloved part of the universe; that she was innocent even as the rocks are innocent, and unpolluted as the first waters" (119).

126

Such moments contribute strength to Meridian's activism for social change on behalf of southern blacks; her mystical sense of the interrelationship of all life makes her work inevitable. It is this aspect of Meridian that Truman Held cannot understand. Finding Meridian living in poverty in Chicokema early in the novel (though late in its narrative chronology), Truman comments that he has never understood her intermittent paralysis: "I always think of you as so strong, but look at you!" Meridian replies, Walker writes, "cockily," "I *am* strong, actually, . . . I'm just not Superwoman" (32). Meridian's refusal to be "Superwoman" marks her mature understanding and acceptance of the limits of her energy and power. She is at peace with her work and her way of life, including its poverty and periodic paralysis. She is dependent upon no one except herself, and when Truman says to her, "I hate to think of you always alone," Meridian replies, "But that is my value" (220). Her youthful vision of being "a speck in the grand movement of time" has led her to intense connectedness even in her self-imposed isolation.

It is characteristic of children and adolescents to have dreams and fantasies of adult power and autonomy. Both boys and girls attempt to transcend the relative powerlessness of youth and its restrictions by constructing imaginary adult selves with freedoms typically denied to the young. Yet fantasies of this sort are informed in turn by reality in the sense that they are derived from the options presented to the imagination by actual life experience. Without her mother's talk-story, Kingston could not have her "woman warrior" fantasy, for example; in contrast, Celie, in *The Color Purple,* leads a life so restricted as to preclude empowering visions of an alternate reality until Shug Avery becomes a presence in her life. Men as well as women base their imaginative futures on the available possibilities for their lives, so that the boy growing up in a ghetto may not be able to imagine any adult future other than gang membership, whereas a middle-class boy observes from the adult models presented to him that there are other, wider possibilities for power and influence. Yet the socially

127

acceptable roles for females—presented by way of both actual adult women and the images of them in books and films—are far narrower and more restricted than those for males. The female characters in the contemporary novel by women demonstrate again and again the ways in which even the possibilities for adolescent female fantasies are limited by the social construction of the woman. For Joan Foster in *Lady Oracle,* films teach female sacrifice for love; the young black girls that Meridian observes exist in impossible fantasies based on roles played by white actresses; Isadora Wing derives conflicting—but unanimously dogmatic—definitions of what it means to be a woman from male writers. Even Offred's memories of Lauren Bacall and Katharine Hepburn playing characters who could choose whether or not to be "undone" are of women whose major definition is ultimately their relationships with men.

Given the persistence of traditional female roles in books and films, even into the 1980s, it is not surprising that the romance as a form, with its female heroine seeking rather than avoiding the position of "angel in the house" or Weldon's "A," is so persistent. In the afterword to *Becoming a Heroine,* Rachel Brownstein comments on the difficulty of overcoming this plot. Although, Brownstein notes, "a woman's struggle to define herself against stereotypical images is a theme of current feminist novels and of fiction affected by feminism," the romance "continues to lap seductively at the edges of realism, and even feminism." This persistence suggests "how hard it is to alter formative fictions":

> The fiction of the heroine encourages aspiration and imposes limits. Paradox is at its core: probably that accounts for its power. The beautiful personal integrity the novel heroine imagines and stands for and seeks for herself is a version of the romantic view of woman as a desired object; as the image of the integral self, she is the inverted image of half of a couple. The literary associations that halo the heroine keep her in a traditional woman's place. That self-awareness which distinguishes her from the simple heroine of romance ends by implicating her further in fictions of the feminine.[17]

Characters who, despite their awareness of the need for change, are ultimately caught in "fictions of the feminine" come readily to mind: Mira in *The Women's Room*, Jane Clifford in *The Odd Woman*, Joan Foster in *Lady Oracle*. Despite extraordinary efforts to dream of and act upon alternatives to the traditional life script, such characters find themselves ironically trapped between it and some unimaginable future. Suzanne Juhasz has more recently concurred with Brownstein's point about the persistence of the traditional romance plot, noting that most twentieth-century women writers "have gone on telling love stories, whether or not the heroine has a good career or is striving to get one."[18] In order to free themselves from the "love story," some writers, such as Doris Lessing and Joanna Russ, have used the mode of speculative fiction to propose full-blown alternate worlds—whether utopian or dystopian—as I will discuss in the next chapter. Russ, who like so many contemporary women writers was a student in the 1950s and 1960s, embraced fantasy because of the absence of women's experience in the literature she was taught:

> When I became aware (in college) of my "wrong" experience, I chose fantasy. Convinced that I had no real experience of life, since my own obviously wasn't part of Great Literature, I decided consciously that I'd write of things nobody knew anything about, dammit. So I wrote realism disguised as fantasy, that is, science fiction.[19]

Just as science fiction, so clearly not "real," became an acceptable form for Russ's feminist vision, so adolescent women's fantasies are acceptable fantasies—first because they are secret, and second because they are dreams that young women are supposed to "grow out of," whether they are fantasies of power, such as those of Kingston and of Miriam in *Small Changes*, or of acquiescence to male superiority, such as those of Joan in *Lady Oracle* or of Gemma in *Words of Advice*. Adult fantasies, on the other hand, are essentially unacceptable: they threaten the social order. Isadora Wing's "zipless fuck," like Jane Gray's affair with James in *The Waterfall*, is threatening not only because of its implicit sexual freedom, but also because it moves the character away from conventional means of fulfillment to a situation in which there is no retribution for female autonomy. Because of their awareness that their fantasies are somehow unacceptable, the central characters in these novels respond with guilt and isolation to the fulfillment of their dreams: at the end of *Fear of Flying* Isadora does not know how Bennett will react to her presence in his London hotel room after her trip with Adrian Goodlove; and Jane Gray continually marvels that she has not been punished for her "sins." Despite their ability to view themselves and their experiences ironically, they remain aware of the "old plots" that would have doomed them.

One way of making the adult female fantasy acceptable, as Jong suggests, is to share it and discover its commonality. That contemporary women novelists have accomplished this sharing is evident; but it constitutes a partial solution only for the author, and not necessarily for her characters. A case in point is Kingston, whose *Woman Warrior* rests on the line between fiction and autobiography, and for whom the very telling of the story seems to represent a power and control that her narrator does not overtly demonstrate. Even in works more clearly fictional, such as *The Color Purple,* the ability to use the language to shape one's own story constitutes a subtle though powerful form of autonomy, in part because the storyteller is forced to see herself with an ironic distance that separates self from experience. It is the lack of such a distancing element in such works as *The Women's Room* and Judith Rossner's *Looking for Mr. Goodbar* (1975) that dooms the central characters to failure—and in the latter case death—in their search for freedom and self-fulfillment. So strong are the constraints of society, these authors propose, that only by removing oneself from them completely, by spiritual self-exploration or madness, can the adult female not merely dream of but possess freedom. In an essay written in 1980, Margaret Atwood comments on the persistence of traditional stereotypes of women even during a period of enormous outward change:

> After 10 years of the Women's Movement we like to think that some of the old stereotypes are fading, but 10 years is not a very long time in the history of the world, and I can tell you from experience that the old familiar images, the old icons, have merely gone underground, and not far at that. We still think of a powerful woman as an anomaly, a potentially dangerous anomaly; there is something subversive about such women, even when they take care to be good role models. They cannot have come by their power naturally, it is felt. They must have *got it from somewhere.*[20]

130

What Atwood suggests here is that the author of realistic fiction is to some extent constrained by the social matrix in which her characters and readers exist, and that to be believed, she cannot claim for her characters greater autonomy than actual women can reasonably claim.

The constraints posed by social reality deepen the need for dreams and fantasies; if actual freedom is difficult to attain, it can still be imagined, and from imagination can come either movement out of the socially constructed self or deeper entrapment within it. Nancy K. Miller's comment that "to read women's literature is to see and hear repeatedly a chafing against . . . 'unsatisfactory reality' "[21] rings true in these novels: the "chafing," Miller argues, frequently takes the form of dream and fantasy. But for these to be elements of positive movement, the woman must know the difference between fantasy and reality—must, in other words, have a sense of irony: a double perspective that pits the emerging self against the socially constructed self in creative tension. Two novels in which sexual freedom is a metaphor for a deeper autonomy—*Fear of Flying* and *Looking for Mr. Goodbar*—illustrate this distinction from positions on opposite ends of a continuum of self-knowledge and possibility.

For both Isadora Wing and Theresa Dunn, sexuality is part of both maturity and belonging, and both have adolescent fantasies of perfect men with whom they will share these pleasures. Isadora's fantasy is quite specific: "He had a face like Paul Newman and a voice like Dylan Thomas. He had a body like Michelangelo's *David* . . . [and] a mind like George Bernard Shaw" (94). Theresa's fantasy is of a more generalized Prince Charming who, "if she lost fifteen pounds and turned beautiful, would swoop down and carry her off to his kingdom."[22] Both women, as young adults, have relationships with men that end up making them feel like victims: Isadora's first husband, Brian Stollerman, goes mad and blames Isadora for having him hospitalized; Theresa's college professor, Martin Engle, uses her sexually with no intention of a permanent commitment, despite Theresa's fantasies that he will divorce his wife. Both women are influenced by the notion that acceptance by a man is the key to female self-esteem; as Isadora so bluntly puts it, "if no man loves me I have no identity" (277).

Further, both Isadora and Theresa have more than one "self" with which to perceive reality. But it is precisely at the point of multiple selves that the two women differ dramatically. Isadora has both a fearful, dependent self and an ironic, self-mocking self that sees clearly the artificiality of socially constructed female dependence. These two aspects of Isadora battle for ascendancy throughout *Fear of Flying*, with the ironic self gradually winning control. Theresa's division of self, in contrast, is pathological. Rather than debating with each other in a struggle for integrated selfhood, Theresa's three selves exist in isolation from each other, as evidence of her psychic disintegration. "Theresa" is flanked by "Terry," on the one hand, who carries Isadora's idea of the "zipless fuck" to self-destructive lengths, and on the other hand by "Miss Dunn," the gifted and committed elementary school teacher.

Ironically, Theresa's various selves are socially acceptable, whereas Isadora's are not. As Judi Roller points out, even Theresa's "madness" fits with social expectations for women:

> If Theresa Dunn is mad, she is only mad in a way very acceptable to society. She accepts everything society tells her and incorporates it into her personality. The part of her that is capable of enjoying sex cannot be part of the same person who is a teacher or who is loved by James Morrisey. . . . She is not permitted to have women friends. She is not allowed to live, and she must be punished. So she obediently separates herself into all her different parts.[23]

*Looking for Mr. Goodbar* provides a paradigm of traditional prescriptions for women's social behavior. School teachers, like "Miss Dunn," are asexual; love and sexual pleasure do not coexist; and promiscuous women like "Terry" deserve whatever happens to them. Gary White, who murders Theresa after meeting her in a singles bar, "had a very clear sense of himself as the victim of the woman he had murdered" (1), and in a very real way Theresa's murder can be considered a suicide: as he is about to hit her with a lamp, she thinks, "do it do it do it and get it over w——" (280). With the death of "Terry," Theresa and Miss Dunn also die. Isadora, in contrast, flaunts social norms, both by being a poet and by being sexually adventurous. Her first psychiatrist—when she is

132

fourteen—urges her to "ackzept being a vohman," but Isadora sees that being the women she is creates conflict between two selves: "If you were female and talented, life was a trap no matter which way you turned. Either you drowned in domesticity (and had Walter Mittyish fantasies of escape) or you longed for domesticity in all your art" (157). But instead of dividing herself into parts, as does Theresa, Isadora manages integration by giving full rein to both the woman and the artist, and allowing each to accept the other.

These two novels also illustrate different approaches to boundaries. Though afraid of flying, Isadora does so; indeed, the novel is filled with her movement and travel: to Vienna with Bennett and the other psychiatrists, around Europe with Adrian, and finally to London to rejoin Bennett. The trip with Adrian is not a solution, but she travels toward experience, not to escape it. When, toward the end of *Fear of Flying,* Isadora attempts to make sense of her life, she does it by going to herself—specifically, to the notebooks she has kept for the past four years: "journal jottings, shopping lists, lists of letters to be answered, drafts of irate letters never sent, pasted-in newspaper clippings, ideas for stories, first drafts of poems" (287). As she reads the pages, which come to seem like a novel about her life, she realizes that there is no need to blame herself for the apparent chaos of her life: "You did not have to apologize for wanting to own your own soul. Your soul belonged to you, for better or worse" (288). The point at which Isadora claims the freedom to determine her own life is encapsulated in the statement "I knew I did not want to be trapped in my own book" (288). And the structure of the novel, ending as it does without any resolution except the certainty of change, underscores the fact that Isadora is not, in fact, trapped in her own book. *Looking for Mr. Goodbar,* on the other hand, has the enclosed ending of death, which, along with marriage, is one of the two approved fates for women in the traditional novel. What for Isadora is movement toward change is for Theresa merely restlessness. She moves—or considers moving—from one apartment to another in New York, as though a change in location might constitute a change in herself. Her dreams are of being closed in, and trapped. She dreams of being locked in a "tiny closet" with Martin Engle (46). Late in the novel she has a series of dreams in which she is first "on her knees in a cold, dark place" and then crawling home through what turns out to be a tunnel (258); in the third dream she is telling these dreams to a psychiatrist who has her strapped to his couch and keeps saying, "We're going to straighten you out, Theresa. We're going to have to straighten you out" (259). But Theresa cannot bring herself to seek help from either psychiatry or a women's consciousness-raising group; and writing, which is for Isadora a process of clarification, results for Theresa only in a blank page:

> She brought the pen to the first page of the notebook and again wrote the date, but then she was paralyzed; where should she begin? How could you begin a diary not long before your twenty-seventh birthday without ever saying anything about what happened before? And what could she say about what happened before? What was there to say about her life? (268–69)

Theresa's inability to find anything to say about her life is emblematic of the emptiness at its core: having parceled herself out into Terry and Miss Dunn, there is nothing left of Theresa.

The positive form of the remaking of one's self in the contemporary women's novel is typically seeking and finding a career that represents autonomy outside the boundaries of domesticity. Most often, the central character becomes an artist of some sort, the profession serving as both a metaphor for self-creation and the tangible embodiment of dreams and fantasies. Isadora Wing is a poet, as is Jane Gray in *The Waterfall;* Godwin's Violet Clay and Elaine Risley, in Atwood's *Cat's Eye* (1988), are painters; Anastasia Carpenter, in Marilyn French's *Her Mother's Daughter* (1987), is a photographer. In *The Color Purple,* Celie's sewing, like Shug's singing, is an art form that represents command over her life. Patricia Meyer Spacks has compared the artist to the adolescent in terms of the need that both have for transcendental visions:

> Like the adolescent, the artist is a dreamer and a revolutionary; like the adolescent he often finds his accomplishment inadequate to his imaginings. But his dream, setting him apart, helps him to escape the burden of the real. (205)

Adolescence is inevitable, whereas one chooses to be an artist; nonetheless, Spacks asserts, in both situations the individual is "trying to transform reality by refusing to accept the given conditions of life as definitive" (205). When the artist is a woman, she continues:

> Both the function of aspiration and the nature of frustration assume characteristic forms. In many ways woman artists' self-depictions corroborate the more indirect testimony offered by fictional accounts of female adolescence. (205)

In the contemporary novel, becoming an artist may be fraught with initial frustrations, but achievement as a professional normally represents not only the fruition of youthful dreams, but more importantly the crossing of restrictive boundaries to claim a mature, autonomous self.

Conversely, when a woman is unable to develop her artistic potential, the circumstance embodies a personal limitation that is far more important than the failure to reach professional goals. The women depicted in these novels as having unfulfilled artistic ambitions are commonly members of generations before that of the central character. In *Violet Clay,* the narrator's grandmother, a pianist, gives up a Carnegie Hall audition to get married, and exchanges her artistic dream for the alternative promoted by the women's magazines of the day: "the accomplished wife and mother who turns her gifts to the enhancement of Home."[24] Her decision is prompted in part by her "secret fears that [she] might not succeed" in the audition (39), and similar fears provide nightmares for Violet when she imagines going to New York to become a painter. Violet's nightmares involve a taxi she attempts to take to visit art galleries with her portfolio; either the taxi goes on and on without a driver, or the charge is exorbitant, or she is forced to submit to the driver's sexual advances. Violet is able to identify the source of these nightmares as her own failure to pursue her youthful aspirations—"I had snatched my security before I'd made a real try for my dream" (26)—and eventually finds the courage to develop herself as a painter. Violet Clay is given a second chance, but Pauline Breedlove, in *The Bluest Eye,* is prevented by poverty and race from having a first one. Morrison describes the young

135

Pauline as having artistic instincts and impulses; she is enchanted by colors, and she loves to "arrange things":

> To line things up in rows—jars on shelves at canning, peach pits on the step, sticks, stones, leaves. . . . Whatever portable plurality she found, she organized into neat lines, according to their size, shape, or gradations of color. Just as she would never align a pine needle with the leaf of a cottonwood tree, she would never put the jars of tomatoes next to the green beans. (88–89)

But there is no recognition nor encouragement of Pauline's talents: "She missed—without knowing what she missed—paints and crayons" (89). Because of the circumstances of her life. Pauline is able to exercise her artistry only in keeping the home of the white family for whom she works meticulously clean, her half-formed dream made subservient to the needs of others.

The women who succeed as artists, in acting upon their dreams, create not only art, but also spaces for themselves as adult women. Violet Clay moves to her uncle's cabin in the Adirondacks to come to terms with her past idealism and to confront her future as a painter. Just before she leaves New York, her friend Milo comments on her work in terms that suggest her personal as well as artistic potential: "It's the way you leave light in and around things so they have room to breathe. Perhaps even to change, or move. . . . there's the suggestion of stretch, of going somewhere" (257). In *The Waterfall*, Jane Gray's dream-like relationship with James frees her from her marriage to Malcolm and enables her to recognize the necessity of her poetry:

> I would write, because writing is the thing that one can do anywhere, in a hotel bedroom, in solitary confinement, in a prison cell, a defense more final, less destructible, than the company of love. I could feel it stirring in me. Descending. I could see the changes in the color of the air, the faintly approaching presences of words. (233)

Poetry, Jane realizes, is a part of her: it exists wherever she is, and is under her control, as relationships are not. In *Her Mother's Daughter*, French chronicles the several attempts that Anastasia makes to define a self apart from the heritage of her self-sacrificing mother. Her first major effort is to become "Stacey" when she goes to college: "too classy and too smart to be considered a tramp, and thus requiring some new category—bohemian, rebel, free spirit."[25] Anastasia's rejection of her mother's punishing self-lessness includes a rejection of her gender: "I was not going to be a woman, I had decided that. Since I clearly was not a man, my only alternative was to be beyond sex, or at least gender. I deluded myself that was how others saw me too" (355). "Stacey" is a delusion, not a solution: "She became a finished product, in the full sense of that phrase: polished, and complete" (355). The artificiality of Stacey as an identity is made clear when Anastasia speaks of living "in a dark little room behind the store that sells her replicas" (356). It is her career as a photographer that allows Anastasia to take risks, to identify with feminism, and ultimately to sustain a relationship with Clara, who loves her for what she is rather than what she pretends or tries to be.

Art leads similarly to feminism and freedom in Atwood's *Cat's Eye*. Returning to Toronto, the scene of her childhood, for a retrospective show of her work, Elaine Risley re-enters imaginatively the nightmarish feeling of that childhood, plagued by three friends: Carol, Grace, and especially Cordelia. The ghost of Cordelia, who set herself up as the disapproving judge of Elaine's behavior and appearance, hovers in the air of Toronto, forcing Elaine to re-live a childhood in which misery led her to self-mutilation and silence. Thinking back, Elaine wonders what her mother thought about the obvious signs of her unhappiness:

> She must have realized what was happening to me, or that something was. Even toward the beginning she must have noted my silences, my bitten fingers, the dark scabs on my lips where I'd pulled off patches of the skin. If it were happening now, to a child of my own, I would know what to do. But then? There were fewer options, and a great deal less was said.[26]

Despite her mother's inattention, Elaine manages to survive her internalization of Cordelia's taunting without significant scars; indeed, by the time they are teenagers, she has shifted the balance of power, and Cordelia's own emotional problems manifest themselves in poor academic performance, while Elaine, like her brother Stephen, is an excellent student. The last time Elaine sees Cor-

137

delia, she is in a rest home—"a discreet, private loony bin" (373)—after a suicide attempt. Following a painful meeting in which the heavily sedated Cordelia tries to enlist Elaine's aid in escaping from the rest home, Elaine leaves her, but the ghost of Cordelia haunts Elaine: "The last time I saw Cordelia, she was going through the door of the rest home. That was the last time I talked to her. Although it wasn't the last time she talked to me" (384). Elaine dreams about Cordelia, and during the visit to Toronto continually believes that she sees her and hears her voice.

It is in her art that Elaine exorcises the ghosts of her past: Cordelia, Carol's mother Mrs. Smeath, and her own mother. While taking her Grade Thirteen exams, Elaine realizes that she will be an artist rather than a biologist:

> In the middle of the Botany examination it comes to me, like a sudden epileptic fit, that I'm not going to be a biologist, as I have thought. I am going to be a painter. I look at the page, where the life cycle of the mushroom from spore to fruiting body is taking shape, and I know this with absolute certainty. My life has been changed, soundlessly, instantaneously. (270)

Instead of the precise diagrams of botanical illustration, Elaine the artist creates surrealistic paintings inspired by dream and memory. She memorializes her unconventional mother wearing an apron; in her self-portrait, three little girls—Carol, Grace, and Cordelia—are in the background; the stern Mrs. Smeath is pictured in her underwear, "her one large breast sectioned to show her heart. Her heart is the heart of a dying turtle, reptilian, dark-red, diseased" (369).

The fact that Elaine paints women, and her early involvement with a feminist art show, lead critics to call her a feminist painter, a label she resists. Her childhood experiences have taught her how cruel women can be to each other; "Sisterhood is a difficult concept for me, I tell myself, because I never had a sister. Brotherhood is not" (361). When the young reporter in Toronto asks her about feminism, she replies acerbically, "I hate party lines, I hate ghettos. Anyway, I'm too old to have invented it and you're too young to understand it, so what's the point of discussing it at all?" (94).[27]

Yet Elaine feels keenly the absence in her own life of the female friendships she sees around her—the kind of relationship that she and Carol, Grace, and Cordelia should have had as children. On the plane leaving Toronto, she watches with envy the two elderly women beside her, friends taking a trip together, enjoying themselves like children:

> They're rambunctious, they're full of beans; they're tough as thirteen, they're innocent and dirty, they don't give a hoot. Responsibilities have fallen away from them, obligations, old hates and grievances; now for a short while they can play again like children, but this time without the pain. (446)

And Elaine silently addresses Cordelia: "This is what I miss, Cordelia: not something that's gone, but something that will never happen" (446). Through dreams and memories of her childhood, Elaine has both created her paintings and come to terms with the ghost of Cordelia, who, ironically, has turned out to be more tormented than tormentor.

Dreams and fantasies come unbidden, as responses to the human need to resolve and order both past and future reality. Madness, too, is a method of coping with experience by an unwilled act of disassociation from what most people consider reality. Yet there is a fine line between what are called "normal" and "abnormal" behavior and perceptions. When, in *Cat's Eye*, Elaine visits Cordelia at the Dorothy Lyndwich Rest Home, she says, "How did you end up in the nuthatch anyway? You aren't any crazier than I am" (376). On one level Elaine is merely trying to comfort Cordelia, but she also articulates the truth that sanity and normality are matters of perception and degree. In Gilman's "The Yellow Wallpaper," the narrator's husband's prescriptions for her "cure" in fact intensify her disorientation, yet the reader, guided by her narrative voice, is led to perceive that a culture that denies her autonomy and expression cannot be considered truly sane. In both *Surfacing* and *The Four-Gated City*, the central characters willingly and deliberately disassociate themselves from what their respective so-

139

cieties consider rational behavior, and call into ironic question the concept of normalcy. Atwood's nameless narrator and Martha Quest make their fantasies acceptable by using them deliberately as stages on the way to autonomy.

Both *Surfacing* and *The Four-Gated City* take place against the backdrop of societies in chaos. The United States that the *Surfacing* narrator leaves for her native Canada is in the throes of the Vietnam War; the London to which Martha Quest goes from Africa is filled with craters left by the bombs of World War II and frantic efforts to return to lives that people can regard as normal. The atrocity of war is evidence of society gone insane, against which individual madness becomes a kind of sanity. Atwood's narrator and Martha are embarking on the quest that Martha's last name represents, but unlike the traditional male quest, they must go into themselves rather than outward to experience, and the journey is a solitary one despite the sympathetic presences of Joe and Lynda, respectively. Finally, both novels embody a critique of the rational as opposed to the intuitive, the artificial as opposed to the natural, the institutional as opposed to the individual—with fantasy and madness as metaphors for individual growth and integration.

Atwood's narrator moves from one kind of fantasy to another in *Surfacing*. The first fantasy is the fabric of lies about marriage, motherhood, and divorce that she has adopted as a socially acceptable past—a fabric so tightly woven that she herself believes it to be true. Not until she dives to look for evidence of her missing father does her mind admit the reality of the abortion, and she realizes that she has been living in "a paper house."[28] The fact that she is able finally to visualize the circumstances of her abortion and remember the indifference of her married lover frees her to enter into the fantasy of rebirth. Having constructed a rational though unreal past, she now understands the "failure of logic" (171). She becomes increasingly alienated from Anna, Davis, and Joe, and section 2 of the novel ends with her realization that "everything is waiting to become alive" (186). In the final section of the novel, the narrator's disassociation from the "real" world is mirrored in her language, which is at once increasingly less referential to this world, and more assured. Annis Pratt, writing of the rebirth journey in women's novels, speaks of the character working through "inauthentic role behaviours" to a "world of the unconscious" in which the narratives are "puzzling, bizarre, even 'crazy.'"[29] The more "crazy" Atwood's narrator becomes in this final section, the more she exerts control over herself and her environment.

For the narrator to become psychically reborn, she requires the possibility of the actual birth of a child as symbolic negation of her abortion; and this possibility in turn requires that Joe become an acceptable lover. As the narrator becomes increasingly less human and more animal, so too does Joe. The last night in the cabin, Joe "unzips his human skin" (189), and when she takes him outdoors to make love, she perceives him as "thick, undefined, outline but no features, hair and beard a mane." He is less human than part of nature: "his beard and hair fall over me like ferns, mouth as soft as water" (190). But before the narrator can fully accept him or herself, she must retreat further into herself and away from the structures of civilization. Nameless to the reader throughout the novel, she does not respond when Anna calls her name: "I no longer have a name. I tried for all those years to be civilized but I'm not and I'm through pretending" (198). Finally left alone, she comments on the irony of her situation: "From any rational point of view I am absurd; but there are no longer any rational points of view" (199). What to others would appear to be insane behavior is for the narrator necessity, with its own logic. Just before the vision of her mother feeding the birds, the narrator abandons the logic of speech, refusing to end her sentences:

> The animals have no need for speech, why talk when you are a word
> I lean against a tree, I am a tree leaning
> I break out into the bright sun and crumple, head against the ground
> I am not an animal or a tree, I am the thing in which the trees and animals move and grow, I am a place (212–13)

Finally, having envisioned her father as well as her mother, she is prepared to emerge from the self-imposed madness in which she has conjured their images: "they have gone finally, back into the earth, the air, the water, wherever they were when I summoned them" (219). She has a "rational" view of herself and how her "irrational" behavior would be perceived by others:

> That is the real danger now, the hospital or the zoo, where we are put, species or individual, when we can no longer cope. They would never believe it's only a natural woman, a state of nature, they think of that as a tanned body on a beach with washed hair waving like scarves; not this, face dirt-caked and streaked, skin grimed and scabby, hair like a frayed bathmat stuck with leaves and twigs. A new kind of centerfold. (222)

With this vision of herself, the narrator is able to laugh, and to move intuitively toward a life that the rest of the world would regard as sane, but always with the awareness that she need not be a victim of others' construction of her reality.

Like the narrator in *Surfacing*, Martha Quest in *The Four-Gated City* must shed assumed selves before undertaking the journey into herself that results in her ability to survive personal and political chaos. One of these selves is the flippant, self-righteous "Matty" that she has adopted as a defensive *persona* and whom she now regards as "an intolerably tedious personage."[30] The other is the name of her second husband, Hesse, "a name acquired like a bracelet" (38). By the time she enters the Coldridge household, Martha has a keen sense of her need to remain alert to what she will become, aware that complacency would blunt her perceptions. At lunch with the capable Phoebe, Martha the "traveller" thinks to herself:

> If I eat, if I start this routine of meals, sleep, order, the fine edge on which I'm living now is going to be dulled and lost. For the insight of knowledge she now held, of the nature of separation, of division . . . was clear and keen—she understood . . . understood *really* (but in a new way, was in the grip of a vision), how human beings could be separated so absolutely by a slight difference in the texture of their living that they could not talk to each other, must be wary, or enemies. (82)

At first in Mark Coldridge's house, Martha is wary of his wife Lynda, who is in and out of mental institutions. Martha has been hired to be capable; Lynda is clearly incapable of normal life. But as Martha begins gradually to realize, Lynda's madness is merely an intensification of the more intuitive aspects of her own mind. As Elizabeth Abel puts it, "By discovering in Lynda an aspect of her own identity, Martha enters a relationship which differs from that of the novel's adult male characters, who react to Lynda with a mixture of compassion and detachment, clearly distinguishing her 'madness' from their 'sanity.'"[31] Lessing targets in particular the male psychiatric establishment, with its sharp lines between the sane and the insane, and its rigid categorizing of types of insanity. Shortly before her mother's visit to London, when Martha feels that she is coming apart emotionally, she considers seeking psychiatric help, and asks Lynda about her own doctor, Dr. Lamb:

> She said: "What is Dr. Lamb like as a person?"
> "Oh, they are all the same!"
> "They can't be."
> "Well, that's one of their points, you see: it shouldn't matter what they are like as people."
> "But that's ridiculous."

Lynda understands how ridiculous is the objective, scientific pose of anyone dealing with the human mind, and cautions Martha against psychiatry: "I shouldn't if I were you" (223).

This and other, similar conversations with Lynda are the beginning of what Catharine Stimpson has termed "a friendship beyond friendliness" between the two women,[32] as Martha turns her mind to Lynda's way of viewing the world. When Martha becomes conscious of her ability to overhear the thoughts of other people, and mentions this to Lynda, it is as if Lynda has been waiting for a long time to welcome Martha into her own reality: "'Oh,' she exclaimed, 'you do? I was waiting for you to . . .'" (371). And so Martha and Lynda begin to work together to find reasons for their perceptions of reality—perceptions considered "mad" by the rest of the world. The two read, talk, share fantasies—and arrive at no conclusions. But the experience of searching is finally more important than the finding of answers:

> It was as if the far-off sweetness experienced in a dream, that unearthly impossible sweetness, less the thing itself than the need or hunger for it, a question and answer coming together on the same fine

143

high note—as if that sweetness known all one's life, tantalisingly in-
tangibly, had come closer, a little closer, so that one continually sharply
turned one's head after something just glimpsed out of the corner of an
eye, or tried to sharpen one's senses to catch something just beyond
them. (374)

The elusiveness of any "truth" about their private visions provides
a beauty in sharp distinction to the fixed diagnoses of the doctors;
Martha reaches empathetic understanding with Lynda, and in the
process takes on a nurturing role that she has not been able to
have with either her daughter or her mother. As Stimpson says,
"Though she does not go mad, Martha must experience the sensa-
tions of insanity in her rites of passage toward a greater comprehension of the mind" (203); but Martha also gains a more
thorough comprehension of the heart.

The *Surfacing* narrator's perception that set against the madness
of the world, hers is a great sanity, is held as well by Martha and
Lynda, who possess some truths not commonly shared or acknowledged by society. Ironically, according to a letter written by
Francis Coldridge's son following the "Catastrophe"—that unidentified disaster that has destroyed much of Britain—Martha
and Lynda were able to predict this event; Lynda has said to
Francis, "Well, yes, for one thing, it looks as if this country is
going to have some kind of accident—probably fairly soon, but
we don't know when" (626). Francis, like others, cannot make
himself take this pronouncement seriously—cannot accept the
existence of the powers of the mind that would make such fore-
knowledge possible. The nurturance that Martha and Lynda have
developed for each other they attempt to extend to a society that
will not listen. But Martha survives the Catastrophe to shepherd a
group of people to an island off the coast of Scotland, where until
she dies she takes care of the children of this group of refugees
from societal madness.

*Surfacing* is concerned with individual regeneration; *The Four-
Gated City*, with social destruction and rebirth. But Atwood and
Lessing share the conviction that what the dominant culture considers madness may in fact be the obverse; an acceptable fantasy
that reveals a transcendent reality. In contrast to the limiting or

144

misleading fantasies fostered by mass culture, which have the potential to trap women in socially constructed selves, the violence of metaphoric madness, like the sword of the woman warrior, may provide the dislocation necessary for the ultimate empowering vision to emerge.

CHAPTER FIVE

# Alternate Realities

Science fiction and fantasy writer Ursula K. Le Guin, in her acceptance speech for the National Book Award in 1972, comments on the necessity for non-realistic fiction in the late twentieth century:

> Sophisticated readers are accepting the fact that an improbable and unmanageable world is going to produce an improbable and hypothetical art. At this point, realism is perhaps the least adequate means of understanding the incredible realities of our existence. . . . The fantasist, whether he uses the ancient archetypes of myth and legend or the younger ones of science and technology, may be talking as seriously as any sociologist—and a good deal more directly—about human life as it is lived, and as it might be lived, and as it ought to be lived. For after all, as great scientists have said and as all children know, it is above all by the imagination that we achieve perception, and compassion, and hope.[1]

Le Guin's perception that periods of disturbance in the social order, when society appears to have abandoned logic in favor of chaos and absurdity, are best reflected in non-realistic fiction, is a familiar one. When accustomed order and values seem threatened

146

by rapid social change, the fiction writer has essentially two alternatives: to recapture imaginatively—even nostalgically—the values and patterns of a previous era now seen as static and idyllic, or to project a future (or, indeed, another world altogether) that is clearly different from the present: either a utopia in which order has been restored along the lines of values and priorities that represent ideality for the author, or a dystopia—a cautionary tale warning of even more threatening and disruptive social patterns if radical changes are not made in the present. Edward Bellamy's *Looking Backward* (1888) and Charlotte Perkins Gilman's *Herland* (1915) are familiar examples of the utopian response, whereas George Orwell's *1984* (1949) and Margaret Atwood's *The Handmaid's Tale* (1986) are dystopian visions of futures readily extrapolated from the realities of the authors' social contexts.

The frequent use of fantasy—including the utopia and the dystopia—in the contemporary novel by women constitutes both a response to the perceived absurdity of contemporary patriarchy and an impulse to envision an alternate reality that either corrects or intensifies the ills of the present. Jong's *Serenissima* and Weldon's *The Rules of Life* are essentially playful fantasies that depict women achieving a measure of ascendance over the circumstances of their lives. Jessica Pruitt, the actress who is the central character in *Serenissima,* is transported by Jong's fantasy to the sixteenth century and the company of William Shakespeare for a sensuous experience that restores both her personal and her professional creativity. In *The Rules of Life,* set in the year 2002,[2] Weldon allows Gabriella Sumpter to speak from her grave to a priest of the Great New Fictional Religion about the rules to which she has adhered in her sixty-one years of life, and those she has not, claiming for herself a quirky, eccentric independence. The frequently ironic tone of both novels challenges the concept of socially determined "rules" for women's behavior as both characters defy even the rules of time and mortality. Time is defied also—though in a far bleaker way—in the dystopian futures of *The Handmaid's Tale* and Lessing's *The Memoirs of a Survivor.* The "Catastrophe" that concludes *The Four-Gated City*—a socio-political disruption that has caused the central characters to become refugees from England—

147

is played out slowly in *The Memoirs of a Survivor,* as social order is gradually replaced by chaos and barbarity. In *The Handmaid's Tale,* the apocalyptic moment has already occurred, establishing a totalitarian regime in which rigorous adherence to selected Biblical precepts makes women the slaves of biological function. Piercy's *Woman on the Edge of Time* and Russ's *The Female Man* each offer glimpses of both utopian and dystopian futures. In Piercy's novel, Consuelo is able to travel telepathically to the beneficent world of 2137, where Luciente shows her an egalitarian culture that, with its emphasis on nurturance, is reminiscent of Gilman's *Herland;* but Consuelo also discovers a possible dystopian future in which, as in *The Handmaid's Tale,* the most threatening features of contemporary society have gained ascendance and women have become objects. In *The Female Man,* Russ juxtaposes Janet's all-female world of Whileaway, which also resembles Herland, to Alice-Jael's world of armed warfare between men and women.

By offering alternative visions of possible human futures—with particular significance for women's lives—Piercy and Russ underscore the fact that these contemporary fantasies by women pose essential challenges to tradition and to what Weldon calls "the rules of life." Even in dystopian fictions, the authors describe, by implication, life as it *might* and *ought* to be lived, which Le Guin proposes as the task of the fantasist. Such challenges to the status quo make these texts inherently ironic. Because the essence of irony is contrast between one meaning or reality and another, speculative fictions, insofar as they are referential to what Le Guin calls "the incredible realities of our existence," force us to consider the validity of the world posited by the fantasist as set against that which we perceive to be "true" about our own world. Both sets of realities necessarily coexist, superimposed upon one another, accomplishing the doubled effect of ironic meaning. Sometimes the writer makes this superimposition of meanings or realities overt. In *The Handmaid's Tale,* for example, Atwood announces in the first sentence that the experiences her narrator is about to describe exist in tension with another, prior set of experiences: "We slept in what had once been the gymnasium."[3] As this first chapter proceeds, Atwood continues to suggest the imposition of present upon past in a manner that simultaneously builds suspense about

148

the narrator's current circumstances and plays upon the reader's own memories of the past:

> The floor was of varnished wood, with stripes and circles painted on it, for the games that were formerly played there; the hoops for the basketball nets were still in place, though the nets were gone. A balcony ran around the room, for the spectators, and I thought I could smell, faintly like an afterimage, the pungent scent of sweat, shot through with the sweet taint of chewing gum and perfume from the watching girls, felt-skirted as I knew from pictures, later in miniskirts, then pants, then in one earring, spiky green-streaked hair. Dances would have been held there; the music lingered, a palimpsest of unheard sound, style upon style, an undercurrent of dreams, a forlorn wail, garlands made of tissue-paper flowers, cardboard devils, a revolving ball of mirrors, powdering the dancers with a snow of light. (3)

In a similar manner, Lessing begins *The Memoirs of a Survivor* by superimposing the present upon the past: "We all remember that time."[4] Lessing, like Atwood, is on the verge of plunging the reader into a dystopian future by first referring to what she assumes to be a commonly shared past.

The fact that irony is achieved through implicit juxtaposition of more than one time or reality is most overt in fictions wholly constructed as fantasies, but it can be observed as well in novels in which fantasy is part of a realistic plot structure. The contrast between Pecola Breedlove's fantasy of blue eyes and the narrator's perception of her terrible isolation at the end of *The Bluest Eye*, for example, forces the reader to observe the ironic distance between dream and reality, the models of white culture and the severe limitations of Pecola's life. Similarly, the narrator's imaginative reversals of the processes of civilization in *Surfacing* call into question the values of contemporary society, especially as those values impose upon women masks of artificiality. The writer who declares independence from the rules of realism for most or all of a novel, however, is free to insist more directly on the ironic distance between life as it *might* or *could* be lived and life as it *is* lived. To highlight this point, it is useful to return briefly to a consideration of the most widely read kind of contemporary women's fantasy: the popular, formulaic romance novel.

149

# Feminist Alternatives

As a number of scholars have pointed out, the popular romance is essentially a conservative document, reinforcing gender-role stereotypes and leaving its heroine inside the marriage plot. Yet as Janice Radway has proposed, these fantasies of love and acceptance may be viewed superficially as feminist because the heroines possess qualities of assertiveness and independence not commonly associated with traditional female behavior. In particular, the heroine frequently expresses dissatisfaction with the system of male dominance, so that she appears to resist the roles established for her. However, the heroine of the popular romance ultimately finds her satisfaction within traditional patriarchal structures; what Radway terms the "fairy-tale fantasy concluding the narrative" negates the quasi-feminist impulses expressed earlier in the narrative. These novels, Radway concludes, are:

> reactionary in their assertion that the feminist goals of individual fulfillment and independence can be achieved through the maintenance of traditional male-female relations. We simply cannot overlook the fact that the feminist protest is not sustained. The novel may temporarily express a subconscious desire for a re-ordering of relations between men and women, but that subversive desire is always turned aside in the end in a way that shows it to have been unnecessary at the outset.[5]

The popular romance thus reinforces the rules rather than challenging them in any fundamental way, so that the narrative ultimately denies the possibility of ironic duality.

The feminist fantasy, in contrast, commonly demonstrates the opposite pattern, in which the female heroine begins in the realm of traditional culture and moves away from its rules and restrictions. Contemporary reality continues to exist as a palimpsest on which an alternative reality is superimposed, and the central character is aware, as is the reader, of the contrast between them. Such patterns of superimposition can be observed also in fictions that are essentially realistic—in which fantasy is an element of the plot rather than its controlling principle. In *Surfacing,* for example, even as the narrator abandons all of the trappings of civilization and prepares for her own rebirth by living like an animal in the woods, she is aware of the ironic contrast between her dirt-caked body and the culturally preferred female body, "a tanned body on a beach with washed hair waving like scarves." Instead of adhering to this stereotype, she is "a natural woman . . . a new kind of centerfold."[6] At the end of *Surfacing*, the narrator re-enters her "own time" (223), but she has been irrevocably altered by her fantasy, just as Martha Quest, in *The Four-Gated City*, emerges from her explorations with Lynda of the mind's untapped powers an essentially different person, but living in a culture that has, itself, not changed. The author who begins with the premise of an alternate reality for her characters to inhabit, thus departing from the rules imposed by realism, claims an even greater freedom from the enclosed plot of the popular romance in which the heroine finally capitulates to traditional values and expectations. Whether the vision is utopian or dystopian—or both in the same novel—the fiction is fundamentally radical rather than conservative.

The very use of such terms as "radical" and "conservative" raises again the issue of the extent to which these novels should be considered political documents, or to be arising from political ideologies. This question is not as much beside the point as it might first appear, because utopian and dystopian fictions in particular have a long tradition in being closely allied with their authors' ideological stances. Gilman's *Herland*, for example, describes a culture in which Gilman's own social beliefs—in the values of female nurturance and the repressive nature of traditional religion—are played out in the dialogues between the residents of Herland and their three male visitors. B. F. Skinner's *Walden Two* (1948) is based on Skinner's theories of behavioral psychology, and Orwell's *1984* had its origin in the author's fears of a totalitarian government. Indeed, to describe the best or the worst society that one can imagine is necessarily to involve oneself in the political structures as well as the values that would govern such a society. Yet the situation is clearly more complex than this. First, a novel of whatever sort is a work of art, and reading it with an eye to the ideology it appears to reflect or espouse is merely one way in which an art form may be approached. More importantly, few authors are eager to be regarded as using the novel solely or even largely to promote an ideological stance, for this reduces them from artists to propogandists. Both Margaret Atwood and Doris

Lessing have rejected even the label of feminist, even though Atwood's *Surfacing* and *The Handmaid's Tale* and Lessing's *The Golden Notebook* and her *Children of Violence* series are widely regarded—even canonized—as feminist texts. Lessing's resistance to labeling has been even more intense than that of Atwood. Elizabeth Dipple has recently discussed Lessing's "demurrals against the current directions of feminism" and her "abandonment of party or ideological politics as a subject worthy of serious commitment," and has pointed out that in such recent novels as *The Good Terrorist* (1985) Lessing takes a position that is "heavily satirical and dismissive of women or men who gives their lives to the falsity of political rhetoric when there are other things to preoccupy a forward-looking mind."[7]

Yet it is impossible to ignore the socio-political implications of contemporary dystopian fantasies in particular. The gradual disintegration of services and commodities in the London of the future that Lessing describes in *The Memoirs of a Survivor* are reminders of the fragility of a standard of living taken for granted by citizens of industrialized nations, and Lessing's grim depictions of polluted air and bands of homeless young people are similar to the alternate future that Consuelo msitakenly enters in *Woman on the Edge of Time*, in which the air is so polluted that even on the one hundred and twenty-sixth floor of a New York apartment building there is no point in having windows. The realistic as well as the utopian/dystopian parts of Piercy's novel embody serious social commentary as well: as a poor Chicana woman, Connie is labeled insane when the conditions of her life lead her to self-defensive violence. *The Handmaid's Tale*, set in the 1990s and drawing upon social and technological realities of the 1980s, has seemed to most readers chillingly possible despite its bizarre and futuristic elements. Linda Kauffman has argued that a novel like *The Handmaid's Tale* must be approached through feminist analysis because it is "less about the 'fearsome future' than about the 'fearsome present.'" Atwood, Kauffman notes:

> dismantles received ideas and unquestioned assumptions about religion, sex, politics, women's cultures—and feminism itself. Atwood au-

daciously creates a heroine who is in a very real sense responsible for the Gileadean coup: she is apathetic politically, complacent about women's struggle for equal rights, absorbed solely in her individual existence. All around her she sees racial hatred, religious intolerance, and sexual repression intensifying daily. If *The Handmaid's Tale* were solely a tragic tale of one woman's suffering, it would merely reinforce the emphasis bourgeois ideology places on the individual, but [it] focus[es] equally on the decimation of a culture and a race.[8]

The fact that these novels depict eventualities that can be readily extrapolated from observable social and environmental realities decreases the space between fantasy and realism, which in turn makes the irony of contrast more palpable.

Russ's *The Female Man*, more closely allied to science fiction by its use of time travel and parallel universes, seems on the surface less referential to contemporary reality. By concatenating past and future, and dividing the narrative perspective among four separate female consciousness, Russ constructs an apparently disjointed narrative that strikes the reader initially as bizarre. But *The Female Man* addresses and exposes as absurd a number of the myths and clichés regarding woman's nature and role by combining straightforward narrative with satire and parody. Jeannine, like a character from a black-and-white movie, alternately believes in and is frustrated by the notion that marriage is a woman's sole source of fulfillment. The women in "The Great Happiness Contest" brag about their contentment as homemakers or "superwomen" in ways that recall the debates about the necessity for feminist activism, while random male voices enunciate the clichés of chauvinism. Russ's novel is thus a compendium of references to contemporary feminist issues, which are thrown into relief by the perspectives of Janet Evason and Alice-Jael Reasoner, who represent alternate futures that are themselves possible outgrowths of current tensions between the genders.

Weldon's *The Rules of Life* and Jong's *Serenissima* also violate conventional notions of time and space, though in quite different ways, and both novels have central characters who break the "rules" in order to live on their own terms. Weldon's and Jong's visions are essentially utopian in that they show women freeing themselves from social restraints—particularly those regarding aging and sexuality—to find fulfillment. When Gabriella Sumpter, in *The Rules of Life*, speaks from her grave in the year 2002 of the satisfaction she has gained from determining on her own which rules to abide by and which to break, her chatty, meticulous advice about such mundane matters as how to remove stains from various fabrics ties her to the world of feminine reality, while the circumstances under which she narrates her story are metaphoric of her freedom from this reality. Jong's Jessica Pruitt, in *Serenissima*, travels to the past for her great erotic adventure and then returns to a recognizable present in 1985 with an infant boy as the sole evidence that her journey has been real rather than imaginary.

The use of fantasy as a dominant mode in all of these novels suggests that the re-visioning of contemporary reality requires the radical and even violent use of the imagination. By creating alternative pasts, presents, and futures for their central characters to inhabit, the authors launch a fundamental critique of the values and assumptions of the culture they inhabit, even when the alternative reality they create is a bleak dystopian vision. These novels further underscore the fact that the mind constructs its own reality: with the single exception of *Woman on the Edge of Time*, the central characters narrate their own stories, suggesting that the alternate realities they inhabit for part or all of the novel are to be understood as their own visions. Offred's continual reminders that her story is a "reconstruction," for example, indicates that the version we read of her experiences in the Republic of Gilead is partial, incomplete—perhaps even inaccurate, depending as it does on the words of a single observer. In *The Rules of Life*, Gabriella announces that there are no rules in fiction, thus implicitly claiming the freedom to tell of her life in any manner she chooses; and in *Serenissima*, Jessica acknowledges the impossibility of knowing what is "true": "How can I tell any longer what is real and what is not, what is life and what is death, or even what century or what place I shall be buried alive in—if burial is to be my fate."[9] By acknowledging the elusive nature of truth or reality, these narrators refuse to be bound by a version of it that is controlled by someone else, and insist, as women, on the validity of their own visions, however equivocal.

It is a common observation that utopian fictions, in particular, have little narrative tension, or dramatic action, precisely because the ideality of the culture envisioned in the novel precludes the kind of conflict that normally gives rise to dramatic suspense. James W. Bittner, for example, has written that "except for the drama of ironic clashes between a reader's actual world and an imagined utopian world, drama is otherwise missing from many utopian narratives because their static societies often make little room for the extraordinary individual." [10] It is true that such works as *Walden Two* are little more than exposition, with little real dramatic action, but in the feminist utopia, the drama of what Bittner calls "ironic clashes" replaces the ordinary drama of ideological or personal conflict precisely because of the author's feminist intent. Ironic drama, that is, deliberately supplants other sorts of dramatic action because the author's intent is to delineate a culture in which such active conflict can be seen as the product of patriarchy and oppression. In *Herland,* for example, the ironic difference between the Herland inhabitants' calm, reasoned self-possession and the bewildered agitation of their three male visitors poses not merely an alternative social order but also a concept of relationships that is devoid of competition and jealousy. Janet Evason's Whileaway, in *The Female Man*, is a similar place, as is the Mattapoisett, Massachusetts, of 2137 in *Woman on the Edge of Time;* in both societies, there is more conflict than in Gilman's pacific Herland, but most of the inhabitants' energy is devoted to preventing or solving conflict rather than perpetuating its origins in "we-they" dichotomies. The drama of irony is dominant also in the dystopian *Handmaid's Tale.* The stasis in Atwood's novel results not from the calm of ideality, as in the utopia, but rather from the imposition of strict rules by those who govern in the Republic of Gilead. There is little overt action in Offred's account of her life; as Linda Kauffman notes, "her entire existence as a handmaid consists of waiting: waiting for the monthly 'ceremony' during which the Commander tries to impregnate her; waiting for the results; and, if they are positive, waiting to deliver the baby" (236). Offred's enforced idleness—

which is reinforced by the fact that alternating chapters take place at night, when she is alone with her thoughts—is sharply at variance with both her past life and the reader's busy imagination, as it compares past, present, and future realities and possibilities.

The drama of ironic contrast is further achieved in some of these novels by the appending of a final section that pulls the reader out of the lives of the characters and forces her or him to view them from the perspective of an institutionalized bureaucracy that dehumanizes them. The "Historical Notes" section at the end of *The Handmaid's Tale* functions in this way, presenting Offred as a problem in historical verification rather than an actual person; as Professor Pieixoto remarks, she was "one of many, and must be seen within the broad outlines of the moment in history of which she was a part" (305). The contrast between the personal, individual voice in which Offred has seemed to speak for nearly three hundred pages and the distanced, even jocular tone of the academic conference at which she is merely a curious case study—an artifact—jolts the reader into questions about the nature of individual identity and worth.[11] Similarly, Piercy concludes *Woman on the Edge of Time* with "Excerpts from the Official History of Consuelo Camacho Ramos," a sampling from more than a hundred pages of documents from various psychiatric facilities that present Connie as consisting of a set of clinically diagnosable disorders. As does Atwood, Piercy forces us to observe the contrast between two kinds of perceptions: though Connie's is not a first-person narrative, the narrative perspective has consistently been hers throughout the novel, convincing us that she is a victim of poverty and ethnic discrimination, but the reports of the authorities depict her as a schizophrenic of "unidff. type 295.90."[12] Most pointed of all the comments in these reports is the statement that Connie's brother is "a reliable informant who expresses genuine concern for his sister" (381), whereas Luis Camacho has been presented throughout the novel as an insensitive man who is primarily concerned that Connie not disturb his upper-middle-class life; he has rejected his ethnic heritage to the point of insisting that his name be pronounced "Lewis," and he shuns Connie as a reminder of his origins.

The documents and letters in the "Appendix" to *The Four-Gated City* similarly serve an ironic purpose, but in this case the attached ending of the novel vindicates rather than calling into question the personhood of the central character. Dating from the years between 1995 and 2000, the letters and fragments of letters provide a partial accounting of the unspecified "catastrophe" that has turned Great Britain into "Destroyed Area II," and the two longest letters—from Francis Coldridge to his stepdaughter Amanda, and from Martha to Francis—focus on the psychic powers that Martha and Lynda have developed by the end of the novel. Whereas in *Woman on the Edge of Time* the closing documents assert the authority of the mental-health establishment over the individual, in Lessing's novel Martha and Lynda are presented as ascendant over the authorities; society has gone mad, not the two women. Francis reports to Amanda that shortly before the catastrophe he spend several days with Martha and Lynda, during which they gradually persuaded him that they, like others, had gifts of foresight and telepathy, and knew of the approaching cataclysm. Although at the time Francis resisted this information, his late-twentieth-century letter makes clear that by the time he is writing it such powers are understood to be commonplace. Having reminded Amanda of the various forms of espionage in existence after the Second World War, he speaks somewhat apologetically of the ignorance of his own time regarding the human mind:

> Imagine, then, the possible dent in this structure [of spies, counter-spies, wiretapping] made by a group of people with ordinary telepathic powers—very well, such thoughts are familiar to you, but I'm writing down, for the benefit of researchers, the reactions of someone only twenty-five years ago, on first considering these very obvious—to you—facts. To imagine the possibilities of ordinary telepathy—I remember it entertained us during dinner. . . . [W]e sat laughing, imagining how in human beings themselves were growing . . . powers which could make all this machinery useless, out of date, obsolete.[13]

Martha's letter to Francis, written in the summer of 1997, reports on the evolution that Francis's letter merely predicts. From her island retreat near Scotland, sensing her impending death, Martha

157

writes of the extraordinary children born on the island in the years since the catastrophe—children who are not only by nature peaceful, but who also have capacities to "see" and "hear" beyond normal sensory abilities. These clearly superior children have become the "guardians" of their elders, and assure them that the entire human race is on the verge of improvement. Martha writes of one particular child:

> Joseph, the black child, will come to your settlement near Nairobi, and you will look after him. So he says. He says more like them are being born now in the hidden places in the world, and one day all the human race will be like them. People like you and me are a sort of experimental model and Nature has had enough of us. (648)

The fact that two later letters from relocation bureaucrats speak of Joseph as subnormal rather than advanced does not detract from Martha's final triumph; Lessing has provided a glimpse of a possible utopia in which the human being has evolved past conflict and the need for it—a fitting conclusion to a five-novel series with the overarching title *Children of Violence*.

Rachel Blau Du Plessis has proposed that glimpsing or exploring the future is one way of "writing beyond the ending" of the traditional novel, citing *The Four-Gated City, Woman on the Edge of Time*, and *The Female Man* as recent examples of the use of this narrative strategy. Du Plessis suggests that by foregoing what she terms the "pleasurable illusion of stasis" that characterizes the ending of the traditional plot, the author enters into a new relationship with the reader in two ways. First, by proposing a future that could be that of the reader as well, the narrative engages the reader in a way that the tidy, historical narrative does not:

> Most novels begin in the past and end just at, or just before, the present, with a highly choreographed, controlled glance at the future. The present (where the reader sits reading) and the future (outside of both book and reader) are felt to be unsullied, untouchable, and in about the same political and moral key as today. But if a novel travels through the present into the future, then social or character development can no longer be felt as complete, or our space as readers perceived as untrammeled.[14]

158

Secondly, because such narratives normally carry a freight of ideology, they challenge assumptions and force revisions in thinking:

> In line with the general use of the narrative as a teaching story, elements like character and plot function mainly as the bearers of propositions or moral arguments, whose function is to persuade. . . . The fiction establishes a dialogue with habitual structures of satisfaction, ranges of feeling, and response. (179)

The concept of such a "dialogue" is similar to what I have earlier identified as the essential irony of such texts: the contrast between a future (or occasionally a past) reality and that inhabited by the reader setting up a tension that can be resolved only outside of the text itself—or not resolved at all.

Such a dialogue or ironic tension is not, of course, limited to novels that explore times or societies unlike our own. The continually revised narrative in novels such as Drabble's *The Waterfall* and Godwin's *Violet Clay,* and the gradual revision of personal history in *Surfacing* and Weldon's *Words of Advice* set up similar tensions and refuse to conclude with a "pleasurable illusion of stasis," as the central characters are still, at the end, questioning and becoming. In speculative fictions, however, the possibilities for change and difference are potentially limitless, which is one of the reasons why these forms are increasingly attractive to women writers. Writing of the literary utopia generally, Peter Ruppert makes the point that these fictions are "open" in two ways. Not only do they invite varying interpretations, but they also, and more importantly, propose that social reality is not fixed, but instead subject to alteration:

> This kind of "openness" aims at producing a heightened sense of awareness in the reader, an awareness that allows her to see all forms of organization—social, political, aesthetic—as contingent and provisional. The effect of this critical distancing is to remind us that whatever "is"—whether it be the social arrangements exposed in the text or our own present moment in history—is historical, provisional, and therefore changeable.[15]

It is not only utopian visions that insist upon the potential for change in a set of social arrangements; the bleak dystopias described in *Woman on the Edge of Time, The Female Man, Memoirs of a Survivor,* and *The Handmaid's Tale* similarly provide readers with the sense that alternative realities are possible. Indeed, the grim futures depicted in these novels may be even more immediately believable and persuasive than those of utopias because the ills they portray spring from those we can identify in our own "moment in history": destruction of the environment, dangerous advancements in technology, and repressive governments justifying their actions on the basis of religious zeal.

The aspect of human experience that the contemporary woman writer of either utopian or dystopian fiction is most concerned to explore—and to propose as mutable—is gender relationships. From Gabriella Sumpter in *The Rules of Life,* who dictates the terms of her own relationships, to Offred in *The Handmaid's Tale,* for whom precisely the reverse is true, the heroines of these novels either participate in or observe relationships between genders that do not adhere to traditional patterns or expectations. Whether the arrangements of these relationships are positive or negative for the characters, it is significant that gender issues are somehow central to each of these novels, because this suggests that for the woman writer such issues are fundamental to any social order rather than peripheral to it. This has been true of women's speculative fiction at least since *Herland,* in which, despite the numerous benefits Gilman ascribes to the all-female society of Herland, it is only by the introduction of men that she is able to provide her narrative with the sort of drama she wanted. As Du Plessis puts it, "although the work talks about changes in narrative, it still offers unwitting proof that 'Love, Combat, or Danger' (all, in Gilman's view, requiring men) might well remain necessary for interesting literature" (181). While few contemporary women writers would argue that "Combat or Danger" are essential to literature, love, with its attendant questions about gender, is central to their works. The alternatives to traditional male-female relationships these authors explore range widely: androgyny, lesbianism, adultery, even outright gender warfare—all suggest that in a society in which one gender dominates the other, any vision of a better or a worse

160

world must address and work through intimate relationships as a foundation for issues of more public concern.

Fay Weldon's short novel *The Rules of Life* is an appropriate beginning point for a more detailed discussion of the novels considered in this chapter, because it is, in a sense, a metafiction. Just as Atwood, in *The Handmaid's Tale*, investigates the nature of truth and fiction in the many-layered "reconstruction" of Offred's tale, so Weldon explores the concept that people invent or create the stories of their own lives, so that "fact" is transmuted into "fiction" that masquerades in turn as "fact." Gabriella Sumpter quite literally speaks to us from her grave; or rather, she speaks to the central narrator, whose task it is to transcribe and report on the tapes made of the reminiscences of the recently deceased, or "rewinds," as they have come to be called, by the "pinner priests" of the Great New Fictional Religion. The narrator, who is of the order of "pulp priests" of the GNFR, works in the Temple, once the British Museum, in the year 2002, listening to tapes of Gabriella's voice made shortly after her death, and moves emotionally from initial disapproval of her "selfish and morally frail" life to the point of falling in love with her. The voice of the narrator alternates with that of Gabriella as he tells the reader the story of telling *her* story.

Weldon calls into question the existence of any fixed "truth," including the ultimate authority of religious belief. The "God" whom the priests serve is known as the Great Screen Writer in the Sky—abbreviated GSWITS—and the priests do not serve this deity with blind faith. Indeed, as the narrator says, "we do acknowledge that the GSWITS has had many a bad idea in his time. Virtue lies in trying to make the best of His mistakes."[16] In his initial disapproval of Gabriella, the narrator resents the fact that the GNFR regards her as something of a saint because "she went where the script dictated," and he considers beginning the *Revised* Great New Fictional Religion, which would have higher standards:

161

Let us simply accept that the GSWITS allocated to us mortals is a mere B-feature writer, with the unhappy tendency of his kind to introduce disasters—cyclones, volcanic eruptions, earthquakes or man-made explosions—to get himself out of plot difficulties. The effort of his creation must therefore be to see that He takes his task seriously, and improves his standards. (21–22)

The narrator-priest thus inverts the traditional relationship between man and God by proposing that it is man's responsibility to raise the standards by which God operates—to improve upon his plot. In contrast to the narrator's concern for upholding rules and standards (he is, appropriately, married to a woman named Honor), Gabriella is intent upon breaking rules—or rather on selecting those that she considers "Valid Rules":

She had observed in life that the mass of ordinarily accepted rules—for example, that too many cooks spoil the broth, or if you can't stand the heat you should get out of the kitchen, or that a woman needs a man as a fish needs a bicycle, were simply not true: mere patterns of words, cement grouting for the shaky construction of our existence, cosmetic rather than structural. (13)

Gabriella's perception that most rules are "mere patterns of words" is matched by her view that there are no rules in fiction, so that "if she wished to start with her death and end with her birth, she would" (12). By acknowledging that her life, at least in the telling of it, is a fiction, Gabriella tacitly recognizes the Great New Fictional Religion, in which people live out parts of the plot devised by the Great Screen Writer in the Sky.

Gabriella believes that her life has been successful because she has not married nor had children. "The best one can do," she says, "while living, is not, by marrying, to burden others with our existence, and not, irresponsibly, by having children, to pass life on" (15). Believing that erotic love is "the only thing that makes life worth living at all" (15), Gabriella has had a series of affairs with married men, always being careful to keep the upper hand in such relationships. One of Gabriella's Valid Rules—"the greatest and most reliable of them all"—is that "Nothing is fair" (15), and she has seen little point in being fair to others. Shortly before she dies,

162

she has the arthritic seamstress Frieda Martock make a white silk shift for her burial, even though the process is quite painful for Miss Martock: "If there is no sacrifice, the God does not descend. He likes blood" (17). The narrator, observing the enormous disparity between rich and poor in the year 2002, tends to agree with Gabriella about the general unfairness of life: "Notions of socialism and a fair society faded along with Christianity: the eighties finally saw them off. The GSWITS, I fear, is a great admirer of Dickens" (75).

The rules that Gabriella is most firm about are those governing the proper care of fabrics, and throughout *The Rules of Life* Weldon uses this appropriately feminine metaphor to represent the fabric of life, which, when stained, can sometimes be made pure again and sometimes not. Gabriella constantly dispenses advice about how to clean scorched linen, how to remove grass stains from fur, and how to clean a lace bedspread. Despite her sexual indiscretions, she believes her life to be without moral stain; yet at the same time she recalls, as a child, reacting to a priest's admonition to remain pure by going home and pouring ink on her white dress: "I wanted to be stained" (24). What Gabriella wants is indulgence without blame or guilt, and when her life ends at the age of sixty-one she believes she has achieved this—or so her self-assured voice suggests to the narrator until the final segment of the tape. Her longest-lasting affair has been with Timothy Tovey, a career diplomat who, according to Gabriella, has married someone else for money while continuing to love her. Yet Gabriella's story, to use Weldon's metaphor, begins to unravel at the end, first when she pulls from her imagination the thread that is Timothy Tovey and finds that his "fabric" has not been treated with the proper care:

> Someone has washed him badly, made the water too hot. The colours have run. It need never have happened. Any person can be washed, if proper care and attention is paid, even those which say "Dry Clean Only"—which is mostly only a manufacturer's convenience—oh, my poor head! What is a word, and what is a label, and what is a principle, and who can we trust? (72)

163

With these fundamental questions, the tape ends, and the narrator later visits Timothy Tovey, who tells him that it was impossible for him to marry Gabriella because she had proven that she was "badly brought up" when she complained to his mother about the manner in which her nightgown had been washed.

The "truth" of Gabriella's story is further called into question, as is Offred's story, by the fact that it is a transcription of tapes by a man who is far from objective about her. The narrator suspects at one point that the pinner priests have "misrecorded her on purpose" because of their own cynicism (38); alternatively, he wonders whether his own mastery of the equipment may be faulty, or whether his own attitudes may have altered what she says: "Perhaps in some way my own personality plays into the text? I may be a more cynical person than I suppose. Nothing, they say, can ever truly be known" (38–39). When Gabriella uses the word "sub-text," the narrator wonders whether the pinner priests have put words in her mouth, because "concepts such as 'sub-text' must be strange to her" (67).

Weldon's amusing fantasy, which begins and ends with the phrase "strange days, indeed," is far less comprehensive in its investigations of cultural mores and malaise than is *The Handmaid's Tale*, but it similarly questions our ability to know the "truth," even about ourselves, and certainly about the "rules of life." Gabriella Sumpter, however, seems to have triumphed, at least during her own lifetime, in the sense that she believed her own story and lived life on her own terms. In a way, she has written her own script, even to the point of dying painlessly while she was still physically attractive.

*Serenissima* shares with *The Rules of Life* the central character's concern with aging and sexuality, and Jong, like Weldon, creates a fantasy that questions the nature of truth—including fictional truth. Jessica Pruitt, as an actress, is well aware of the roles that people play in life, not merely on the stage, and she narrates the story of writing the script for her own life with the consciousness of being a storyteller who, like Offred in *The Handmaid's Tale*, can convey only a partial truth. Early in the novel Jessica announces the precariousness of her task: "What storyteller is adequate to

164

her story? The story carries us along, bottles on the tide, each with our secret message and the fervent hope that it does not turn out to be blank."[17] By asserting the primacy of the story over the storyteller, Jong claims a measure of authenticity for her tale of time travel, but at the same time the first-person narrative provides Jessica with the illusion of control over her own story. By moving from actress to participant in the drama she will then re-enact for the screen, Jessica is empowered to accept herself rather than assuming the identity of a character in order to *have* an identity. "I," she says, "was always fleeing myself—the very opposite of the writer's craft." On the stage, the actress is "insulated from past and future," seeking in the role she plays "home, mother, completion, peace" (5–6). It is by immersion in the past—her own past history and the Venice of 1592—that Jessica is able to come to terms with her future.

At the age of forty-three, though professing to be thirty-four—"simply reversing the digits like a dyslexic" (10)—Jessica has come to Venice to judge a film festival and then to star in a "filmic fantasy" of Shakespeare's *Merchant of Venice* to be titled *Serenissima,* the nickname given the city of Venice by its inhabitants. The film will mark the end of one phase of her career—that in which she can play younger women: "It was my last chance to play the lover before I entered that desperate no woman's land between *innamorata* and grandma, that terrifying no woman's land from forty to sixty that all actresses wander into sooner or later" (7). In *Serenissima,* Jessica is to play her namesake from Shakespeare's play: "It was ironic that I had been named for Shylock's daughter, named for her by a WASP mother who also loved Shakespeare" (6). Jessica is not new to Venice: her "WASP mother," before her suicide at the age of fifty, had married a Venetian, and Jessica and her brother had spent summers there. The trip to Venice is therefore a return for Jessica, and it becomes a quest for her lost mother and her own lost child. Through Jessica Pruitt's words, Jong presents Venice as the ideal location for experience that erases the line between reality and fantasy. Venice, Jessica remarks, is itself a "chimera": "that city of illusions where reality becomes fantasy and fantasy becomes reality. Perhaps it is because Venice is both

165

liquid and solid, both air and stone, that it somehow combines all the elements crucial to make our imaginations ignite and turn fantasies into realities" (8). By emphasizing this mystical quality of Venice, Jong prepares the reader to accept as real what seems to be Jessica's fantasy, and sets up the ironic tension governing the events of the novel.

Venice also suggests to Jessica the concept of multiple selves, a concept that is amplified as the novel proceeds:

> Each time one comes to Venice, it reflects back another self, another dream, as if it were partly your own mirror. The air is full of the spirits of all those who have lived here, worked here, loved here. The stones themselves are thick with history. They whisper to you as you walk the deserted streets at night. (8)

Into this city with its layers of history comes the actress accustomed to having two selves: living a life and playing a part, and as the film festival ends and she remains in Venice with a fever, awaiting the script of *Serenissima*, she becomes another Jessica, in 1592, the companion and lover of William Shakespeare. Rather than submerging Jessica completely in the Venice of 1592, Jong allows her a dual consciousness: as Jessica Shalach, daughter of a Jewish merchant, she is aware of also being Jessica Pruitt, a film star in the 1980s:

> How to describe living two lives at once? It is, after all, my sullen craft, my soaring art, to live one life in the quotidian (buying food, cleaning house, caring for kin) while I lead a more heroic life on the stage— speaking the lines of queens and courtesans, lovers and heroines. To hold two characters in mind at once, one's self and one's not-self, this is my art. . . . I remember the life of Jessica Pruitt as in a dream. Jessica Shalach is my present. But human beings are so made as to wake and dream all in one day and think nothing of it. (149)

By reminding us that both dreaming and waking are part of normal lives, Jong draws more closely together the two Jessicas, allowing both to exist simultaneously. Somewhat later in the novel Jessica Shalach dreams of her other life as Jessica Pruitt and wonders how it is that both realities can co-exist: "[D]o New York and

L.A. really exist if I am here in 1592? Can both times exist simultaneously—parallel universes, time flowing forward in one and backward in another, and I the only wanderer, the only vagabond who can pass between them?" (193). The implicit answer to Jessica's question must be affirmative, not only because by the end of the novel Jessica Pruitt is once again in the Venice of the 1980s with the baby that she and Will Shakespeare have saved from its dying mother, but also because in her time as Jessica Shalach, Jessica Pruitt has been released from her mother's death, and has saved a child to atone for the daughter she has lost in a custody battle with her former husband.

As a further level of fantasy, Jessica's dreams of her mother and daughter while she is in the world of 1592 serve as an imaginative healing, and, together with her restorative love for Will, provide her with the resolve to change her life. In one dream, her mother and her daughter are dancing together, reciting Shakespeare's sonnet 19: "All is well, I say to myself in the dream. All is well" (195). Finally, her mother appears to her to release her from the burden of her death that Jessica has borne since she was fifteen, "a ghostly companion" (5). Ultimately, Jessica's fantasy escapade with Will Shakespeare, a life stripped to the essentials of love and survival, allows her to determine that she will, as Jessica Pruitt, take command of her own life. Like the narrator in *Surfacing*, who removes layers of civilization and its weight of female role-playing, Jessica requires removal from her accustomed world in order to see it clearly and re-enter it on her own terms. In a statement that encapsulates Jong's narrative method in the novel, Jessica thinks, "Sometimes freedom is just a matter of changing perspective" (199). Empowered by this change in perspective, she determines to return to New York and fight for her daughter: "Antonia deserved better than a mother who gave up a fight" (199).

The concept that life is a script to be played out and rewritten when necessary—which Weldon treats playfully in *The Rules of Life*—exists on several levels in *Serenissima*, and is the source of much ironic doubling. The film script of *Serenissima* that Jessica Pruitt awaits in Venice turns out to be the story that she has lived with Shakespeare in 1592, so that life has preceded art. Bjorn

167

Perrson, the director, has a policy of never giving actors the script in advance of shooting the film, so Jong precludes the possibility that Jessica has dreamed a story that she has previously read. Further, Jessica Shalach knows the scripts of plays that Shakespeare has not, in 1592, yet written, and in a sense Jong has written part of the script of Shakespeare's life, placing him in Venice during a period in which scholars are uncertain of his whereabouts. In addition to these overarching uses of the concept of scripting, Jessica foretells her own eventual command of her life's script in a comic scene during the film festival. Pursued by a Russian film star who is bent on seducing her, Jessica must finally use physical force to extricate herself:

> He drags me to [the bed] and begins clawing at me in what seems like a rape pantomime drawn from a B movie. I have played this scene before myself. And I know it has only three possible scenarios: the girl gets raped, the girl gets killed, the girl gets killed and raped. Rewrite the script! I command myself. That is your whole life's task, after all, to rewrite these hackneyed scripts and make them real, true, authentically heroic. (66)

By the end of *Serenissima*, Jessica has ceased merely mouthing the words of heroines, and has resolved to become "authentically heroic" in her own script. She has been both metaphorically and literally reborn: Jessica Shalach succumbs to the plague in 1592, and her coffin washes up on a beach in Venice in 1985, where she emerges as Jessica Pruitt, ready to play a role for the cameras in a drama she has already experienced, and thus to turn her life into art.

If Atwood and Jong view a return to elemental survival, unencumbered by the artifices of society, as a cleansing preparation for rebirth into that society, Lessing, in *Memoirs of a Survivor*, turns that proposition on its head. In this essentially dystopian novel, the goods, services, and bureaucratic structures of London disintegrate gradually, revealing a barbarism that is finally more threatening in its implications about human nature than is the virtual absence of a social order. In contrast to the "catastrophe" that has occurred by the end of *The Four-Gated City*, the breakdown in

168

*Memoirs* occurs so slowly that one merely keeps readjusting the definition of normality to absorb the changes. Indeed, Lessing's central theme in the novel is the human capacity to create an acceptable reality even out of objectively unacceptable components. As the unnamed narrator states near the beginning of the novel:

> There is nothing that people won't try to accommodate into "ordinary life." It was precisely this which gave that time its peculiar flavour; the combination of the bizarre, the hectic, the frightening, the threatening—an atmosphere of siege or war—with what was customary, ordinary, even decent. (19)

Only occasionally does "the game we were all agreeing to play" give way to reality, and people recoil from these glimpses into the lives they have fabricated, even as food grows scarce and bands of homeless people roam the streets. Such a dystopian vision, like that of *The Handmaid's Tale*, is derived so carefully from contemporary reality as to seem almost a depiction of actual life.

Yet alongside this bleak, decaying London is a parallel world into which the narrator is able to step through the wall of her flat. It is a set of high-ceilinged rooms that represent a kind of salvation that the narrator has longed for: "this place held what I needed, knew was there, had been waiting for—oh, yes, all my life, all my life" (13). It is into this parallel universe that the narrator and her "family" ultimately escape from the inexorable collapse of a society, led by a shadowy female deity whom the narrator describes as "the one person I had been looking for all this time" (216). The existence of this world, and the narrator's final entrance into it, suggest that social disintegration is not answerable by a rational solution, but that fantasy is the only response.[18] Indeed, it is possible to read this parallel world as existing only in the narrator's own imagination, and her final entrance into it as the ultimate abandoning of conscious, rational thought in favor of the psychological realm. Betsy Draine has suggested that the movement into the parallel world behind the wall is a movement "from Marx to Jung"—from a belief in human historical evolution to a belief in psychological evolution.[19] Such a reading is consonant with Martha's and Lynda's psychological explorations in *The Four-Gated*

169

*City,* and with Martha's description of an evolving race of psychologically superior people in the closing section of that novel.

The focal point of *Memoirs of a Survivor,* however, is the development of Emily, the "half-grown girl" who is mysteriously delivered to the narrator's flat and left for her to care for. The man who brings Emily says merely, "She's your responsibility" (15), a statement that takes on more than its superficial meaning as the story unfolds and Emily grows into a parody of socially constructed womanhood. The narrator, Lessing suggests, about whom we know very little, may not be personally responsible for Emily's ready capitulation to traditional female roles, but the culture she represents has formulated these norms. Emily is twelve when she is delivered to the narrator, and fourteen when the novel ends, but she effectively develops from a child to a mature woman in these two years, acting out several traditional female stereotypes as she grows older.

At first, Emily appears to be a well-behaved child, announcing her full name as "Emily May Cartright" (16) and promising to be "ever so tidy": "I'm really very good, you know, I won't make a mess, I never do" (17). Accompanied by her dog-cat Hugo, a pet of uncertain species, Emily has an "invincible obedience" (23) that causes the narrator to think of her as younger than twelve; she offers to cook and to clean, and is "ever so handy and capable" (26). Yet the narrator senses that this childish obedience is a facade: "Her taste in reading was adult: seeing her there, with what she had chosen, made her bright child's manner even more impossible, almost as if she were deliberately insulting me" (27). Emily's observations of other people have an adult sharpness and perception that startles the narrator; their accuracy makes her realize how automatically people subject one another to "the defensive inspection, the rapid, sharp, cold analysis" (31).

Rather abruptly, this child-woman becomes involved with successive gangs of youths who camp on the streets near the flat during their movements out of the city. She becomes flippant about her escapades to the narrator, who makes no attempt to discipline her even when she returns one evening drunk and disheveled, announcing defiantly that she has not lost her virginity, "though it was a close thing, I grant you" (39). Emily's adolescent rebellion continues with a refusal to buy and wear new clothes, a compulsion to eat and daydream, until the need to be accepted by a gang of boys as an attractive female plunges her into dieting, "preparing her to take her place as a woman among other women" (55). Lessing's narrator sees Emily's rehearsal of adult female images as an inevitable if frightening process:

> The way this child, this little girl, had found the materials for her dreams in the rubbish heaps of our old civilisation, had found them, worked on them, and in spite of everything had made her images of herself come to life . . . but such old images, so indestructible, and so *irrelevant*— (58)

The ironic juxtaposition of Emily's need to prepare herself rapidly for mating rituals and the irrelevance of those rituals in a society struggling with bare survival reveals Lessing's insistence that such behaviors are changeless despite alterations in the social order. Female gender roles that in Atwood's Republic of Gilead are maintained by edict are in *Memoirs of a Survivor* perpetuated by instinct. At the age of thirteen, Emily appears to be seventeen or eighteen, and "had mated herself in imagination with romantic heroes and chief executives and harem tyrants" (60).

Of the novel's structure, Mona Knapp has remarked that it hinges on the stages in Emily's relationship with Gerald, the young leader of one of the roaming bands of youths, with whom she experiences love, jealousy, separation, and reconciliation. Knapp outlines the stages as sections of the narrative:

1. Emily alone (to p. 84)
2. Emily and Gerald (84 ff.)
3. Emily and June (102 ff.)
4. June and Gerald (142 ff.)
5. Emily alone once more (169 ff.)
6. Emily and Gerald reunited (213 ff.)

Knapp remarks of this scheme that it is "dangerously similar to the classic girl-meets-boy novel," and that "the archetype of feminine behavior acted out by [Emily] is woefully traditional and undynamic."[20] But Lessing has in fact encapsulated the traditional romance plot within her dystopian novel in order to demonstrate how enduring this plot actually is—how, in the midst of social upheaval and decay, a woman may not only adhere to the traditional script for her life, but may experience it in accelerated form if time is short: between the ages of twelve and fourteen Emily seems to pass from childhood to womanhood and even on to middle age. Lessing describes her as "the eternal woman" (171) and "the jaded woman of our dead civlization," knowing that love was "an illness to be endured, a trap which might lead her to betray her own nature, her good sense, and her real purposes" (201). So Emily plays out the role of the subordinate "wife" in Gerald's communal family, enduring his unfaithfulness, taking him back—a parody that is rendered grotesque because of her age, even though, at fourteen, she has "the eyes of a mature woman of about thirty-five, or forty" (201).

The parallel world that the narrator enters a number of times during the novel seems at first a personal refuge for her, but sometimes it is in fact inhabited—haunted might be a better term—by Emily's parents and by Emily herself as a product of their terrifyingly conventional marriage and parenting. If this alternate world represents the recesses of the narrator's own psyche, these scenes may be viewed as her attempt to establish an understandable origin for Emily; within the paradigm of the traditional life script that Lessing plays out in the novel these scenes deepen the sense that Emily's is a life chosen for her rather than one of her own choosing. The narrator witnesses in these rooms behind the wall of her own living room several scenes from Emily's childhood, first when she is four years old and already realizes that she has little power over her life:

> Her face was old and weary. She seemed to understand it all, to have foreseen it, to be living through it because she had to, feeling it as a thick heaviness all around her—Time, through which she must push herself till she could be free of it. For none of them could help themselves—not the mother, that feared and powerful woman; not the nurse, bad-tempered because of her life. (45)

172

Another scene, glimpsed when Emily is five or six, reveals the mother bemoaning to a visitor the entrapment of her life as a homemaker: the lack of time for herself, the repetitions of house-keeping, the demands of the children—especially Emily, "who knew she was the chief culprit, the one being complained of" (68). Lessing's description of Emily's mother's malaise could have been quoted directly from *The Feminine Mystique:*

> She was trapped, but did not know why she felt this, for her marriage and her children were what she personally had wanted and had aimed for—what society had chosen for her. Nothing in her education or ex-perience had prepared her for what she did in fact feel, and she was isolated in her distress and her bafflement, sometimes even believing that she might perhaps be ill in some way. (70)

Ultimately, the narrator traces Emily's mother's rejection of her to the mother's own emotionally deprived childhood as she dis-covers the woman, as a small child, weeping from loneliness: "up went the little arms, desperate for comfort, but they would be one day those great arms that had never been taught tenderness" (151). The scene is, as Lorna Sage puts it, one of "infinite regress": "Each generation has stamped its own discipline, its own wretch-edly acquired boundaries, on the next. The 'personal' is not the unique: its claustrophobia derives precisely from its repetitions."[21]

The most grotesque image of Emily that the narrator sees in the world beyond the wall—and one that unites the concept of Emily as a child-woman with Lessing's emphasis on women's cultural conditioning—is the image of Emily at fourteen, against the pris-tine whiteness of a schoolgirl's room, wearing the vulgar scarlet evening dress of an adult woman. Not only does the scene solidify the contrast between virginity and blatant sexuality; it also under-scores the notion of woman-as-object:

> It was a dress of blatant vulgarity. It was also, in a perverted way, non-sexual, for all its advertisement of the body, and embodied the fan-tasies of a certain kind of man who, dressing a woman thus, made her a doll, ridiculous, both provocative and helpless; disarmed her, made her something to hate, to pity, to fear—a grotesque. (187)

173

The dress and its implications are similar to the section of *The Handmaid's Tale* in which Offred's Commander gives her a pink and purple evening dress to wear on their clandestine trip to the nightclub/whorehouse. The Commander articulates the point that Lessing's narrator has made when he says to Offred, "Nature demands variety, for men. It stands to reason, it's part of the procreational strategy." Offred, freed for the night from her red Handmaid's uniform, responds mockingly, "So now that we don't have different clothes, . . . you merely have different women" (237). No such sense of irony is available to Emily, however; faced with the disapproving figure of her mother, who dislikes her as much in her adult garb as she had in diapers, Emily disappears in a puff of red smoke, "like a morality tale of flesh and the devil" (188).

The disintegration of this bizarre image of Emily is followed by the final disintegration of the society surrounding the narrator, Emily, and Hugo, the strange pet whose loyalty comes to seem the only humane pulse in the increasing barbarity of life. When the narrator finally senses that the moment is right for an escape to one of the worlds behind the wall, "into another order of world altogether" (217), she signals a repudiation of contemporary civilization and the Edenic beginning of a new order. If, as Claire Sprague has proposed, the communal life that Emily and Gerald have attempted to establish with the roving bands of children on the streets of London makes them "a new Adam and Eve," and the novel itself "a failed creation myth," [22] it is ironic that the narrator ushers into the new world behind the wall a version of the traditional nuclear family: Emily, the disillusioned woman; Gerald, the ineffectual father figure; and several rebellious children. Only Hugo seems transformed—"a splendid animal, handsome, all kindly dignity and command" (217)—as if to suggest that human beings alone are incapable of re-ordering the world.

In fictions that are not overtly speculative—that remain tied to a recognizable reality, however skewed or exaggerated—the utopian or dystopian fantasies they contain are frequently hinted to be dreams or hallucinations of the central characters. In *Serenissima*, for example, except for the presence of the infant in Jessica's room at the end, her adventure with Will Shakespeare can be in-

174

terpreted as feverish dreams brought on by her illness. The parallel universe beyond the wall in *Memoirs of a Survivor* may be viewed as a mental sanctuary for an elderly woman enduring the stress of social disintegration. By creating such ambiguity, Jong and Lessing heighten the drama of ironic juxtaposition. Early reviewers of Piercy's *Woman on the Edge of Time* were quick to see, mistakenly, the utopian and dystopian visions that are part of the novel as drug-induced hallucinations or products of Consuelo Ramos' mental condition as diagnosed by the various mental institutions in which she is confined. But such readings ignore the fact that *Woman on the Edge of Time* is a successful blending of realistic and speculative modes; the story of Consuelo's life as a poor Mexican-American woman in New York and in its institutions for social misfits is, as Margaret Atwood has put it, "rendered in excruciating, grotty, Zolaesque detail, pill by deadening pill, meal by cardboard meal, ordeal by ordeal, and as a rendition of what life in a New York bin is like for those without money or influence it is totally convincing and depressing."[23] Just as convincing, though in a different way, are the utopian and dystopian segments of the novel—visions of alternate futures between which those in the present of the novel seem able to choose, if only they are made aware of the necessity of choice.

On the surface, Connie Ramos would seem to be an unlikely guide or medium to a utopian future. She is a thirty-seven-year-old welfare recipient who has been deserted by her husband and rejected by her successful brother. When her relationship with a black, blind pickpocket ends with his death, her depression and consequent drinking cause her to accidentally break her daughter's wrist, whereupon her daughter is removed from her care and Connie is judged to be mentally ill and is committed to a mental institution—caught in the double bind of being found guilty of child abuse and at the same time judged incapable of rational thought or action. As Piercy's novel opens, Connie is institutionalized once more for having injured her niece's pimp while defending her from his attack. Yet Piercy makes it clear that Connie is a victim of the social system; her only crimes are poverty and her Mexican heritage. Moreover, Connie is well aware of the ab-

175

surdity of her dilemma. Early in the novel, for example, longing for Mexican food, Connie notes that the Mexican restaurants in New York are too expensive for her: "Ridiculous to live in a place where the taste of your own soul food was priced beyond you. She got to eat Chinese oftener than Mexican" (29). Part of the ironic fabric of the novel is Piercy's choice of a woman in Connie's circumstances to be visionary and time traveler.

This irony is deepened by the fact that Luciente, Connie's guide to the utopia of 2137, finds her gifted and attractive. At their first meeting, Luciente tells her, "You're an unusual person. Your mind is unusual. You're what we call a catcher, a receptive" (41). Moreover, Luciente immediately comprehends the difference between the way he regards her and the way she is regarded by her own culture: "Believe me, Connie, I have respect for you. We've been trying to get through for three months before I chanced on your mind. You're an extraordinary top catcher. In our culture you would be much admired, which I take it isn't true in this one?" (42). Connie has been vaguely aware of having powers of mental prescience before this, but their only value has been to enable her to predict when her husband was going to hit her. This woman who is so poor that she is thrilled to find an abandoned ballpoint pen on the subway is welcomed by the community of Mattapoisett, Massachusetts, in the year 2137, where wealth and ethnic origins are not issues.

Sheila Delany, in *Writing Woman*, makes a useful distinction between two kinds of utopias: the programmatic and the ideological. She places *Woman on the Edge of Time* in the former group, which she describes as follows:

> [The programmatic utopia] stresses a comprehensive social critique and serious social planning, attempts to demonstrate what should change and what might realistically replace present arrangements; it tends to propose social reforms that give scope to human variability.[24]

Though certainly utopian, the culture of Mattapoisett is dynamic rather than static; there is conflict, and there are problems to work through as the community evolves. The utopia that Piercy imagines can be seen as growing out of the period in which the novel was written; as Delany puts it, it is "a heady blend of late 1960s and early 1970s countercultures: R. D. Laing, group therapy, natural health foods, marijuana, ecology, anarchism, socialism, New Left and Yippie politics, and the radical wing of the women's liberation movement" (175). Mattapoisett, and by implication the rest of North America, embodies an ideology long a part of the "American dream" in that it is pastoral and communal. Education is accomplished by an apprenticeship system, government is decentralized, and there are few hierarchies. Yet the culture has not abandoned technology: much communication is electronic, human embryos are grown *in vitro,* and various machines take the drudgery out of life. Of great interest to Connie, who "visits" Mattapoisett while in a mental institution, the society of 2137 has its "madhouses," too, but they are places that one enters voluntarily, "to collapse, carry on, see visions, hear voices of prophecy, bang on the walls, relive infancy—getting in touch with the buried self and the inner mind" (66). In short, it is a culture that values mental states other than those we consider "normal."

As in most feminist utopias, the nuclear family does not exist, because it is associated with patriarchal concepts of power and ownership. Parenting is by choice, not necessity, and men may choose to take hormones that allow them to nurse infants. In fact, the utopia that Piercy envisions is powerfully androgynous, even linguistically: the pronoun "per," from "person," refers to both male and female. Connie initially assumes Luciente to be a man rather than a woman, and one may have lovers—called "pillow friends"—of either gender. Connie, who in New York in 1976 considers herself an aging woman at thirty-seven, is welcomed into the easy sexuality of Mattapoisett by Bee, a pillow friend of Luciente, and it is clear that through Bee the whole community is making love to her: "We all care for you. But you're of a society with many taboos. It's easier for me to hold you for all of us" (189). In the absence of exclusive, power-based relationships, jealousy cannot exist. The juxtaposition of this world with the one of 1976 throws into sharp relief the ills of contemporary society, especially as they affect women.

Much of the dynamism of Piercy's utopia is its precariousness: it is a *possible* future, not necessarily *the* future, and it can, as Luciente puts it, "wink out" if those in Connie's present fail to make

177

the proper choices about politics, the environment, and human development. One chapter in *Woman on the Edge of Time* is devoted to an alternate future in which Connie lands by mistake, and it is characteristic of Piercy's purpose that much of the horror of this dystopia is related to gender relationships. In contrast to the environmentally pure Mattapoisett, the New York of the future is an urban nightmare of pollution and high-rise compartmentalization. Everything in this culture is artificial: a window is actually a changeable picture; food is made from coal, algae, and wood byproducts, artificially flavored; and wealthy people achieve longevity through repeated organ transplants. Gildina 547-921-45-822-KBJ, the woman whose apartment Connie has inadvertently entered, has through plastic surgery, implants, and shots been made into a "cartoon of femininity" (288), and participates in a form of socially sanctioned prostitution in which women are under contarct to men for specified periods of time: "Contract sex," Gildina explains. "It means you agree to put out for so long for so much" (289).

Piercy's dystopian vision has certain parallels with that of Atwood's *The Handmaid's Tale*. Both feature an enforced prostitution, though the object of it in *Woman on the Edge of Time* is not procreation but sexual pleasure. Piercy's New York of the future and the Republic of Gilead are highly stratified societies, with extremes of wealth and poverty. Connie learns from Gildina about the "richies"—"the Rockmellons, the Morganfords, the Duke-Ponts" (297)—who may live two hundred years, and the "duds," who are farmed for organ transplants. Women in both societies are closely guarded and monitored to be sure that they do nothing except the function they are assigned, and even their emotions are artificially induced: the Handmaids are supposed to feel ritualized joy at birthings and anger at Salvagings; Gildina takes pills: "risers, soothers, sleepers, wakers, euphors, passion pills, the whole works" (292). Like Atwood ten years later, Piercy extrapolates from the technological and ideological possibilities of her own time to project a world in which women are truly objects.

While a visitor to this alternate future, Connie realizes that she is witnessing the eventuality that Luciente and her friends are fighting to prevent: "So that was the other world that might come

178

to be. That was Luciente's war, and she was enlisted in it" (301). Connie's resolve is strengthened by the advice of Bee, her Mattapoisett lover: "There's always a thing you can deny an oppressor, if only your allegiance. Your belief. Your co-oping. Often even with vastly unequal power, you can find or force an opening to fight back. In your time many without power found ways to fight. Till that became a power" (328). Connie's only arena for rebellion is the hospital to which she is confined, but her resistance is overt rather than passive, and her targets are appropriate for one enlisted in Luciente's war: the doctors who have placed an experimental implant in her brain as a means of controlling her behavior—an experiment they intend to repeat on other patients. The poison that Connie puts in the coffee in the doctors' lounge kills four of them, and the act insures that Connie will never be released from institutions, but she has found a channel for her anger, and has regained some of her self-esteem: "I'm a dead woman now too. I know it. But I did fight them. I'm not ashamed. I tried. . . . to you who will be born from my best hopes, to you I dedicate my act of war. At least once I fought and won" (375). Connie Ramos has won a small battle in the large war to achieve Luciente's future, and *Woman on the Edge of Time*, in its presentation of alternate future societies, reminds the reader that the future depends on the present.

*The Female Man* also presents utopian and dystopian alternatives, and Russ, like Piercy, proposes that present actions create future probabilities, but she does so in a far more complex manner by insisting on parallelism and relativity instead of direct historical progression:

> The Past one visits is never one's own Past but always somebody else's; or rather, one's visit to the Past instantly creates another Present (one in which the visit has already happened) and what you visit is the Past belonging to that Present—an entirely different matter than your own Past. And with each decision you make (back there in the Past) that new probable universe itself branches, creating simultaneously a new Past and a New Present, or to put it plainly, a new universe.[25]

Universes, in Russ's terms, are personal and individual rather than objective historical realities; they are states of mind. And because

179

the four central "characters" in *The Female Man* are aspects of a single central consciousness, Russ suggests that each of us may contain more than one world. Whileaway, from which Janet Evason comes, and the world of Alice-Jael, which consists of Manland and Womanland, are societies of the future, but not necessarily outgrowths of the reader's present. Whileaway, Russ notes, is "a name for the Earth ten centuries from now, but not *our* Earth, if you follow me. . . . Whileaway, you may gather, is in the future. But not *our* future" (7). *The Female Man*, like *Woman on the Edge of Time*, is a cautionary tale, but what Piercy achieves by stark realism, Russ achieves by parody and hyperbole, using these devices to undescore the power of language and the imagination to create alternate realities.

The paradox of the title *The Female Man* has several ironic manifestations in the novel. Jeannine, who inhabits the 1930s, is, as Rachel DuPlessis notes, a female man "because she is male-identified. She 'turns into a man' by subsuming herself in male demands, by identifying with her oppression and oppressor. Thus she is a 'man'—seeing herself completely through male eyes."[26] Joanna, who bears the given name of the author, "is closest to ourselves":

> the woman who stands in a puddle of water, grasping two alternating electrical currents, trying to fuse them. She lives in an oscillating contradiction: between woman and man, feminist and phallocrat, joy and rage. . . . Joanna did not turn into a member of the male gender or sex, but she did turn into a generic man—or, as one might translate the term, a human, a person. (183)

Janet is to some extent able to circumvent the gender issue because Whileaway is an all-female society like Herland. When she lands on our Earth and is confronted with blatant sexism, she responds with decisive force born, it seems, of simple disbelief. Jael, the fourth component of this multiple consciousness, adopts a "male" role in two ways. Bearing the name of a Biblical warrior (but with the paradoxical last name of Reasoner), she is an assassin, engaged in on-going physical warfare between Manland and Womanland. She also reserves stereotypical sexual-aggressive roles by keeping a beautiful young man as a sexual plaything, completely subjugated to her whims.

Whileaway, more like Piercy's Mattapoisett than like Gilman's Herland, is not a static, pacific society. Janet Evason ("son" of Eva) is a Safety and Peace officer who has fought four duels—"I've killed four times" (2)—and the author comments that "Whileawayans are not nearly as peaceful as they sound" (49). Yet in the nine centuries following the plague that killed all the men on Whileaway, the women have developed a technologically sophisticated yet still pastoral culture that is characterized primarily by its energy:

> the incredible explosive energy, the gaiety of high intelligence, the obliquities of wit, the cast of mind that makes industrial areas into gardens and ha-has, that supports wells of wilderness where nobody ever lives for long, that strews across a planet sceneries, mountains, glider preserves, culs-de-sac, comic nude statuary, artistic lists of tautologies and circular mathematical proofs (over which afficionados are moved to tears), and the best graffiti in this or any other world. (54)

Russ is less concerned than Piercy or Gilman to provide a complete picture of her utopia; Whileaway is closer to what Delany calls the "ideological" utopia, which concentrates on "a few key areas of social concern" (*Writing Woman,* 158). As in other feminist utopias, a central issue is family structure and child-rearing. The women of Whileaway marry, but are not sexually monogamous. A Whileawayan woman bears a single child (sometimes twins) at the age of thirty, and enjoys an extended period of maternity leave from her job, spending the next five years in a common nursery with other mothers and children of the same age. Parenting effectively ends at this point, because at the age of five, children are sent away to district schools, where until puberty they are instructed in the practical skills needed by the society. Russ notes that Whileawayans have a saying: "When the mother and child are separated they both howl, the child because it is separated from the mother, the mother because she has to go back to work" (49). Russ's utopia thus provides for both intense maternal nurturance and the woman's commitment to her career, and she

181

simultaneously humanizes Whileaway by acknowledging the pain of separation.

Apart from the enforced schooling of childhood, social organization in Whileaway is relatively loose and non-bureaucratic. From puberty until the age of seventeen, at which time they become part of the labor force, young people roam the world, following their own curiosity; at twenty-two they achieve "Full Dignity" and are allowed to join families and participate in the adult world, part of which involves developing a "network of informal associations of the like-minded which is Whileaway's substitute for everything else but family" (51). Old age is respected: the old are free to dream, to create, to enjoy "a freedom they haven't had since adolescence" (53), so aging is eagerly anticipated rather than feared.

Part of the charm of Whileaway is that, even though Russ offers alternatives to some of the problems that women face in contemporary society, the people are neither perfect nor perfectly happy. Ideality creates stasis, and Russ envisions a dynamic culture. The very patterns of life seem designed to prevent contentment:

> Whileawayan psychology locates the basis of Whileawayan character in the early indulgence, pleasure, and flowering which is drastically curtailed by the separation from the mothers. This (it says) gives Whileawayan life its characteristic independence, its dissatisfaction, its suspicion, and its tendency toward a rather irritable solipcism. (52)

The same pattern of indulgence and withdrawal is seen as the source of Whileaway's lack of sexual monogamy: "the reluctance to form a tie that will engage every level of emotion, all the person, all the time" (53). Russ cites statements by a venerated Whileawayan philosopher, Dunyasha Bernadetteson, as warnings against an ideal happiness. Without irritations and dissatisfactions, she has said, "we would all become contented slobs" (52); "we would become so happy we would sit down on our fat, pretty behinds and soon we would start starving, *nyet?*" (53–54). The casual, flippant tone of the philosopher's remarks is characteristic of the humorous approach to life in Whileaway, where little is forbidden and there is only a handful of taboos: "sexual relations with anybody considerably older or younger than oneself, waste, ignorance, offending others without intending to" (53).

In stark contrast to the easy high spirits of Whileaway is the world of deliberate, grim conflict represented by Alice-Jael Reasoner, whose code name "Sweet Alice" is ironic in light of her hard-edged, high-tech deadliness. As in *Woman on the Edge of Time*, the essential difference between utopian and dystopian visions is expressed in terms of the natural versus the artificial, and the readers's first encounter with Jael is in a New York apartment with a window that is actually a series of changeable pictures. Alice-Jael is herself presented as unnatural: her head and hands move "like puppets controlled by separate strings"; her teeth seem to be "one fused ribbon of steel"; and her laugh is "the worst human sound I have ever heard": "a hard screeching yell that ends in gasps and rusty sobbing, as if some mechanical vulture on a gigantic garbage heap on the surface of the moon were giving one forced shriek for the death of all organic life" (158–59). DuPlessis observes that Alice-Jael is the embodiment of the ruthlessness of our own time: "However revolting Jael is—and she is not pleasant—she is the mirror image of the glib, patronizing, and equally murderous patterns of the socially acceptable relations between the sexes" (184). Manland and Womanland are armed camps, complete with guards and military code names, and Jael embodies the essence of women's anger at men for centuries of subjugation. Jael's culture is founded on perpetual warfare; when "The War Between the Nations" was over, "people began shopping for a new war," and found that "there was only one war left" (164).

Child-rearing in Manland is the obverse of the nurturance, freedom, and practical training that characterizes Whileaway. Except for a wealthy few, who have their own children, Manlanders purchase infants from Womanland and set them, at the age of five, on a course of training that determines which can be "real-men." Those who fail early undergo sex-change operations and become known as "the changed"; those who fail later on forego surgery and become "the half-changed": "impressionists of femininity who keep their genitalia but who grow slim, grow languid, grow emotional and feminine" (167). In this all-male society the

183

"changed" and the "half-changed" are the sexual objects of the "real-men," who shun real women. The goal of Manland is Total Masculinity, and Jael muses about what might happen if that goal were ever reached:

> I suspect we real women still figure, however grotesquely, in Manland's deepest dreams; perhaps on that morning of Total Masculinity they will all invade Womanland, rape everyone in sight (if they still remember how) and then kill them, and after that commit suicide on a pyramid of their victims' panties. (170–71)

Sexuality, in Jael's world, is still the major power play, as is demonstrated in her conversation with one of the leaders of Manland, whose underlying hatred of women surfaces in his attempt to rape her during what is supposed to be a negotiating conference. Jael, the warrior, unsheathes the claws on the ends of her fingers and kills him, not so much in self-defense as in exultant anger. At the end of the novel Jael tries to convince Janet that the war she is fighting has made possible Janet's world of Whileaway, but Janet refuses to believe this, thereby rejecting the concept of historical continuity and refusing to bring the utopia and the dystopia together in the same universe.

As these five quite different novels demonstrate, both the utopian and the dystopian visions of women's speculative fiction have common elements that point to critiques of our own time. Whether in positive or negative terms, these authors address the nature and structure of the family, the natural as opposed to the artificial— especially the arbitrary imposition of gender roles—women's sexual freedom, ways of resolving conflict, and the importance of the imagination. Rather than maps for social change, these fictions represent transcendence over the status quo, and even the bleaker visions urge the possibility—even the inevitability—of change. Marge Piercy has noted that one of the reasons she admires Joanna Russ's work is that she "demand[s] that you read [her] work actively."[27] The central activity of reading speculative fiction is constant comparison between two sets of realities, and feminist fantasies, by refusing to be confined to the reader's observable world, force a re-vision of that world through the medium of ironic drama.

# Conclusion

In 1972, near the beginning of the period that this study covers, and before many of the novels considered here were written or published, Joanna Russ wrote a curiously prophetic passage in concluding her essay "What Can a Heroine Do? or Why Women Can't Write." Anticipating some of the concerns she would express in *How To Suppress Women's Writing* and the themes she would explore in *The Female Man*, Russ ends her essay by expressing her sense of the dangers and promises of a period of transition:

> When things are changing, those who know least about them—in the usual terms—may make the best job of them. There is so much to be written about, and here we are with nothing but the rags and tatters of what used to mean something. One thing I think we must know— that our traditional gender roles will not be part of the future, as long as the future is not a second Stone Age. Our traditions, our books, our morals, our manners, our films, our speech, our economic organization, everything we have inherited, tells us that to be a Man one must bend Nature to one's will—or other men. This means ecological catastrophe in the first instance and war in the second. To be a Woman, one must be first and foremost a mother and after that a server of Men; this means overpopulation and the perpetuation of the first two disasters. The roles are deadly. The myths that serve them are fatal.

185

# Conclusion

Women cannot write—using the old myths.
But using new ones—?[1]

Russ assumes in these remarks a close relationship between literature and the social order, understanding that literature perpetuates the myths and values by which we live, and she calls upon
women writers to devise new mythologies adequate to reverse the
destructive patterns of the past.

With the exception of a few utopian visions, such as Piercy's
Mattapoisett and Russ's own Whileaway, women's fiction of the
past twenty years cannot be said to have created systematic new
mythologies to replace those of the past. However, women writers
have taken the step that necessarily precedes such formulations,
which is to undermine the old mythologies of gender relationships
by questioning and revising them: challenging the stereotypes,
fairy tales, traditions, and histories that have prescribed the plots
of women's lives and estimates of their power and authority. By
doing so, they have insisted on the relativity and mutability of
truth and reality. Fictions as disparate as Fay Weldon's witty parodies and the tragedy of Morrison's *The Bluest Eye* are equally re-
lentless in deconstructing the received wisdom of a culture by revealing the terrible ironic distance between official cultural images
and pronouncements and actual human realities.

It is in fact this questioning of received tradition that is the hall-
mark of women's fiction during the past twenty years. Conventional gender relationships, cultural maxims and truisms, and
even the nature of identity itself—all have become the objects of
the ironic eye of the novelist. To accomplish the task of revision,
women writers of this period have questioned and revised the
form of the novel itself. They have appropriated and altered traditional fictional genres—the epistolary novel, the tale, the fairy tale,
utopias, and dystopias—and have written narratives in which the
validity of the author's or narrator's own perceptions is called into
question and revised or reconstructed. What Godwin refers to in
*Violet Clay* as "The Book of Old Plots" is revealed for what it is: a
collection of outworn stories once used to dictate the scripts of
women's lives, a fiction that must be transcended so that a woman

186

may, in Carolyn Heilbrun's words, "write her own life in advance of living it."

Yet it has been equally important for these writers to show the continuing power of the old plots, and to acknowledge the weight of tradition and habit. Joan Foster is caught in the plots of popular romances in *Lady Oracle;* in *The Odd Woman* Jane Clifford lives in the world of the classic English novels she teaches; and Jane Gray remains distrustful of her freedom from the enclosed plots of the novels that haunt her in *The Waterfall.* More tragically, Theresa Dunn, in *Looking for Mr. Goodbar,* mistakes promiscuity for freedom and dies as merely another female stereotype. Dreams and fantasies may empower, but they may also be false or misleading, as they are for Pecola Breedlove in *The Bluest Eye* and Mira in *The Women's Room.* The fact that these characters are unable to fully script their own lives testifies to the difficulty of altering entrenched mythologies, and one reason why *The Handmaid's Tale* is so compelling is that Atwood demonstrates how precariously balanced is the feminist agenda over the waters of regressive tradition.

The struggle to imagine lives, selves, ways of being that transcend tradition, however, permeates these novels just as it does those in which an individual character in some measure breaks free of inhibiting forces. To acknowledge the power of old texts, old scripts, is simultaneously to claim power for the text one is writing, and when, as is the case in these novels, the old texts are viewed ironically, the power they lose in the process is transferred to the new texts, as the ironist claims superiority over the subject of her irony. To demonstrate the destructive influence of female images promulgated by literature, film, and other media is at the same time to demystify those images by showing them to be culturally defined constructs, products of historical moments, which can be rendered absurd. The very fascination with language itself that figures in all of these novels demonstrates the authors' distrust of the power of words to define and confine women's experience. Moving, frequently, from silence to language, the central characters approach language as the cultural artifact it in fact is, measuring and weighing words, clichés, and maxims—what Weldon terms "the rules of life"—rather than accepting them as valid.

187

## Conclusion

Along with this careful examination of the artifacts of received tradition goes imagining beyond that tradition—the dreams and fantasies of alternate worlds, alternate lives, different values. Such imagining is the task of feminist critics as well as the works they study; in *Subject to Change,* for example, Nancy K. Miller writes, "the hope I express for a female future is a desire for *all that we don't know* about what it might mean to be women beyond the always already provided identity of Women with which we can only struggle."[2] Part of the struggle that feminist scholarship has had during the past twenty years—and a good part of its richness as well—stems from its own attempts at self-definition while at the same time trying to avoid the trap of adopting the authoritarian model that would belie the values of feminism itself. Like the central character in one of these novels, feminist scholars seek a new order that will not merely replicate the systems of authority they seek to overturn—freedom without anarchy, order without oppression.[3]

Given the enormous differences in setting, style, and thematic emphasis among the novels considered in this study, what, if any, general outlines for alternate lives for women emerge from them? Are there common impulses, hopes, or designs that could begin to outline what Miller calls "a female future"? Obviously, each of the imagined utopias sets forth a version of ideality, but what do these visions share with the implications of dystopian visions and realistic accounts of contemporary women? Most obvious, it seems to me, is a common plea for recognition that the emotional, intuitive powers of women neither negate nor contradict their intellectual abilities. The very fact that the insistence on dreaming and imagining so frequently co-exists with the cool rationality of the ironic stance suggests that the capacities of feeling and thinking are to be equally valued. In Russ's Whileaway, women very capably run a complex culture, but at the same time afford themselves ample opportunity for creativity and nurturance. This same theme is conveyed negatively, in the splitting into separate selves of characters such as Theresa Dunn and Jane Gray, and the identification with the intellect that precludes emotional commitment for Jane Clifford in *The Odd Woman.* Wholeness, these authors suggest,

188

would necessitate abandoning the stereotypes of women as primarily emotional beings who deny their essential selves when they move into the intellectual realm.

Another common element is a celebration of women's sexuality and the desire for sexual freedom—not the self-destructive promiscuity of Terry Dunn, but an ability to engage in sexual activity without regard to gender, as in Piercy's utopian Mattapoisett and Walker's *The Color Purple,* and without the guilt that afflicts Jane Gray and that numerous mothers in these novels attempt to instill in their daughters. The joy of sexual pleasure, as presented, for example, in *Serenissima* and *The Female Man,* is contrasted to sexual degradation in *The Handmaid's Tale, The Memoirs of a Survivor,* and *Looking for Mr. Goodbar.* But sexuality is conceived more broadly in these novels; it includes childbirth, especially in *The Waterfall;* nurturance, in the utopian sections of *The Female Man* and *Woman on the Edge of Time;* and a general acceptance of biological femaleness, seen most clearly in *Surfacing* and *Fear of Flying.*

Concomitant with the desire for acceptance of women's intellectual and biological nature—as norms rather than aberrations—is a reformulation of the concept of power. The questioning and rejection of culturally defined formulations of womanhood that are so pervasive in these novels are essentially attempts to deny the authority of the patriarchy. Through ironic revisions of cultural history and mythology, these authors present traditional systems of power as destructive and finally ineffective, and propose instead various versions of non-hierarchal cultures based in the values of nurturance and individual fulfillment. With the exception of Whileaway and Mattapoisett, these novels do not contain fully realized alternative social systems, but the dystopian visions in *The Handmaid's Tale, Woman on the Edge of Time,* and *Memoirs of a Survivor* imply their opposites by pointing up the failure of societies organized, as Russ puts it, so that men "must bend Nature to one's will—or other men," resulting in ecological disaster and war. The novels that do not have such visionary components nonetheless make strikingly similar suggestions about the nature of power and authority. In the alternate reality implied in these works, poverty and the color of one's skin would not be invita-

189

tions to coercive power, as they are in *The Bluest Eye, The Color Purple,* and *Woman on the Edge of Time.* The psychiatric establishment, in *Woman on the Edge of Time* as well as in *The Four-Gated City* and *Fear of Flying,* is presented as cold and unfeeling, and also serves as a metaphor for other institutions that deny autonomy and individuality.

The most fundamental and pervasive characteristic of a new social order suggested by the contemporary novel by women, however, is a re-ordering of the relationship to language itself. Recognizing the power of language to confine and define, to claim power, to coerce and subjugate, these novelists suggest not merely the need for a non-sexist language, but more importantly women's full participation in the determination of meaning. And it is here that the devices of irony and fantasy come into full play, for it is the purpose of irony to cast doubt on assumed meaning and of fantasy to reformulate meaning in accordance with a new reality—an alternate world which, once imagined, becomes a possible, a potential place to live.

## Notes to Introduction

1. Carolyn G. Heilbrun, *Writing a Woman's Life* (New York: W. W. Norton, 1988), 44.

2. Nora Johnson, "Housewives and Prom Queens, 25 Years Later," *New York Times Book Review,* 20 March 1988, 1.

3. This percentage was claimed by the publisher of the Harlequin romances in a 1981 publicity blurb, and is cited by Kay Mussell in *Fantasy and Reconciliation: Contemporary Formulas of Women's Romance Fiction* (Westport, Conn.: Greenwood Press, 1984), 4–5.

4. Janice A. Radway, *Reading the Romance: Women, Patriarchy, and Popular Literature* (Chapel Hill: University of North Carolina Press, 1984), 78–79.

5. Margaret Atwood, *Lady Oracle* (1976; reprint, New York: Ballantine, 1987), 241.

6. Suzanne Juhasz, "Texts to Grow On: Reading Women's Romance Fiction," *Tulsa Studies in Women's Literature* 7, no. 2 (Fall 1988): 246.

7. For studies of Austen's use of irony and her connection with the philosophical ideas of the feminist movement of her day, see the following: Lilian R. Furst, *Fictions of Romantic Irony* (Cambridge: Harvard University Press, 1984), 49–67; Rachel M. Brownstein, "Jane Austen: Irony and Authority," in *Last Laughs: Perspectives on Women and Comedy,* ed. Regina Barreca (New York: Gordon and Breach, 1988), 57–70; and Margaret Kirkham, *Jane Austen, Feminism, and Fiction* (New York: Methuen, 1986).

8. Hélène Cixous, "Castration or Decapitation," trans. Annette Kuhn, *Signs* 7, no. 1 (Autumn 1981): 53.

9. Doris Lessing, *The Memoirs of a Survivor* (1974; reprint, New York: Bantam, 1976), 107.

Notes to Chapter One

1. Erica Jong, "Blood and Guts: The Tricky Problem of Being a Woman Writer in the Late Twentieth Century," in *The Writer on Her Work,* ed. Janet Sternburg (New York: Norton, 1980), 175.

2. Rachel M. Brownstein, *Becoming a Heroine: Reading about Women in Novels* (1982; reprint, New York: Penguin, 1984.) xviii.

3. Margaret Drabble, *The Waterfall* (1969; reprint; New York: Fawcett, 1977), 248.

4. Marge Piercy, *Small Changes* (Greenwich, Conn.: Fawcett, 1973), 29.

5. Margaret Drabble, "A Woman Writer," in *On Gender and Writing,* ed. Michelene Wandor (London: Pandora Press, 1983), 159.

6. Although, as Jong points out, in the early years of the movement, the release of pent-up anger in the women's novel sometimes threatened to divert attention from anything else: "In many cases, the rage tended to eclipse the writing. . . . Rage became almost as compulsory to the generation of writers who came of age in the late sixties and early seventies as niceness and meekness had been to an earlier generation." ("Blood and Guts," 172)

7. Nora Johnson, "Housewives and Prom Queens, 25 Years Later," *New York Times Book Review,* 20 March 1988, 1.

8. Fay Weldon, "Me and My Shadows," in *On Gender and Writing,* 164.

9. Margaret Atwood, however, has expressed reservations about too close a connection between politics and art. Of women writers who become involved in the women's movement, she notes that "their involvement may be good for the movement, but it has yet to be demonstrated that it's good for the writer." Atwood's reservations have to do in part with the fact that many women writers began work too early to have benefited from the movement, so that "it would be fairly galling for these writers . . . to be hailed as products, spokeswomen, or advocates of the Women's Movement," and partly because she resists—quite correctly— a feminist literary criticism that would assess works on the basis of their adherence to an ideology. ("On Being a 'Woman Writer': Paradoxes and Dilemmas," in *Second Words: Selected Critical Prose* (Boston: Beacon Press, 1984), 190−91.

192

10. Annette Kolodny, "A Map for Rereading: Or, Gender and the Interpretation of Literary Texts," *New Literary History* 11, no. 3 (1980): 454.

11. Joanne S. Frye, *Living Stories, Telling Lives: Women and the Novel in Contemporary Experience* (Ann Arbor: University of Michigan Press, 1986), p. 51.

12. Elizabeth Janeway, "Women's Literature," in *Cross Sections from a Decade of Change* (New York: William Morrow, 1982), 192–93.

13. Fay Weldon, *Words of Advice.* (1977; reprint, New York: Ballantine, 1978), 183.

14. Judi M. Roller, *The Politics of the Feminist Novel* (Westport, Conn.: Greenwood Press, 1986), 36.

15. Critics have referred to *The Woman Warrior* as both a novel and an autobiography with equal certainty. Kingston herself has described it as "five interlocking short stories," which suggests fiction, but when asked a direct question about fiction versus fact in the work, she was reluctant to commit herself, commenting only that she was pleased to have been told that works such as hers that broke new ground usually defied easy genre classification (Discussions with Kingston at the University of Missouri–Columbia, 8–9 March 1988).

16. Janeway, "Women's Literature," 223.

17. Lilian R. Furst, *Fictions of Romantic Irony* (Cambridge: Harvard University Press, 1984), 9.

18. D. C. Muecke, *Irony,* The Critical Idiom Series, no. 13 (London: Methuen, 1970), 2.

19. Fay Weldon, *Female Friends* (New York: St. Martin's Press, 1974), 17.

20. Erica Jong, *Fear of Flying* (1973; reprint, New York: Signet 1974), 3.

21. Wayne C. Booth, *A Rhetoric of Irony* (Chicago: University of Chicago Press, 1974), 41.

22. Bertrice Bartlett, "Reading Negations and Ironies" (Paper presented at the Northeast Modern Language Association, Rutgers University, April 1985), 3.

23. Umberto Eco, "Postmodernism, Irony, the Enjoyable" in *Postscript to The Name of the Rose,* trans. William Weaver (New York: Harcourt Brace Jovanovich, 1984), 68.

24. Nancy K. Miller, "Emphasis Added: Plots and Plausibilities in Women's Fiction." *PMLA* 96, no. 1 (January 1981): 46–47.

25. A. E. Dyson, *The Crazy Fabric: Essays in Irony* (London: Macmillan, 1965), x.

26. For example, William Robert Irwin, in *The Game of the Impossible: A Rhetoric of Fantasy*, says that a fantasy is "a story based on and controlled by an overt violation of what is generally accepted as possibility; it is the narrative result of transforming the condition contrary to fact into 'fact' itself" ([Urbana: University of Illinois Press, 1976], 4.)

27. Rosemary Jackson, *Fantasy: The Literature of Subversion* (London: Methuen, 1981), 3–4.

28. Gail Godwin, *Violet Clay* (1978: reprint, New York: Warner Books, 1979), 13.

29. Doris Lessing, *The Four-Gated City* (1969; reprint, New York: Bantam, 1970), 598.

30. Joanna Russ, *The Female Man* (1975; reprint, London: The Women's Press, 1985), 140.

31. Maxine Hong Kingston, *The Woman Warrior: Memoirs of a Girlhood Among Ghosts* (1976; reprint, New York: Vintage, 1977), 24.

32. Marge Piercy, *Woman on the Edge of Time* (1976; reprint, New York: Fawcett Crest, 1977), 66.

33. Barbara Hill Rigney, *Madness and Sexual Politics in the Feminist Novel* (Madison: University of Wisconsin Press, 1978), 119.

34. Kay Mussell, *Fantasy and Reconciliation: Contemporary Formulas of Women's Romance Fiction* (Westport, Conn.: Greenwood Press, 1984), 172–73.

Notes to Chapter Two

1. Marge Piercy, *Small Changes* (New York: Doubleday, 1973), 266–67.

2. Fay Weldon, *Words of Advice* (1977; reprint, New York: Ballantine, 1978), 20. Gemma's statement is also an example of irony, as is the entire story she tells.

3. Margaret Atwood, *Life Before Man* (1979; reprint, New York: Ballantine, 1987), 12–13.

4. Margaret Homans, "'Her Very Own Howl': The Ambiguities of Representation in Recent Women's Fiction," *Signs* 9, no. 2 (Winter 1983): 196.

5. Tillie Olsen, *Silences* (New York: Delacorte, 1978), 42–43.

6. Alicia Suskin Ostriker, *Stealing the Language: The Emergence of Women's Poetry in America* (Boston: Beacon Press, 1986), 211.

7. Hélène Cixous, "The Laugh of the Medusa," trans. Keith Cohen and Paula Cohen, *Signs* 1, no. 4 (Summer 1976): 879.

8. Hélène Cixous, "Castration or Decapitation?" trans. Annette Kuhn, *Signs* 7, no. 1 (Autumn 1981): 45.

9. Deborah Cameron, *Feminism and Linguistic Theory* (New York: St. Martin's Press, 1985), 144. Cameron is here arguing specifically against the theories of Saussure and Whorf, which maintain, respectively, that the meaning of language is absolute and therefore outside the control of an individual language user, and that language is a "mode of action that interpenetrates with experience to the extent that words *are* things" (97).

10. Homans, "'Her Very Own Howl,'" 191.

11. Joanna Russ, *The Female Man* (1975; reprint, London: The Women's Press, 1985), 174−75.

12. Natalie M. Rosinsky, "A Female Man? The 'Medusan' Humor of Joanna Russ," *Extrapolation* 23, no. 1 (1982): 32.

13. Fay Weldon, *Female Friends* (New York: St. Martin's Press, 1974), 108.

14. Margaret Atwood, *The Handmaid's Tale* (Boston: Houghton Mifflin, 1986), 87.

15. Elaine Tuttle Hansen, "The Double Narrative Structure of *Small Changes*," in *Contemporary American Women Writers: Narrative Strategies*, ed. Catherine Rainwater and William J. Scheick (Lexington: University Press of Kentucky, 1985), 213. I am indebted to this essay for its clear, succinct analysis of the way in which Piercy approaches both language and narrative structure in the novel.

16. Doris Lessing, *The Summer Before the Dark* (1973; reprint, New York: Bantam, 1974).

17. Joanne S. Frye, *Living Stories, Telling Lives: Women and the Novel in Contemporary Experience* (Ann Arbor: University of Michigan Press, 1986), 18.

18. Alice Walker, *The Color Purple* (1982; reprint, New York: Washington Square Press, 1983), 181.

19. Margaret Drabble, *The Waterfall* (1969; reprint, New York: Fawcett, 1977), 51.

20. Ellen Cronan Rose, *The Novels of Margaret Drabble: Equivocal Forms* (Totowa, N.J.: Barnes and Noble, 1980), 61.

21. Joanne V. Creighton, *Margaret Drabble* (London: Methuen, 1985), 63.

22. Gail Godwin, *Violet Clay* (1978; reprint, New York: Warner Books, 1979), 39−40.

23. In *Living Stories, Telling Lives*, Joanne Frye analyzes the way in which Godwin uses the narration of Violet's own story as a means of uniting the two selves of woman and artist (111−39). I would extend Frye's excellent study of the novel by pointing out that a major way in which

Godwin accomplishes this narrative strategy is by using ironic discourse, much as Weldon does in *Female Friends* and Drabble does in *The Waterfall*, to allow her character to step out of and thus revise her own story.

24. Lilian R. Furst, *Fictions of Romantic Irony* (Cambridge: Harvard University Press, 1984), 9.

25. William Robert Irvin, *The Game of the Impossible: A Rhetoric of Fantasy* (Urbana: University of Illinois press, 1976), 61—62.

26. For analyses of feminist attitudes toward naming, see Nancy M. Henley, "This New Species That Seeks a New Language: On Sexism in Language and Language Change," and Nan Van Den Bergh, "Renaming: Vehicle for Empowerment," both in *Women and Language in Transition*, ed. Joyce Penfield (Albany: State University of New York Press, 1987).

27. One reviewer of the novel stated that "The real meaning of Offred . . . is Afraid; though since it is not her real name, she is also Not Afraid" (Patrick Parrinder in the *London Review of Books*, 20 March 1986; quoted in Carol Ann Howells, *Private and Fictional Words: Canadian Women Novelists of the 1970s and 1980s* [London: Methuen, 1987], 58—59.) Roberta Rubenstein suggests that the name "encodes her indentured sexuality: both 'offered' and the property 'of-Fred.'" (*Boundaries of the Self: Gender, Culture, Fiction* [Urbana: University of Illinois Press, 1987], 109.)

28. Margaret Atwood, *Surfacing* (New York: Simon and Schuster, 1972), 39.

29. Maxine Hong Kingston, *The Woman Warrior: Memoirs of a Girlhood Among Ghosts* (1976; reprint, New York: Vintage, 1977), 127.

30. Marge Piercy, *Woman on the Edge of Time* (1976; reprint, New York: Fawcett Crest, 1977), 17.

31. The issue of whether Piercy means for this to be an actual utopia or the product of Consuelo's hallucinations has sparked lively controversy among critics, as I will discuss in a later chapter. See, e.g., Sheila Delaney, "Ambivalence in Utopia: The American Feminist Utopias of Charlotte P. Gilman and Marge Piercy," in *Writing Woman: Women Writers and Women in Literature, Medieval to Modern* (New York: Shocken Books, 1983), 157—80; Margaret Atwood, "Marge Piercy: *Woman on the Edge of Time, Living in the Open*," in *Second Words: Selected Critical Prose* (Boston: Beacon Press, 1984), 272—78.

32. Doris Lessing, *The Four-Gated City.* (1969; reprint, New York: Bantam, 1970), 224.

33. Elizabeth Abel, " (E)Merging Identities: The Dynamics of Female Friendship in Contemporary Fiction by Women," *Signs* 6, no. 3 (Spring 1981): 419.

34. Alice Walker, *Meridian* (1976; reprint, New York: Washington Square Press, 1977), 44.

35. Elizabeth Fifer, "The Dialect and Letters of *The Color Purple*," in *Contemporary American Women Writers: Narrative Strategies*, ed. Catherine Rainwater and William J. Scheick (Lexington: University Press of Kentucky, 1985), 158. Fifer also points to the irony of the fact that Nettie, better educated than Celie, writes in a standard English that Celie does not speak, so that it is Nettie's letters that must be "translated" when Celie finally finds them.

36. King-Kok Cheung, "'Don't Tell': Imposed Silences in *The Color Purple* and *The Woman Warrior*," *PMLA* 103, no. 2 (March 1988): 162–63.

37. Suzanne Juhasz, "Towards a Theory of Form in Feminist Autobiography: Kate Millett's *Flying* and *Sita; Maxine Hong Kingston's *The Woman Warrior*," in *Women's Autobiography: Essays in Criticism*, ed. Estelle C. Jelinek (Bloomington: Indiana University Press, 1980), 223; and Hélène Cixous, "Castration or Decapitation?" 53.

38. Most critics approach *The Woman Warrior* as an autobiography, and there are surely bases for its experience in Kingston's own life as a Chinese-American woman. Kingston herself, however, has called the book "five interlocking short stories" (discussion at the University of Missouri–Columbia, 9 March 1988). Mere classification of a work should of course not be the goal of the literary critic; what is significant is, as I pointed out in the introductory chapter, that the line between fiction and autobiography is blurred in works by contemporary women authors. See chap. 2, "Politics, Literary Form, and a Feminist Poetics of the Novel," in Joanne Frye's *Living Stories, Telling Lives.*

39. Rubenstein, *Boundaries of the Self,* 176.

40. Juhasz, "Towards a Theory of Form in Feminist Autobiography," 231. In a *Belles Lettres* interview, Kingston has expressed her own fears about publishing *The Woman Warrior:* "At first I said to myself, 'I must write this.' Then I tried to fool myself by thinking that I didn't have to publish it. I even started thinking that the work could be published after my death, and then everything would be fine. All of that was fooling myself so that I could keep going. Then I did publish it, thinking that it was only in English and therefore my parents and most of their friends would not be able to read it. When it was published in Chinese, I felt very much afraid. Some people read one chapter and didn't continue, feeling that it was too horrible. So they never saw that in *The Woman Warrior* there is a reconciliation of beauty" (Angeles Carabi, "Special Eyes: The Chinese-

American World of Maxine Hong Kingston," *Belles Lettres* [Winter 1989]: 11).

41. Homans, "'Her Very Own Howl,'" 198.

42. This comment echoes Miriam, in Piercy's *Small Changes*, who, realizing that "women were supposed to be dull and good," decides that she would rather, like men, be "bad and exciting" ([Greenwich, Conn.: Fawcett, 1973], 97).

43. Rubenstein, *Boundaries of the Self*, 77; and Howells, *Private and Fictional Words*, 63.

44. In this respect, Atwood uses a technique similar to that of Marge Piercy in *Woman on the Edge of Time:* one of the visits that Consuelo makes to the future is not to the utopia to which Luciente has invited her, but rather to a dystopia that could be a natural result of current tendencies.

45. Margaret Atwood, "Witches," in *Second Words*, 333 (italics mine).

46. Linda Hutcheons, "From Poetic to Narrative Structures: The Novels of Margaret Atwood," in *Margaret Atwood: Language, Text, and System*, ed. Sherrill E. Grace and Lorraine Weir (Vancouver: University of British Columbia Press, 1983), 17.

47. Margaret Atwood, "An End to Audience?" in *Second Words*, 348.


Notes to Chapter Three

1. George Gusdorf, "Conditions and Limits of Autobiography," in *Autobiography: Essays Theoretical and Critical*, ed. James Olney (Princeton: Princeton University Press, 1980), 35.

2. Judith Kegan Gardiner, "On Female Identity and Writing by Women," *Critical Inquiry* 8, no. 2 (Winter 1981): 347. Gardiner is careful to distinguish gender identity from the more general issue of selfhood: "The problems of female identity presented in women's poetry and prose are rarely difficulties in knowing one's gender; more frequently, they are difficulties in learning how to respond to social rules for what being female means in our culture" (359).

3. Margaret Miller, "Threads of Identity in Maxine Hong Kingston's *Woman Warrior*," *Biography* 6, no. 1 (Winter 1983): 15.

4. Doris Lessing, *The Four-Gated City* (1969; reprint, New York: Bantam, 1970), 17.

5. Margaret Atwood, *Surfacing* (New York: Simon and Schuster, 1972), 50–51.

6. Sherrill Grace, *Violent Duality: A Study of Margaret Atwood* (Montreal: Vehicule Press, 1980), 3.

7. Tom Staicar, foreword to *The Feminine Eye: Science Fiction and the Women Who Write It* (New York: Frederick Ungar, 1982), vii.

8. Thomas F. Dillingham, "Joanna Russ" *Beacham's Short Fiction of America*, Vol. 3 (Washington, DC: Beacham Publishing, 1987), 1212.

9. Joanna Russ, *The Female Man* (1975; reprint, London: The Women's Press, 1985), 151.

10. Natalie M. Rosinsky, "A Female Man? The 'Medusan' Humor of Joanna Russ," *Extrapolation* 23, no. 1 (1982): 32.

11. Gail Godwin, "Towards a Fully Human Heroine: Some Worknotes," *The Harvard Advocate* (Winter 1973): 26.

12. Gail Godwin, *The Odd Woman* (1974; reprint, New York: Warner Books, 1980), 9.

13. Susan E. Lorsch, "Gail Godwin's *The Odd Woman:* Literature and the Retreat from Life," *Critique: Studies in Modern Fiction* 20, no. 2 (1978): 22.

14. Rachel Blau DuPlessis, *Writing Beyond the Ending: Narrative Strategies of Twentieth-Century Women Writers* (Bloomington: Indiana University Press, 1985), 4–5.

15. Gail Godwin, *Violet Clay* (1978; reprint, New York: Warner Books, 1979), 73.

16. Godwin, "Towards a Fully Human Heroine: Some Worknotes," 27. Godwin also uses her mother's experience in *The Odd Woman*, in which Jane Clifford's mother, Kitty, has written stories for a publication titled *Love Short Stories*. Godwin has elaborated on her mother's brief career as a writer of pulp-magazine stories in a more recent essay: "My Mother, the Writer: Master of a Thousand Disguises," *New York Times Book Review*, 11 June 1989, 7, 50–51.

17. Margaret Atwood, *Lady Oracle* (1976; reprint, New York: Ballantine, 1987), 238.

18. It is interesting to note that although their central characters are female, both Atwood and Godwin acknowledge that men as well as women write the "women's" romance. In *Violet Clay*, Violet's only close friend at the beginning of the novel is Milo Hamilton, who, as "Arabella Stone," writes some of the Gothic romances that Violet illustrates.

19. Marge Piercy, *Small Changes* (Greenwich, Conn.: Fawcett, 1973), 37.

20. Elaine Tuttle Hansen, "The Double Narrative Structure of *Small Changes*," in *Contemporary American Women Writers: Narrative Strategies*, ed. Catherine Rainwater and William J. Scheick (Lexington: University Press of Kentucky, 1985), 215.

199

21. Erica Jong, *Fear of Flying* (1973; reprint, New York: Signet, 1974), 277.

22. Joan Reardon, "*Fear of Flying:* Developing the Feminist Novel," *International Journal of Women's Studies* 1, no. 3 (May/June 1978): 307.

23. Ann Barr Snitow, "The Front Line: Notes on Sex in Novels by Women, 1969–1979," *Signs* 5, no. 4 (Summer 1980): 705.

24. Ursula K. Le Guin, "The Hand That Rocks the Cradle Writes the Book," *New York Times Book Review*, 22 January 1989, 37.

25. Hélène Cixous, "The Laugh of the Medusa," trans. Keith Cohen and Paula Cohen, *Signs* 1, no. 4 (Summer 1976): 880.

26. Hélène Cixous, "Castration or Decapitation?" trans. Annette Kuhn, *Signs* 7, no. 1 (Autumn 1981): 51. The article was originally published in France in 1975.

27. Annis V. Pratt, "Spinning Among Fields: Jung, Frye, Levi-Strauss," in *Feminist Archetypal Theory: Interdisciplinary Re-Visions of Jungian Thought*, ed. Estella Lauter and Carol Schreier Rupprecht (Knoxville: University of Tennessee Press, 1985), 129.

28. Fay Weldon, *Words of Advice* (1977; reprint, New York: Ballantine, 1978), 9.

29. Fay Weldon, *Female Friends* (New York: St. Martin's Press, 1974), 309.

30. Agate Nesaule Krouse, "Feminism and Art in Fay Weldon's Novels," *Critique: Studies in Modern Fiction* 20, no. 2 (1978): 8.

31. Michael F. Harper, "Margaret Drabble and the Resurrection of the English Novel," *Contemporary Literature* 23, no. 2 (1982): 154–55.

32. Nancy S. Hardin, "An Interview With Margaret Drabble," *Contemporary Literature* 14, no. 3 (Summer 1973): 293.

33. Margaret Drabble, *The Waterfall* (1969; reprint, New York: Fawcett, 1977), 161.

34. Caryn Fuoroli, "Sophistry or Simple Truth? Narrative Technique in Margaret Drabble's *The Waterfall*," *Journal of Narrative Technique* 11, no. 2 (Spring 1981): 112.

35. Cixous, "Castration or Decapitation?" 53.

36. Ellen Cronan Rose, "Feminine Endings—And Beginnings: Margaret Drabble's *The Waterfall*," *Contemporary Literature* 21, no. 1 (Winter 1980): 96.

37. Anne Golomb Hoffman, "Acts of Self-Creation: Female Identity in the Novels of Margaret Drabble," in *Faith of a (Woman) Writer*, ed. Alice Kessler-Harris and William McBrien (Westport, Conn.: Greenwood Press, 1988), 26.

200

Notes to Chapter Four

1. Fay Weldon, "Me and My Shadows," in *On Gender and Writing*, ed. Michelene Wandor (London: Pandora Press, 1983), 162.

2. Roberta Rubenstein, *Boundaries of the Self: Gender, Culture, Fiction* (Urbana: University of Illinois Press, 1987), 233–34.

3. Mickey Pearlman, ed., *American Women Writing Fiction: Memory, Identity, Family, Space* (Lexington: University Press of Kentucky, 1989), 5.

4. Patricia Meyer Spacks, *The Female Imagination* (New York: Knopf, 1975), 402.

5. Marilyn French, *The Women's Room* (1977; reprint, New York: Harcourt Brace, 1978), 29.

6. Erica Jong, "Blood and Guts: The Tricky Problem of Being a Woman Writer in the Late Twentieth Century," in *The Writer on Her Work*, ed. Janet Sternburg (New York: Norton, 1980), 178.

7. Margaret Drabble, *The Waterfall* (1969; reprint, New York: Fawcett, 1977), 172.

8. Erica Jong, *Fear of Flying* (1973; reprint, New York: Signet, 1974), 283.

9. Gail Godwin, *The Odd Woman* (1974; reprint, New York: Warner Books, 1980), 428.

10. Margaret Atwood, *Lady Oracle* (1976; reprint, New York: Ballantine, 1987), 379.

11. Margaret Atwood, "That Certain Thing Called the Girlfriend," *New York Times Book Review*, 11 May 1986, 1.

12. Margaret Atwood, *The Handmaid's Tale* (Boston: Houghton Mifflin, 1986), 38.

13. Alice Walker, *Meridian* (1976; reprint, New York: Washington Square Press, 1977), 75.

14. Toni Morrison, *The Bluest Eye* (1970; reprint, New York: Washington Square Press, 1972), 90.

15. Maxine Hong Kingston, *The Woman Warrior: Memoirs of a Girlhood Among Ghosts* (1976; reprint, New York: Vintage, 1977), 24.

16. Joanne Frye, "*The Woman Warrior:* Claiming Narrative Power, Recreating Female Selfhood," in *Faith of a (Woman) Writer*, ed. Alice Kessler-Harris and William McBrien (Westport, Conn.: Greenwood Press, 1988), 297.

17. Rachel M. Brownstein, *Becoming a Heroine: Reading About Women in Novels* (1982; reprint, New York: Penguin, 1984), 294–95.

18. Suzanne Juhasz, "Texts to Grow On: Reading Women's Romance Fiction," *Tulsa Studies in Women's Literature* 7, no. 2 (Fall 1988): 249.

19. Joanna Russ, *How to Suppress Women's Writing* (Austin: University of Texas Press, 1983), 127.

20. Margaret Atwood, "Witches," in *Second Words: Selected Critical Prose* (Boston: Beacon Press, 1984), 329.

21. Nancy K. Miller, "Emphasis Added: Plots and Plausibilities in Women's Fiction," *PMLA* 96, no. 1 (January 1981): 46.

22. Judith Rossner, *Looking for Mr. Goodbar* (1975; reprint, New York: Pocket Books, 1976), 22.

23. Judi M. Roller, *The Politics of the Feminist Novel* (Westport, Conn.: Greenwood Press, 1986), 55.

24. Gail Godwin, *Violet Clay* (1978; reprint, New York: Warner Books, 1979), 39.

25. Marilyn French, *Her Mother's Daughter* (New York: Ballantine, 1987), 355.

26. Margaret Atwood, *Cat's Eye* (New York: Doubleday, 1988), 160.

27. Elaine's resistance to feminist labeling is a direct echo of Atwood's own stance on being ideologically categorized. In "On Being a 'Woman Writer': Paradoxes and Dilemmas," written in 1976, Atwood notes: "Time after time, I've had interviewers talk to me about my writing for a while, then ask me, 'As a woman, what do you think about—for instance—the Women's Movement,' as if I could think two sets of thoughts about the same thing, one set as a writer or person, the other as a woman. But no one comes apart this easily; categories like Woman, White, Canadian, Writer are only ways of looking at a thing, and the thing itself is whole, entire and indivisible. *Paradox:* Woman and Writer are separate categories; but in any individual woman writer, they are inseparable" (*Second Words: Selected Critical Prose* [Boston: Beacon Press, 1984], 195.)

28. Margaret Atwood, *Surfacing* (New York: Simon and Schuster, 1972), 169.

29. Annis V. Pratt, "*Surfacing* and the Rebirth Journey," in *The Art of Margaret Atwood: Essays in Criticism,* ed. Arnold E. Davidson and Cathy N. Davidson (Toronto: Anansi, 1981), 142.

30. Doris Lessing, *The Four-Gated City* (1969; reprint, New York: Bantam, 1970), 38.

31. Elizabeth Abel, "(E)Merging Identities: The Dynamics of Female Friendship in Contemporary Fiction by Women," *Signs* 6, no. 3 (Spring 1981): 418.

32. Catharine R. Stimpson, "Doris Lessing and the Parables of Growth," in *The Voyage In: Fictions of Female Development*, ed. Elizabeth Abel, Marianne Hirsch, and Elizabeth Langland (Hanover: University Press of New England, 1983), 203.

Notes to Chapter Five

1. Ursula K. Le Guin, "National Book Award Acceptance Speech," in *The Language of the Night: Essays on Fantasy and Science Fiction*, ed. Susan Wood (New York: Putnam, 1979), 57–58.

2. There is an unresolved discrepancy in the novel regarding the date of its action: the narrator announces on the first page that he is writing in the year 2004, and remarks later that Gabriella Sumpter has been dead three months, yet Gabriella's headstone says she was born in 1941 and died in 2002. Since Gabriella says that she died at the age of 61, the death date of 2002 would seem to be the accurate one.

3. Margaret Atwood, *The Handmaid's Tale* (Boston: Houghton Mifflin, 1986), 3.

4. Doris Lessing, *The Memoirs of a Survivor* (1974; reprint, New York: Bantam, 1976), 3.

5. Janice A. Radway, "Gothic Romances and 'Feminist' Protest," *American Quarterly* 33, no. 2 (Summer 1981): 160.

6. Margaret Atwood, *Surfacing* (New York: Simon and Schuster, 1972), 222.

7. Elizabeth Dipple, *The Unresolvable Plot: Reading Contemporary Fiction* (New York: Routledge, Chapman and Hall, 1988), 238.

8. Linda Kauffman, "Special Delivery: Twenty-first-Century Epistolarity in *The Handmaid's Tale*," in *Writing the Female Voice: Essays on Epistolary Literature*, ed. Elizabeth C. Goldsmith (Boston: Northeastern University Press, 1989), 239.

9. Erica Jong, *Serenissima: A Novel of Venice* (Boston: Houghton Mifflin, 1987), 219.

10. James W. Bittner, "Chronosophy, Aesthetics, and Ethics in Le Guin's *The Dispossessed: An Ambiguous Utopia*," in *No Place Else: Explorations in Utopian and Dystopian Fiction*, ed. Eric S. Rabkin, Martin H. Greenberg, and Joseph D. Olander (Carbondale: Southern Illinois University Press, 1983), 246.

11. Both times that I have taught *The Handmaid's Tale*, my students have reported feelings of shock, indignation, and anger upon encountering Professor Pieixoto's remarks at the end. Having come to trust and

identify with Offred's narrative, they resist this final dehumanizing of her. Because they are less familiar than I am with the academic conference, their reaction is also not mitigated by a perception that Atwood doubles the irony by writing a parody of such conferences in the "Historical Notes" section.

12. Marge Piercy, *Woman on the Edge of Time* (1976; reprint, New York: Fawcett Crest, 1977), 378.

13. Doris Lessing, *The Four-Gated City* (1969; reprint, New York: Bantam, 1970), 623.

14. Rachel Blau DuPlessis, *Writing Beyond the Ending: Narrative Strategies of Twentieth-Century Women Writers* (Bloomington: Indiana University Press, 1985), 178.

15. Peter Ruppert, *Reader in a Strange Land: The Activity of Reading Literary Utopias* (Athens: University of Georgia Press, 1986), 55–56.

16. Fay Weldon, *The Rules of Life* (New York: Harper and Row, 1987), 13.

17. Erica Jong, *Serenissima*, 5.

18. As several critics have pointed out, *Memoirs of a Survivor*, published in 1974, immediately preceded Lessing's Canopus series, and so forms a sort of coda to her more-or-less realistic fiction and an entry point to her more overtly speculative fiction.

19. Betsy Draine, "Changing Forms: Doris Lessing's *Memoirs of a Survivor*," *Studies in the Novel* 11 (1979): 56.

20. Mona Knapp, *Doris Lessing* (New York: Frederick Ungar, 1984), 124–25.

21. Lorna Sage, *Doris Lessing* (London: Methuen, 1983), 75–76.

22. Claire Sprague, *Rereading Doris Lessing: Narrative Patterns of Doubling and Repetition* (Chapel Hill: University of North Carolina Press, 1987), 167.

23. Margaret Atwood, "Marge Piercy: *Woman on the Edge of Time, Living in the Open*," in *Second Words: Selected Critical Prose* (Boston, Beacon Press, 1984), 273. Atwood, who ten years later would publish her own foray into the future, *The Handmaid's Tale*, is particularly annoyed in this essay with those reviewers who found what they termed the "science fiction" parts of the novel irrelevant to its social realism. "Piercy is not that stupid," she writes: "If she had intended a realistic novel she would have written one. *Woman on the Edge of Time* is a utopia, with all the virtues and shortcomings of the form, and many of the things reviewers found irksome are indigenous to the genre rather than the author." (273)

24. Sheila Delany, *Writing Woman: Women Writers and Women in Literature, Medieval to Modern* (New York: Schocken Books, 1983), 158. The

"ideological" utopia, in which Delany includes Gilman's *Herland*, is more narrowly focused in its social concerns, and tends to simplify and standardize human behavior in the culture it depicts.

25. Joanna Russ, *The Female Man* (1975; reprint, London: The Women's Press, 1985), 7.

26. Du Plessis, *Writing Beyond the Ending*, 182–83.

27. "A Symposium on Contemporary American Fiction," *Michigan Quarterly Review* 27, no. 1 (Winter 1988): 105 (special issue on contemporary American fiction, ed. Nicholas Delbanco).

Notes to Conclusion

1. Joanna Russ, "What Can a Heroine Do? Or Why Women Can't Write," in *Images of Women: Feminist Perspectives*, ed. Susan Koppelman Cornillon (Bowling Green, Ohio: Bowling Green Popular Press, 1972), 20.

2. Nancy K. Miller, *Subject to Change: Reading Feminist Writing* (New York: Columbia University Press, 1988), 118.

3. Some crucial evidences of this struggle can be found in the special double issue of *Tulsa Studies in Women's Literature* titled *Feminist Issues in Literary Scholarship* (3 [1984]), and in Laurie Finke's response to the essays in this issue: "The Rhetoric of Marginality: Why I do Feminist Theory," *Tulsa Studies in Women's Literature* 5, no. 2 (Fall 1986): 251–72.

## BIBLIOGRAPHY

Abel, Elizabeth. "(E)Merging Identities: The Dynamics of Female Friend-ship in Contemporary Fiction by Women." *Signs* 6, no. 3 (Spring 1981): 413–35.

———, ed. *Writing and Sexual Difference*. Chicago: University of Chicago Press, 1982.

Attebery, Brian. *The Fantasy Tradition in American Literature: From Irving to Le Guin*. Bloomington: Indiana University Press, 1980.

Atwood, Margaret. *Cat's Eye*. New York: Doubleday, 1988.

———. "An End to Audience?" In *Second Words: Selected Critical Prose*, 334–57. Boston: Beacon Press, 1984.

———. *The Handmaid's Tale*. Boston: Houghton Mifflin, 1986.

———. *Lady Oracle*. 1976. Reprint. New York: Ballantine, 1987.

———. *Life Before Man*. 1979. Reprint. New York: Ballantine, 1987.

———. "Marge Piercy: *Woman on the Edge of Time, Living in the Open*." In *Second Words: Selected Critical Prose*, 272–78. Boston: Beacon Press, 1984.

———. "On Being a 'Woman Writer': Paradoxes and Dilemmas." In *Second Words: Selected Critical Prose*, 190–204. Boston: Beacon Press, 1984.

———. *Surfacing*. New York: Simon and Schuster, 1972.

———. "That Certain Thing Called the Girlfriend." *New York Times Book Review*, 11 May 1986, 1, 38–39.

———. "Witches." In *Second Words: Selected Critical Prose*, 329–33. Boston: Beacon Press, 1984.

Bartlett, Bertrice. "Reading Negations and Ironies." Paper presented at the Northeast Modern Language Association, Rutgers University, April 1985.

207

# Bibliography

Beards, Virginia K. "Margaret Drabble: Novels of a Cautious Feminist." *Critique: Studies in Modern Fiction* 15, no. 1 (1973): 35–47.

Bittner, James W. "Chronosophy, Aesthetics, and Ethics in Le Guin's *The Dispossessed: An Ambiguous Utopia.*" In *No Place Else: Explorations in Utopian and Dystopian Fiction,* edited by Eric S. Rabkin, Martin H. Greenberg, and Joseph D. Olander, 244–70. Carbondale: Southern Illinois University Press, 1983.

Booth, Wayne C. *A Rhetoric of Irony.* Chicago: University of Chicago Press, 1974.

Brownstein, Rachel M. *Becoming a Heroine: Reading about Women in Novels.* 1982. Reprint. New York: Penguin, 1984.

———. "Jane Austen: Irony and Authority." In *Last Laughs: Perspectives on Women and Comedy,* edited by Regina Barreca, 57–70. New York: Gordon and Breach, 1988.

Cameron, Deborah. *Feminism and Linguistic Theory.* New York: St. Martin's Press, 1985.

Campbell, Jane. "Margaret Drabble and the Search for Analogy." In *The Practical Vision: Essays in English Literature in Honour of Flora Ray,* edited by Jane Campbell and James Doyle, 133–50. Waterloo, Ontario: Wilfrid Laurier University Press, 1978.

Carabi, Angeles. "Special Eyes: The Chinese-American World of Maxine Hong Kingston" (Interview). *Belles Lettres* (Winter 1989): 10–11.

Cheung, King-Kok. "'Don't Tell': Imposed Silences in *The Color Purple* and *The Woman Warrior.*" *PMLA* 103, no. 2 (March 1988): 162–74.

Cixous, Hélène. "Castration or Decapitation?" Translated by Annette Kuhn. *Signs* 7, no. 1 (Autumn 1981): 41–55.

———. "The Laugh of the Medusa." Translated by Keith Cohen and Paula Cohen. *Signs* 1, no. 4 (Summer 1976): 875–93.

Cott, Nancy F. *The Grounding of Modern Feminism.* New Haven: Yale University Press, 1987.

Creighton, Joanne V. *Margaret Drabble.* London: Methuen, 1985.

Delany, Sheila. "Ambivalence in Utopia: The American Feminist Utopias of Charlotte P. Gilman and Marge Piercy." In *Writing Woman: Women Writers and Women in Literature, Medieval to Modern,* 157–80. New York: Schocken Books, 1983.

Dillingham, Thomas F. "Joanna Russ." *Beacham's Popular Fiction of America,* Vol. 3. Washington, DC: Beacham Publishing, 1987: 1204–1213.

Dipple, Elizabeth. *The Unresolvable Plot: Reading Contemporary Fiction.* New York: Routledge, Chapman, and Hall, 1988.

# Bibliography

Donovan, Josephine, ed. *Feminist Literary Criticism: Explorations in Theory.* Lexington: University Press of Kentucky, 1975.

Drabble, Margaret. *The Waterfall.* 1969. Reprint. New York: Fawcett, 1977.

———. "A Woman Writer." In *On Gender and Writing,* edited by Michelene Wandor, 156–59. London: Pandora Press, 1983.

Draine, Betsy. "Changing Forms: Doris Lessing's *Memoirs of a Survivor.*" *Studies in the Novel* 11 (1979): 51–62.

DuPlessis, Rachel Blau. *Writing Beyond the Ending: Narrative Strategies of Twentieth-Century Women Writers.* Bloomington: Indiana University Press, 1985.

Dyson, A. E. *The Crazy Fabric: Essays in Irony.* London: Macmillan, 1965.

Eakin, Paul John. *Fictions in Autobiography: Studies in the Art of Self-Invention.* Princeton: Princeton University Press, 1985.

Eco, Umberto. "Postmodernism, Irony, the Enjoyable." In *Postscript to The Name of the Rose,* translated by William Weaver, 65–72. New York: Harcourt Brace Jovanovich, 1984.

Elshtain, Jean Bethke. "Feminist Discourse and Its Discontents: Language, Power, and Meaning." *Signs* 7, no. 3 (Spring 1982): 603–21.

Fifer, Elizabeth. "The Dialect and Letters of *The Color Purple.*" In *Contemporary American Women Writers: Narrative Strategies,* edited by Catherine Rainwater and William J. Scheick, 155–71. Lexington: University Press of Kentucky, 1985.

Finke, Laurie. "The Rhetoric of Marginality: Why I Do Feminist Theory." *Tulsa Studies in Women's Literature* 5, no. 2 (Fall 1986): 251–72.

Fox-Genovese, Elizabeth. "The Ambiguities of Female Identity: A Reading of the Novels of Margaret Drabble." *Partisan Review* 46 (1979): 234–48.

French, Marilyn. *Her Mother's Daughter.* New York: Ballantine, 1987.

———. *The Women's Room.* 1977. Reprint. New York: Harcourt, Brace, 1978.

Frye, Joanne S. *Living Stories, Telling Lives: Women and the Novel in Contemporary Experience.* Ann Arbor: University of Michigan Press, 1986.

———. "*The Woman Warrior:* Claiming Narrative Power, Recreating Female Selfhood." In *Faith of a (Woman) Writer,* edited by Alice Kessler-Harris and William McBrien. Westport, Conn.: Greenwood Press, 1988.

Fuoroli, Caryn. "Sophistry or Simple Truth? Narrative Technique in Margaret Drabble's *The Waterfall.*" *Journal of Narrative Technique* 11, no. 2 (Spring 1981): 110–25.

# Bibliography

Furst, Barbara Griffith. "Retrospective: Margaret Drabble." *Belles Lettres* (July/August 1988): 10–11.

Furst, Lilian R. *Fictions of Romantic Irony*. Cambridge: Harvard University Press, 1984.

Gardiner, Judith Kegan. "On Female Identity and Writing by Women." *Critical Inquiry* 8, no. 2 (Winter 1981): 347–61.

Garland, Barbara. "Joanna Russ." *Dictionary of Literary Biography*. Vol. 8, Twentieth-Century American Science Fiction Writers, edited by David Cowart and Thomas L. Wymer. Detroit: Gale Research, 1981. Part 2 (M–Z), 88–93.

Gatlin, Rochelle. *American Women Since 1945*. Jackson: University Press of Mississippi, 1987.

Godard, Barbara. "My (m)Other, My Self: Strategies for Subversion in Atwood and Hebert." *Essays on Canadian Writing* 26 (Summer 1983): 13–44.

Godwin, Gail. "My Mother, the Writer: Master of a Thousand Disguises." *New York Times Book Review*, 11 June 1989, 7, 50–51.

———. *The Odd Woman*. 1974. Reprint. New York: Warner Books, 1980.

———. "Towards a Fully Human Heroine: Some Worknotes." *The Harvard Advocate* (Winter 1973): 26–28.

———. *Violet Clay*. 1978. Reprint. New York: Warner Books, 1979.

Grace, Sherrill. *Violent Duality: A Study of Margaret Atwood*. Montreal: Vehicule Press, 1980.

Gusdorf, George. "Conditions and Limits of Autobiography." In *Autobiography: Essays Theoretical and Critical*, edited by James Olney, 28–48. Princeton: Princeton University Press, 1980.

Hansen, Elaine Tuttle. "The Double Narrative Structure of *Small Changes*." In *Contemporary American Women Writers: Narrative Strategies*, edited by Catherine Rainwater and William J. Scheick, 209–28. Lexington: University Press of Kentucky, 1985.

Hardin, Nancy S. "An Interview with Margaret Drabble." *Contemporary Literature* 14, no. 3 (Summer 1973): 273–95.

Harper, Michael F. "Margaret Drabble and the Resurrection of the English Novel." *Contemporary Literature* 23, no. 2 (1982): 145–68.

Heilbrun, Carolyn G. *Writing a Woman's Life*. New York: W. W. Norton, 1988.

Henley, Nancy M. "This New Species That Seeks a New Language: On Sexism in Language and Language Change." In *Women and Language in Transition*, edited by Joyce Penfield, 3–27. Albany: State University of New York Press, 1987.

# Bibliography

Hoffman, Anne Golomb. "Acts of Self-Creation: Female Identity in the Novels of Margaret Drabble." In *Faith of a (Woman) Writer,* edited by Alice Kessler-Harris and William McBrien, 21–29. Westport, Conn.: Greenwood Press, 1988.

Homans, Margaret. "'Her Very Own Howl': The Ambiguities of Representation in Recent Women's Fiction." *Signs* 9, no. 2 (Winter 1983): 186–205.

Howells, Coral Ann. *Private and Fictional Words: Canadian Women Novelists of the 1970s and 1980s.* London: Methuen, 1987.

Hutcheons, Linda. "From Poetic to Narrative Structures: The Novels of Margaret Atwood." In *Margaret Atwood: Language, Text, and System,* edited by Sherrill E. Grace and Lorraine Weir, 17–31. Vancouver: University of British Columbia Press, 1983.

Irvin, William Robert. *The Game of the Impossible: A Rhetoric of Fantasy.* Urbana: University of Illinois Press, 1976.

Jackson, Rosemary. *Fantasy: The Literature of Subversion.* London: Methuen, 1981.

Janeway, Elizabeth. *Cross Sections from a Decade of Change.* New York: William Morrow, 1982.

Johnson, Nora. "Housewives and Prom Queens, 25 Years Later." *New York Times Book Review,* 20 March 1988, 1, 32–33.

Jong, Erica. "Blood and Guts: The Tricky Problem of Being a Woman Writer in the Late Twentieth Century." In *The Writer on Her Work,* edited by Janet Sternburg, 169–79. New York: Norton, 1980.

———. *Fear of Flying.* 1973. Reprint. New York: Signet, 1974.

———. *How to save your own life.* New York: Holt, Rinehart, 1977.

———. *Parachutes and Kisses.* New York: New American Library, 1984.

———. *Serenissima: A Novel of Venice.* Boston: Houghton Mifflin, 1987.

Juhasz, Suzanne. "Texts to Grow On: Reading Women's Romance Fiction." *Tulsa Studies in Women's Literature* 7, no. 2 (Fall 1988): 239–59.

———. "Towards a Theory of Form in Feminist Autobiography: Kate Millet's *Flying* and *Sita;* Maxine Hong Kingston's *The Woman Warrior.*" In *Women's Autobiography: Essays in Criticism,* edited by Estelle C. Jelinek, 221–37. Bloomington: Indiana University Press, 1980.

Kauffman, Linda. "Special Delivery: Twenty-first-Century Epistolarity in *The Handmaid's Tale.*" In *Writing the Female Voice: Essays on Epistolary Literature,* edited by Elizabeth C. Goldsmith, 221–44. Boston: Northeastern University Press, 1989.

Kingston, Maxine Hong. Discussion at the University of Missouri–Columbia, 8–9 March 1988.

211

# Bibliography

———. *The Woman Warrior: Memoirs of a Girlhood Among Ghosts.* 1976. Reprint. New York: Vintage, 1977.

Kirkham, Margaret. *Jane Austen, Feminism, and Fiction.* New York: Methuen, 1986.

Knapp, Mona. *Doris Lessing.* New York: Frederick Ungar, 1984.

Kolodny, Annette. "A Map for Rereading; Or, Gender and the Interpretation of Literary Texts." *New Literary History* 11, no. 3 (1980): 451–67.

Krouse, Agate Nesaule. "Feminism and Art in Fay Weldon's Novels." *Critique: Studies in Modern Fiction* 20, no. 2 (1978): 5–20.

Le Guin, Ursula K. "The Hand That Rocks the Cradle Writes the Book." *New York Times Book Review,* 22 January 1989, 1, 35–37.

———. "National Book Award Acceptance Speech." In *The Language of the Night: Essays on Fantasy and Science Fiction,* edited by Susan Wood, 57–58. New York: Putnam, 1979.

Lessing, Doris. *The Four-Gated City.* 1969. Reprint. New York: Bantam, 1970.

———. *The Memoirs of a Survivor.* 1974. Reprint. New York: Bantam, 1976.

———. *The Summer Before the Dark.* 1973. Reprint. New York: Bantam, 1974.

Lorsch, Susan E. "Gail Godwin's *The Odd Woman:* Literature and the Retreat from Life." *Critique: Studies in Modern Fiction* 20, no. 2 (1978): 21–32.

Manheimer, Joan. "Margaret Drabble and the Journey to the Self." *Studies in the Literary Imagination* 11, no. 2 (Fall 1978): 127–43.

Miller, Margaret. "Threads of Identity in Maxine Hong Kingston's *Woman Warrior.*" *Biography* 6, no. 1 (Winter 1983): 13–33.

Miller, Nancy K. "Emphasis Added: Plots and Plausibilities in Women's Fiction." *PMLA* 96, no. 1 (January 1981): 36–48.

———. *Subject to Change: Reading Feminist Writing.* New York: Columbia University Press, 1988.

Morrison, Toni. *The Bluest Eye.* 1970. Reprint. New York: Washington Square Press, 1972.

Muecke, D. C. *Irony.* The Critical Idiom Series, no. 13. London: Methuen, 1970.

Mussell, Kay. *Fantasy and Reconciliation: Contemporary Formulas of Women's Romance Fiction.* Contributions in Women's Studies, no. 46. Westport, Conn.: Greenwood Press, 1984.

Nin, Anais. *The Novel of the Future.* New York: Collier Books, 1968.

Olsen, Tillie. *Silences.* New York: Delacorte, 1978.

212

# Bibliography

Ostriker, Alicia Suskin. *Stealing the Language: The Emergence of Women's Poetry in America.* Boston: Beacon Press, 1986.

Pearlman, Mickey, ed. *American Women Writing Fiction: Memory, Identity, Family, Space.* Lexington: University Press of Kentucky, 1989.

Piercy, Marge. *Small Changes.* Greenwich, Conn.: Fawcett, 1973.

———. *Woman on the Edge of Time.* 1976. Reprint. New York: Fawcett Crest, 1977.

Poovey, Mary. "Feminism and Deconstruction." *Feminist Studies* 14, no. 1 (Spring 1988): 51–65.

Pratt, Annis V. "Spinning Among Fields: Jung, Frye, Levi-Strauss." In *Feminist Archetypal Theory: Interdisciplinary Re-Visions of Jungian Thought,* edited by Estella Lauter and Carol Schreier Rupprecht, 93–136. Knoxville: University of Tennessee Press, 1985.

———. "*Surfacing* and the Rebirth Journey." In *The Art of Margaret Atwood: Essays in Criticism,* edited by Arnold E. Davidson and Cathy N. Davidson, 139–57. Toronto: Anansi, 1981.

Rabine, Leslie W. "No Lost Paradise: Social Gender and Symbolic Gender in the Writings of Maxine Hong Kingston." *Signs* 12, no. 3 (Spring 1987): 471–92.

Radway, Janice A. "Gothic Romances and 'Feminist' Protest." *American Quarterly* 33, no. 2 (Summer 1981): 140–62.

———. *Reading the Romance: Women, Patriarchy, and Popular Literature.* Chapel Hill: University of North Carolina Press, 1984.

Reardon, Joan. "*Fear of Flying:* Developing the Feminist Novel." *International Journal of Women's Studies* 1, no. 3 (May/June 1978): 306–20.

Rigney, Barbara Hill. *Madness and Sexual Politics in the Feminist Novel.* Madison: University of Wisconsin Press, 1978.

Roller, Judi M. *The Politics of the Feminist Novel.* Contributions in Women's Studies, no. 63. Westport, Conn.: Greenwood Press, 1986.

Rose, Ellen Cronan, ed. *Critical Essays on Margaret Drabble.* Boston: G. K. Hall, 1985.

———. "Feminine Endings—And Beginnings: Margaret Drabble's *The Waterfall.*" *Contemporary Literature* 21, no. 1 (Winter 1980): 81–99.

———. *The Novels of Margaret Drabble: Equivocal Forms.* Totowa, N.J.: Barnes and Noble, 1980.

Rosinsky, Natalie M. "A Female Man? The 'Medusan' Humor of Joanna Russ." *Extrapolation* 23, no. 1 (1982): 31–36.

Rossner, Judith. *Looking for Mr. Goodbar.* 1975. Reprint. New York: Pocket Books, 1976.

# Bibliography

Rubenstein, Roberta. *Boundaries of the Self: Gender, Culture, Fiction*. Urbana: University of Illinois Press, 1987.

Ruppert, Peter. *Reader in a Strange Land: The Activity of Reading Literary Utopias*. Athens: University of Georgia Press, 1986.

Russ, Joanna. *The Female Man*. 1975. Reprint. London: The Women's Press, 1985.

————. *How to Suppress Women's Writing*. Austin: University of Texas Press, 1983.

————. "What Can a Heroine Do? Or Why Women Can't Write." In *Images of Women in Fiction: Feminist Perspectives*, edited by Susan Koppelman Cornillon, 3–20. Bowling Green, Ohio: Bowling Green Popular Press, 1972.

Sage, Lorna. *Doris Lessing*. London: Methuen, 1983.

Shinn, Thelma J. *Radiant Daughters: Fictional American Women*. Contributions in Women's Studies, no. 66. Westport, Conn.: Greenwood Press, 1986.

Snitow, Ann Barr. "The Front Line: Notes on Sex in Novels by Women, 1969–1979." *Signs* 5, no. 4 (Summer 1980): 702–18.

Spacks, Patricia Meyer, ed. *Contemporary Women Novelists: A Collection of Critical Essays*. Englewood Cliffs, N.J.: Prentice-Hall, 1977.

————. *The Female Imagination*. New York: Knopf, 1975.

Sprague, Claire. *Rereading Doris Lessing: Narrative Patterns of Doubling and Repetition*. Chapel Hill: University of North Carolina Press, 1987.

Staicar, Tom. *The Feminine Eye: Science Fiction and the Women Who Write It*. New York: Frederick Ungar, 1982.

Stimpson, Catharine R. "Doris Lessing and the Parables of Growth." In *The Voyage In: Fictions of Female Development*, edited by Elizabeth Abel, Marianne Hirsch, and Elizabeth Langland, 186–205. Hanover: University Press of New England, 1983.

"A Symposium on Contemporary American Fiction." *Michigan Quarterly Review* 27, no. 1 (Winter 1988): 79–135.

*Tulsa Studies in Women's Literature* 3 (1984). Special issue: "Feminist Issues in Literary Scholarship."

Van Den Bergh, Nan. "Renaming: Vehicle for Empowerment." In *Women and Language in Transition*, edited by Joyce Penfield, 130–36. Albany: State University of New York Press, 1987.

VanSpanckeren, Kathryn, and Jan Garden Castro, eds. *Margaret Atwood: Vision and Forms*. Carbondale: Southern Illinois University Press, 1988.

Walker, Alice. *The Color Purple*. 1982. Reprint. New York: Washington Square Press, 1983.

# Bibliography

————. *Meridian.* 1976. Reprint. New York: Washington Square Press, 1977.

Weldon, Fay. *Female Friends.* New York: St. Martin's Press, 1974.

————. "Me and My Shadows." In *On Gender and Writing,* edited by Michelene Wandor, 160–65. London: Pandora Press, 1983.

————. *The Rules of Life.* New York: Harper and Row, 1987.

————. *Words of Advice.* 1977. Reprint. New York: Ballantine, 1978.

Whittier, Gayle. "Mistresses and Melodramas in the Novels of Margaret Drabble." In *Gender and Literary Voice,* edited by Janet Todd, 197–213. New York: Holmes and Meier, 1980.

# INDEX

*Alice in Wonderland* (Carroll), 96
Atwood, Margaret, 4, 5, 8, 15, 20,
 21, 32–33, 38–39, 47, 56, 67,
 69–74, 75, 130–31, 148, 151–
 53, 156, 161, 168, 171, 175, 178,
 187; *Cat's Eye*, 134, 137–39;
 *Double Persephone*, 82; *Edible
 Woman, The*, 4; *Handmaid's
 Tale, The*, 4, 8, 9, 10, 12, 20, 22,
 27, 28, 30, 32–33, 35, 37, 38–
 39, 41, 44, 46–47, 53, 55, 56,
 60–61, 69–74, 75, 100, 105,
 118–19, 128, 147–49, 152–53,
 154, 155–56, 160, 161, 164,
 169, 171, 174, 178, 187, 189;
 *Lady Oracle*, 6–7, 91–92, 117,
 119–20, 128, 129, 187; *Life Before Man*, 39, 49–50, 57–58,
 117; *Surfacing*, 11, 35, 56, 60,
 79, 80–84, 85, 87, 99, 115, 139–
 42, 144–45, 149, 150–52, 159,
 167, 189; *Two-Headed Poems*, 82
Austen, Jane, 7–8, 15, 19, 23;
 *Pride and Prejudice*, 8; *Northanger Abbey*, 8
Autobiography, 3, 20–22, 65–66,
 77–78, 130

Barth, John, 23
*Bildungsroman*, 76, 93, 108
*Brave New World* (Huxley), 30

Cartland, Barbara, 29
Chopin, Kate, 7, 15; *Awakening,
 The*, 7, 16

*Diary of a Mad Housewife* (Kaufman), 4
Drabble, Margaret, 5, 11, 15, 18,
 20, 21, 24, 34, 36, 40, 43, 51–
 53, 107–9, 134, 159; *Waterfall,
 The*, 9, 11, 16–17, 20, 24, 27,
 28, 33, 40, 43, 51–53, 107–12,
 116–17, 129–30, 134, 136, 159,
 187, 188, 189
Durrell, Lawrence, 23

Eco, Umberto, 29
Eliot, George, 7, 19; *Mill on the
 Floss, The*, 7, 17, 33, 108
*Equality* (Bellamy), 12

Fairy tales, 11, 31, 32, 39, 41, 50–
 51, 92, 101–4, 111–12, 115–16,
 186

217

# Index

Fantasy, 4–5, 6–7, 8, 11–12, 28–37; as related to irony, 29–30; as related to language, 39
*Female Quixote, The* (Lennox), 8
*Female Quixotism* (Tenney), 8
*Feminine Mystique, The* (Friedan), 15, 173
Fern, Fanny (Sara Willis Parton), 4, 19; *Ruth Hall,* 4
French, Marilyn, 4, 115, 136; *Women's Room, The,* 115–16, 129, 130, 187; *Her Mother's Daughter,* 134, 136–37

Gilman, Charlotte Perkins, 23, 84, 151, 160, 181; *Herland,* 12, 32, 84, 147, 148, 151, 155, 160; "Yellow Wallpaper, The," 139
Godwin, Gail, 5, 8, 20, 21, 33, 34, 87-89, 90, 92, 186; *Violet Clay,* 6, 20, 31, 33, 36, 41, 53–54, 83, 89, 90–91, 92, 134, 135–36, 159, 186; *Odd Woman, The,* 6, 88–89, 117, 129, 187, 188; "Towards a Fully Human Heroine: Some Worknotes," 87–88

Hawthorne, Nathaniel, 22, 32, 41; *Scarlet Letter, The,* 32, 41
*Heartburn* (Ephron), 77

*I Know Why the Caged Bird Sings* (Angelou), 77
*Inferno* (Dante), 96
Irony, 4–5, 7–8, 23–28, 29, 37; as related to fantasy, 29–30; as related to language, 39

James, Henry, 23
Jewett, Sarah Orne, 19

Jong, Erica, 11–12, 14–15, 18, 25–26, 77, 95–97, 116, 153–54, 165–66, 168; *Fear of Flying,* 11–12, 15, 25, 36, 95–97, 99, 100, 116–17, 118, 122–23, 128, 129–30, 131–33, 189, 190; *How to save your own life,* 15; *Parachutes and Kisses,* 15; *Serenissima: A Novel of Venice,* 11–12, 100, 147, 153–54, 164–68, 174–75, 189
Joyce, James, 23
*Jude the Obscure* (Hardy), 108

Kingston, Maxine Hong, 10, 11, 15, 35, 55, 58, 60, 65–69, 77, 78–79, 115, 117, 123–26, 127, 129–30; *Woman Warrior: Memoirs of a Girlhood Among Ghosts, The,* 10, 11, 21, 35, 39, 44, 55, 56–57, 58, 60–61, 65–69, 78–79, 115, 117, 123–26, 129, 130

Language, 8, 10–11, 187, 190; women's, 10, 40–51, 66, 97–99; as related to irony, 39, 43–44; as related to fantasy, 39; women's exclusion from, 40, 44–45, 55–61, 72–74

Le Guin, Ursula K., 98, 146–48
Lessing, Doris, 5, 9, 12–13, 15, 32, 48–49, 59, 129, 144–45, 151–52, 157–58, 168–75; *Children of Violence,* 152, 158; *Four-Gated City, The,* 9, 12, 21, 31–33, 35, 59–60, 79–80, 100, 115, 139–40, 142–45, 147–48, 151, 157–58, 168–70, 190; *Golden Notebook, The,* 152; *Good Terrorist, The,* 152; *Memoirs of a Survivor,*

218

# Index

*The*, 12–13, 32, 100, 147–49, 152, 160, 168–75, 189; *Summer Before the Dark, The*, 48–49

*Looking Backward* (Bellamy), 147

*Looking for Mr. Goodbar* (Rossner), 130, 131–34, 187, 188–89

Madness, 11, 35–36, 58–60, 69, 114–17, 120–22, 130, 139–45, 177

Melville, Herman, 22

*Memories of an Ex-Prom Queen* (Schulman), 4

*Memoirs of a Catholic Girlhood* (McCarthy), 77

Miller, Sue, 114

Morrison, Toni, 67, 135; *Bluest Eye, The*, 120–22, 135–36, 149, 186, 187, 190

Mythology, cultural, 8, 39, 41, 50–55, 90, 92–93, 95, 97, 101, 105, 110, 153, 186, 189

Names, 55–57, 59, 61–63, 79–80, 142

Orwell, George, 32, 151; *1984*, 30, 147, 151

Parton, Sara Willis. *See* Fern, Fanny

Piercy, Marge, 5, 38, 47–48, 93–94, 148, 156, 175–79, 180, 181, 184, 186; *Small Changes*, 17, 38, 43–44, 47–48, 50, 57, 79, 91, 92–95, 115, 117, 129; *Woman on the Edge of Time*, 12, 36, 58–59, 100, 148, 152, 154, 155–57, 158, 160, 175–79, 180, 181, 183, 186, 189–90

Popular romance novel, 5–7, 36–37, 90–92, 94, 117, 128–29, 149–50

*Pumpkin Eater, The*, (Mortimer), 4

*Red Shoes, The* (film), 119–20

Russ, Joanna, 9, 34–35, 40, 45–46, 84–87, 129, 148, 153, 179–82, 184, 185–86, 189; *Female Man, The*, 12, 34–35, 44–46, 55, 84–87, 100, 148, 153, 155, 158, 160, 179–84, 185, 186, 188, 189; *How to Suppress Women's Writing*, 40, 45, 185; "When It Changed," 85

Selfhood, 8, 11, 75–80, 100–01, 107–8, 113–14, 132–33, 142, 166–67

Sexuality, 28, 56–57, 64, 67, 80–83, 84, 85, 89, 95–99, 101–3, 106, 108, 118–24, 129–30, 131–33, 140, 154, 155, 160–61, 162–63, 164–65, 168, 170–74, 177–78, 180–81, 183–84, 189

Shakespeare, William, 12, 52, 111, 165; *Merchant of Venice*, 12, 165; *Romeo and Juliet*, 52, 111

*Silences* (Olsen), 40

Speculative fiction, 12–13, 34, 44–45, 84, 146–49, 151–61, 184

*Through the Looking Glass* (Carroll), 96

Twain, Mark, 23, 27

*Walden Two* (Skinner), 151, 155

Walker, Alice, 5, 8, 9, 15, 61, 63,

# Index

65–66, 67; *Color Purple, The*, 8, 10, 21, 29–30, 35, 36, 44, 50–51, 58, 60–66, 69, 72, 117, 127, 130, 134, 189, 190; *Meridian*, 61, 120, 122, 126–27, 128

Weldon, Fay, 5, 9, 18–19, 26–27, 33–34, 36, 47, 101–2, 104, 106–7, 113–14, 128, 147, 148, 153–54, 161–64, 167, 186, 187; *Female Friends*, 24–25, 26–27, 33–34, 40, 43, 46, 104–7; "Me and My Shadows," 113–14; *Rules of Life, The*, 147, 153–54, 160, 161–64, 167; *Words of Ad-*

*vice*, 11, 20–21, 28, 32, 39, 41, 51, 101–4, 107, 117, 129, 159

Wharton, Edith, 15, 16, 114; *House of Mirth, The*, 16

Woman as artist, 6, 31, 52–54, 58, 63, 83, 90–92, 113–14, 133, 134–38, 150–51

Women's movement, 4–6, 9, 14–19, 21, 25, 37, 38, 43, 75–76, 99, 130–31

Woolf, Virginia, 15, 114; *Orlando*, 12

*Writing a Woman's Life* (Heilbrun), 3, 4, 17, 116, 187